THE LOOMIS GANG

THE LOOMIS GANG

By George W. Walter

NORTH COUNTRY BOOKS
311 Turner Street
Utica, New York 13501

THE LOOMIS GANG

Copyright © 1953, 1968
George W. Walter

Paperback Edition
Seventh printing December 1996
Eighth printing 2002

All Rights Reserved

No part of this book may be reproduced
in any manner without written
permission of the publisher.

Library of Congress Catalogue Number 53-7852
ISBN 0-932052-47-9

Printed by
Canterbury Press
Rome, New York
USA

NORTH COUNTRY BOOKS
311 Turner Street
Utica, New York 13501

To
Clarice

FOREWORD

This is the authentic story of a highly intelligent family which was able to create and maintain a feudal empire in upstate New York during the 19th century. The Loomises were akin to the ancient robber barons and ruled for over 100 years until they became an international scandal.

Today the site of the Loomis homestead on a knoll, and overlooking the Nine-Mile Swamp Road between Sangerfield Center and Heads Corners has been obliterated.

For more than a century the cellar ruins and a few of the old trees that once surrounded the site, had remained practically unchanged. Today the trees and the cellar are gone. A recent owner has cleared the plot and made it part of the field.

The Loomises most likely would have wanted it this way. Descendants who reside in Central New York have wished the escapades of the family were forgotten.

There have been several books of fiction based on the exploits of the Loomis family, but the only serious attempts to mirror their lives and exploits have been confined to contemporary newspaper accounts. The basis for many of the articles of the past and present can be traced directly to Amos Cumming's "The Loomis Gang" that appeared in the New York Sun in 1879.

A letter written by A. B. Loomis of Albany on February 17, 1919 to Professor E. S. Loomis of Cleveland, Ohio, compiler of "The Loomis Family in America," clearly indicated that the national family association welcomed an expose of their black sheep: "I thought for a long time it must be there weren't any bad or unfortunate Loomises. At one of the Windsor (Conn.) reunions, some one referred to the horse thieves of Oneida County, N. Y., saying that even they excelled in their particular line.

"I assume it is just as well that there be some record here and there to show who the guilty Loomises were, that the innocent may not be under shadow."

Research for this book began in 1930. Children and grandchildren of the Loomis family have been interviewed as well as many men and women who knew them and visited in their home.

Several well documented stories and chapters have been added since this book was first published in 1953.

Whenever possible I have allowed the Loomises, their friends and enemies to speak for themselves by quoting from newspaper stories, memories, coroner's inquests, affidavits, court records and letters. Each folk and family story has been carefully evaluated and used if found appropriate. It was impossible to use all of the stories. I have wanted the facts to speak for themselves and deliberately have made no effort to champion or condemn the Loomises.

This book would not have been possible without the aid of the men and women who gave me access to court records, vital statistics, scrapbooks, newspaper files and private collections and helped me to locate descendants of many of the participants. Working faithfully with me through the long years have been Thomas L. Hall of Smith's Valley and "Aunt Neva" (Mrs. Geneva) Watson of Hubbardsville; the Misses Ruth Conway and Alma Jones of the reference room, Mrs. L. C. Foucher and Miss Alice C. Dodge, past head librarians of the Utica Public Library; Paul Paine and Miss Frieda Gates, past head librarians of the Syracuse Public Library; the staffs and officials of the Morrisville Public Library; the late Thomas Iams, former Colgate University librarian; the late Orrin Terry and Mr. and Mrs. George E. Westcott, former owners of the Waterville Times; Roger R. Dorrance, former Madison County Clerk; officials of the Oneida County Courthouse in Utica, who allowed me access to records in its Law Library, and many others.

For helpful criticism and advice along the way I am indebted to Dr. Porter G. Perrin of Seattle, Washington; Reed Alvord of Putney, Vermont and the late John F. McNamara of New Hartford.

And last, but not least, to my wife, Clarice Dougherty Walter, who read the original manuscript shortly after I started my research, long before I ever was in love with her.

George W. Walter

Oneida, New York
1968

TABLE OF CONTENTS

		Page
	Foreword	7
I	The Seeds Are Sown	13
II	The Loomises At Home	22
III	Wash Loomis Goes West	33
IV	Cornelia Liked Muffs	38
V	Albany Money	44
VI	Wandering Sheep	51
VII	Grove The Horseman	59
VIII	Filkins Takes The Trail	67
IX	Shoot Plumb!	76
X	The Gang Takes Over	83
XI	The War Years	92
XII	The Syndicate Of Thieves	99
XIII	Underground Stables	111
XIV	Loot From The Loomis Attic	114
XV	Fires In The Night	121
XVI	Unhappy Loomis Women	129
XVII	The Horse Thief	141
XVIII	Death Comes Calling	149
XIX	The Loomises Destroy Evidence	153
XX	"Wash Is Killed!"	158
XXI	Filkins Is Indicted	173
XXII	The Crandall Murder	185
XXIII	The Loomises Seek Revenge	191
XXIV	Clean Out The Loomises	200
XXV	Filkins Stands Trial	210
XXVI	The Confession	218
XXVII	Denio Assumes Leadership	222
XXVIII	Grove Entices Cora Magwood	230
XXIX	Young Grove Loomis	239
XXX	The Family Quarrels	244
XXXI	The Loomis Empire Falls	250
XXXII	The Ghost of Wash Loomis	267
	Bibliography	270

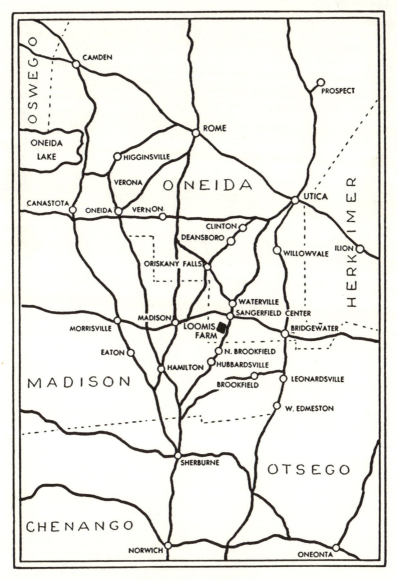

The Loomis Country

CHAPTER I

THE SEEDS ARE SOWN

In that paradise of sunlight and shadows, the Chenango Valley of New York, if you listen closely on a late October evening, so the story goes, you will hear the muffled drumming of horses' hoofs along the empty roads. The sound heralds the return of the earth-bound souls of the Loomis gang on the anniversary of Wash Loomis' murder. The hills resound with hollow laughter as the merry riders gather where the shadows lie thickest at the abandoned Loomis farm above the dark recesses of the Nine-Mile Swamp. After a night of revelry they disappear before the morning sun slants over the eastern hills.

The Loomis family founded a robber empire in upstate New York and maintained it for nearly a hundred years, creating a legend of swashbuckling infamy that became an international scandal during their lifetime. The names of Wash, Grove, Bill, Wheeler, Plumb, Denio and Cornelia Loomis remain emblazoned in the era of turnpike and stagecoach and the golden age of hop-growing. Hundreds of newspaper stories and court records clearly indicate that the Loomises made crime a big business and used highway robbery, counterfeiting, arson and murder as their weapons of terrorism.

The Loomises were bold, resourceful and highly intelligent. Like all great criminal organizations they learned early that the best legal talent was required to help outwit the law, and that judges and juries could be bribed.

While some members of the family tried to live at peace with their neighbors, others stole from their relatives. Their general characteristics were summed up in this statement from a report made by the New York Prison Association and submitted to the State Legislature in January, 1866: "These men, as might be supposed, exert a great political influence, and it is well understood that they are always ready to reward their friends and punish their enemies, both in primary conventions and at the polls. Although, as we have said, they have been repeatedly indicted, yet the number of their indictments bears but a small ratio to the number of their depredations. It usually happens that anyone who is particularly active in bringing any of the gang to justice has his barn or dwelling soon after burned, or his horses are missing from the stable, or his sheep or cattle from the pasture."

The Loomis farm straddled the Oneida and Madison County line some four miles south of Sangerfield Center on the Swamp Road that skirts the western fringe of the Nine-Mile Swamp to Hubbardsville. One building of the many erected by the Loomises remains standing — a small, weather-beaten barn to the left of the road, where the pastureland descends swiftly towards the Swamp. Almost opposite the barn rises a small knoll formerly fringed with gaunt and dying maples. Here, as in some forgotten graveyard over which the trees kept vigil, were the rock-strewn, overgrown ruins of a cellar where the Loomis homestead stood, an imposing structure against a background of wooded hillside. The sunken remains of a dugway, rutted by seasonal torrents and blanketed with weeds and brambles, hugs the southern rim of the wide mouth of the gully separating the property from the adjoining farm. Long ago it formed a connecting link between the older buildings above and the newer ones below.

On the broad, rolling uplands where the dugout reaches its crest, numerous sheep and dairy cattle graze in the old Loomis hay, grain and hop fields. The sagging remains of a split-rail fence partially enclose a ten-acre lot. Near its center a rectangle of loose stones and splinter beams indicates where George Washington Loomis, Sr. built his first barn. The original Loomis house, where five of his children were born, stood nearby, beside the Oxford Turnpike that pursued a rambling course across the high western hills. Traces of this old road are obliterated except for faint depressions on the higher points of land.

From here the Valley unfolds. The farms on the eastern slope of the Chenango hills lay like a quilted pattern of soft color, overshadowed with splashes of green marking the orchards and woodlots. At the northern end of the Valley, where the spires of Sangerfield Center and Waterville protrude above the dense foliage, a silver ribbon of road runs a westerly course. Lost from sight on the lower benches, it reappears shortly, stretching towards Sweet's Corners and Hubbardsville, hazy in the distance.

Below, almost filling the wide floor of the Valley between these far-separated hamlets, lies the Nine-Mile Swamp, choked with cedar and pine, its brooding somberness covering earth and bogs alike. In the old days the hunted found it a natural hiding place when fleeing from the law. The Loomises secreted horses and plunder in its depths and found it a sanctuary when cornered by vigilantes.

The country was emerging from the wilderness when George Washington Loomis, Sr. rode into Sangerfield Center in 1802. Twenty-three years old and a striking figure of manhood, George stood five feet, ten inches in height. His weight of one hundred and eighty pounds did not include the three thousand dollars in gold he was reported to have been carrying when he fled Vermont ahead of a sheriff's posse.

Loomis made his money running stolen horses, according to letters of the late John Mulligan of Sherburne. "G. W. L. covered a wide territory around Randolph, Vermont. The wise and wily Wash did not steal horses. He ran stolen horses to Danbury, Conn. for a commission of 75% just to accommodate strangers. It was pure velvet till the authorities told him, 'You git out'n the state an' don't come back.' "

Loomis chanced one more delivery of horses and was discovered. Riding night and day, he fled through the Winooski Valley and crossed the border near Whitehall. He had several distant cousins in Central New York, but chose to go to Sangerfield Center because his older sister, Clarissa, her husband, Dr. Stephen Preston and son, Medina, had moved there six years earlier from Ashford, Connecticut.

Clarissa Preston probably knew nothing about her brother's escapades. They came from a prominent New England family which boasted strains of English royalty and a long line of New England ancestors distinguished for piety and wealth. The American branch traces back to Joseph Loomis, an English woolen draper who settled in Windsor, Connecticut in 1639 on "The Island" at the junction of the Farmington and Connecticut Rivers. His home, one of the oldest in New England, has always been in possession of the family. In 1874 it was incorporated as the Loomis Institute, consecrated to American education.

The descendants of Joseph Loomis became extensive landowners, fought Indians and raised children. Daniel Loomis the grandfather of George Washington Loomis, was born in Windsor, but moved to Union in Tolland County in 1741. George Washington, seventh child of Lieutenant Daniel and Sarah Crawford Loomis, first saw the light of day August 17, 1779 in the new house his father had built on the Bugbee place.

During his first months in Sangerfield George Washington Loomis traveled about the Valley making acquaintances. Currency being scarce, gallons of whiskey and gin were used for bartering. "Loomis wasn't the kind to waste his gold," Mulligan declared. "He was not the kind who worked for someone else. A good mixer, talkative and well-liked by his neighbors, Loomis made charcoal and potash. There was always a ready market for such products in New York City."

On May 1, 1806 he paid Hervey Prentice $1,700 in cash for 115 acres in Lot Number 10 of the Twentieth Township, which lay on the rolling uplands on the western edge of the Swamp.

During the next few years he cleared more land and earned an enviable reputation for driving the finest horses in the Valley. His younger brothers, Walter and Willard, and older sister, Sarah, came from Connecticut to live with him. Shortly afterward Sarah met and married William Mahan, a Westmoreland farmer. Walter took Nancy Graves of the same village as his wife and moved to Westmoreland. Willard married Clara Howard of Oswego and went there to live.

The opening of the Third Great Western Turnpike running from Cherry Valley to Sangerfield Center and westward brought with it an epidemic of counterfeit money to plague travelers as well as local residents. George and Willard Loomis were members, if not leaders, in the counterfeiting ring. They were detected when George passed a bad ten-dollar note on Captain Stephen Leonard of Sangerfield. They were not convicted.

George Loomis marched with the Madison County militia to Sackets Harbor during the War of 1812; years later, he was awarded fifty-five dollars by the Federal Government for his services.

Before leaving to fight the British he had met Rhoda Marie Mallett. At eighteen Rhoda was considered the most beautiful girl in the Valley. Intimate friends described her as a "very accomplished girl of medium height and slender build, with clear-cut, regular features. She had glossy, black hair, brushed back from her forehead, parted in the middle, and caught in a loose knot at the nape of her neck." One of her granddaughters revealed that "her skin was like pale ivory and her only beauty secret was to wash her face every day with a fine linen handkerchief soaked in dew."

Rhoda, the daughter of Zachariah and Abigail Osburn Mallett, who had emigrated from Stratford, Connecticut about 1800, was well educated and had taught in district schools. She boasted of her French blood and probably instigated the folk tale that her father, of noble lineage, had stolen funds belonging to the French Revolutionary Army and had been forced to flee to the United States to escape the guillotine.

Rhoda idolized her father, though his chief claim to fame seems to have been as a forger and distiller of whiskey. George met her one day when he accompanied Sheriff James Kip to the Mallett farm to serve some papers. When Kip tried to crawl through a window to arrest Mallett, Rhoda knocked him over with a fire shovel. Loomis attempted to intercede, and also was battered on the head. When the natives twitted him about the affair he said, "A girl that will fight for her father will fight for her husband. I'm going to marry that girl." Though there was thirteen years difference in their ages, they were married in 1814, according to John Mulligan.

Under Rhoda's capable management the farm was expanded and improved until by 1823 it consisted of 325 acres valued at $3,250.

Loomis gained a reputation as a money lender who insisted that notes he held be met when due. The papers of Othniel Williams of Clinton, his attorney, show judgments granted for two failures to pay notes.

The Loomises, though growing wealthy, apparently were not content to stay within the law. Phinett Carter, whose family resided in the Nine-Mile Swamp area for over 125 years, remarked, "These Loomises got well-to-do and they wanted to get an easy living and not work. So they got men and women around them that wanted a home, and they had these people do most of the stealing so they could live a life of ease."

Carter also told how Rhoda kept her husband under control "Old man Loomis came home one night intoxicated. That was nothing unusual for most of his neighbors. Whiskey was only from 18 cents to 25 cents a gallon and good and oily. There was no whiskey tax. The night old Loomis came home drunk, his wife put him to bed. Most everyone had a warming pan to put live coals in to warm up the bed. His wife went out and filled the warming pan with snow. Every time she hit him with it he would yell, 'You're burning me:' "

George and Rhoda had a large family. Their first child, Harriet, was born in 1815. Two years later, when a second daughter, Calista Adelia arrived, the joyous event was saddened by the death of their first child. Ten other children followed during the next quarter of a century; William Walter in 1819, Maria Cornelia 1821, George Washington Wheeler 1823, Grove Lawrence 1825, Lucia Ella 1828, Wheeler Theodore 1830, Mary Charlotte 1832, Amos Plumb 1834, Hiram Denio 1836 and a second Harriet in 1838 who died at the age of two years.

These healthy, handsome children all bore a strong family resemblance. They rode good horses almost as soon as they walked, and the boys learned how to use rifles and pistols. The Nine-Mile Swamp cast its spell over them. In those days it stretched some eleven miles from the Center to Dunbar's Mills, now Hubbardsville, and from one to three miles in width, and contained about five thousand acres. The Loomis children made the Swamp their playground, although panthers and lynx and an occasional wolf prowled through its depths.

The small home on the hill became over-crowded as the family increased. A new road had been constructed on the lower benches of the Valley, skirting the western edge of the Swamp. When George and Rhoda decided to erect a larger house, they picked a site on a small knoll overlooking the road, which commanded a ten-mile view of the Valley. The new home, often referred to as the Loomis homestead, was probably built about 1825, the year that Grove Lawrence was born.

The homestead stood two stories in height, with a forty foot frontage and a depth of fifty feet. A long hallway ran the full length of the building; from it opened double parlors, two bedrooms, a middle kitchen with a fireplace, a back kitchen and a spacious pantry. Staircases at the front and rear of the hallway climbed to the second floor, which contained several bedrooms and an unfinished storeroom. An open stairway led to the spacious garret.

The homestead had two main entrances: the front door facing the east opened on a small porch; the side door, off a long but narrow verandah, led into the back kitchen. A third entrance was through the woodshed in the one-story wing added later.

Stories of double-panelled rooms for hiding persons and plunder in the home and cellar and double floors in the garret, are all well authenticated. It is not definitely known whether they were originally constructed with the mansion.

Contrary to legend no secret underground passages led from the cellar to the barns across the road, for it would have been almost impossible to construct them, due to the underlying shale and the great difference in the elevation of the buildings. To illustrate the spread of the tunnel story, an elderly Bridgewater gentleman, considered well-versed in local history, often related how he had visited the Loomis family with a doctor and had been taken by the boys through the tunnel to the barn. A check of the storyteller's birth record disclosed that he was born twelve years after the Loomis homestead had burned to the ground.

L. Sherwood Fitch, a North Brookfield farmer who kept a journal of local happenings, described the Loomis homestead as "a large house, painted white, a fine yard in front of the house with beautiful flower gardens back of the house near a splendid grove of maples, beech and butternut trees. A dugway ran through this grove up onto the hill. When you got through the grove you came to a large meadow of about 200 acres with two large barns with yards for cattle. A little farther up the hill was a large pasture that ran up to what is known as the Loomis Pinnacle. This pinnacle is one of the highest elevations around this part of the country."

On the east side of the Swamp Road stood the large cattle and hay barn and several smaller sheds. A horse barn stood south of the larger barn and near it the hop house.

The Loomises continued to raise the best horses, cattle and sheep in the area. They were also exceptionally fond of dogs, and the large numbers in the yard frequently annoyed visitors and travelers. A man riding on horseback past the Loomis home was set upon by a hound and carried the imprint of its fangs in his boot.

Some time later the sixteen year old son of Horace Terry, a near neighbor, and several companions were hunting in the woods on the Loomis farm. This same hound sprang upon Terry and brought him to the ground. Another hound, a slut, joined in the attack and it took the other boys several minutes to beat off the dogs and rescue their friend.

When Horace Terry informed Loomis of his son's wounds and suggested that something should be done about the vicious hounds, Loomis declared, "I wish my dogs had eaten him up."

Terry brought suit against his neighbor in Justice's Court. Loomis pleaded innocent, pointing out that he had warned the neighboring boys that the slut had puppies in a log in the woods. A jury found a verdict of fifteen dollars for young Terry. Loomis appealed the case, but the verdict was upheld by the Supreme Court in 1837.

On June 18 of that same year the barn of Captain Stephen Leonard of Sangerfield burned to the ground. Leonard, the man to whom the Loomises had given a counterfeit bill several years earlier, had George indicted for arson. After pleading innocent and posting $1,000 bail, George absented himself from so many sessions of court that the District Attorney finally ordered the indictment "to be no longer prosecuted and a nolle prosqui entered." This policy of sacrificing large sums of money in bail in order to avoid a conviction was followed consistently by the family for many years.

CHAPTER II

THE LOOMISES AT HOME

The Loomis children were fitted by background and training for careers of crime which many of them were to follow. Rhoda, who never forgot she had taught school, insisted that each child get the best formal education possible, but she managed to counteract the instruction of the schools by instilling into the minds of her children certain ideas that she had inherited from her father.

The children attended the district school, in Terrytown, a short distance north of their home. Former teachers found them "bright, intelligent children, no different than any other pupils," and "well-mannered and good students." Young Wash became a favorite with his schoolmasters.

Thomas L. Hall of Smith's Valley, Madison County historian emeritus, related what Wash often told his intimate friends about his boyhood. "We went to school when we pleased and stayed out when we pleased. We sometimes traded little things like boys do, and learned quickly to deceive and cheat. Mother smiled approval when she learned of what we did and told us not to get caught nor to allow anyone to get the better of us. We were always supposed to seize the advantage. When we stole little things, Mother approved. As long as we were not caught, she said it was all right. If we got caught, we got licked."

"Mother was always quick to reward us for our cleverness and was unusually severe in punishing our mistakes," Wash also said. "She ruled the household implacably. We children had to obey her and Father was dominated by her. We soon learned obedience to him was a matter of choice. If he wanted us to work on the farm, but we wanted to go fishing instead, we went to Mother. She made him let us have our way."

Older residents of the Valley agreed that the father was ignored by his wife and children. "He (George Loomis) was a genial old man, who was always joking with the young folks and twitting them of their love affairs," Constable James L. Filkins, their most bitter enemy, recalled. "In the fall his pockets were filled with fruit which he distributed liberally."

Rhoda's main ambition was to mould her sons into leaders who would be influential in the town. Her chief hopes were pinned upon Wash, who showed unusual brilliance as an organizer and leader. When his school days were over Rhoda sent him to Hamilton to study law under Judge James B. Eldridge. Though Wash never tried for the bar theoretical knowledge of law proved invaluable in guiding the family through troublesome years.

"We can try a case, but there is no one who can plan it like Wash," remarked J. Thomas Spriggs of Utica, the Loomis family lawyer.

"Wash was a genius," Filkins admitted grudgingly . "He could train a witness in manufactured evidence until he actually made him believe that he was telling the truth."

"Wash was a fine looking man about five feet ten inches tall with blue eyes and jet black hair, black chin whiskers," Fitch jotted down in his picturesque style. "(He) always dressed in broad cloth clothes and high top boots, broad brimmed hat such as cowboys wore on ranches. He was a smart man in every sense of the word and more of a gentleman there never was born in any place. No rough language came out of him. When he looked at a person he could pretty well tell what kind of a person it was."

Wash's magnetic personality attracted many people. "Few could resist the fascination of his manners and conversation," Amos Cummings wrote in The New York Weekly Sun of May 21, 1879. "He was a born diplomat and never resorted to physical force when his ends could be obtained any other way. Among his brothers and sisters, his word was law.

He dressed with exquisite neatness, sported the finest turnout in the country, attended all rural dances and festivals, and was a general favorite with the fair sex."

Fitch recorded in his journal over 135 years ago this story of how Wash acted as an attorney:

"I will tell you one little circumstance that happened to a man by the name of Thomas. He had been in our little village one Fourth of July and while he got a little too much to drink and got a little noisy, so much so, the Constable arrested him and brought him before the Justice. He was pretty drunk, so the Justice told the Constable to take care of the prisoner until morning, then bring him before him in the morning.

"Wash happened to be over to town and saw Thomas and talked with him a little while and Thomas asked Loomis to act as counsel for him. Loomis told him he would if you will keep still and let me do the talking and do as I tell you.

"Thomas says all right, I will keep still.

"They brought him before the Justice and the Justice says, Mr. Thomas you're under arrest for public intoxication. What do you plead to the charge?

"Loomis steps up and says, your honor this man pleads guilty and asks the mercy of the court in his behalf. Your honor this man has done no wrong. Yesterday was Independence Day. This man left his home to celebrate the Independence of our forefathers, and it's a glorious thing to do, something that every American citizen ought to do and no doubt but what he drank too much and perhaps made some noise. I have inquired of the boys about this man and they tell me he has not made a very great amount of noise.

"Your honor this poor man has got a wife and several small children at home. They need every penny that he has got to keep them comfortable. If you fine this man you will take the bread from those poor children. If you send him to jail for a length of time his family will suffer. By that, therefore I ask for the discharge of the prisoner believing that its right and just so this poor man, and Madison County will not be any poorer by your doing so.

"Mr. Thomas have I told everything as it is and if you are discharged you will go home to your family? The Justice says, Mr. Thomas you are discharged. Mr. Loomis says in behalf of the prisoner, I thank you for him also."

Fitch, who either knew very little about punctuation, or cared less, wrote honestly. He added this note to the story:

"For myself I myself do not like to see a man drunk. That was good for Washington. I don't think I ever saw one of the Loomises drunk. They were a pretty temperate lot of men."

Bill, the eldest son, married the daughter of a Higginsville farmer and purchased a place on the west bank of the Side Cut Canal in the Town of Verona. Short and stocky, with a rugged face, thick black hair and full beard and mustache, he lacked the swift energy of Wash and Grove. He probably would liked to have broken his family ties, but they held him in bondage.

Grove's natural fearlessness and daring won him the admiration of the gang, but his ready fists often involved him in trouble. Women succumbed easily to his twinkling blue eyes and glib tongue. "Grove never knew one half as much as Wash," Fitch commented. "He was more of a dude. He was a fine-looking man with black, curly hair, black whiskers, wore patent leather boots or shoes; black coat and pants, a white vest or fancy plaid ruffled shift front, wore a large ring and studs in his shirt. (He) drove a black team of stallions (hitched) to a yellow-geared buggy. He tried to fill Wash's place but could not half do it."

Amos Plumb possessed a deceptive personality. His friends remember him as a genial man with a sense of humor who would do anything for someone he liked. George L. Loomis of Willowvale, a grandson, wrote: "Mother often said Plumb was the most generous and kind-hearted man she ever knew."

W. H. Weller, a Waterville lawyer who defended Plumb on several occasions, said, "Plumb had a cold, steely and expressionless eye and a poker face." His enemies said he was dour and possessed artful, childish cunning. "There is no dependence to be placed upon his word of honor," Filkins stated, "and in a pinch he will show the white feather." Fitch said, "He was a different man than Grove and Wash. (He) was not so much of a gentleman as they were (and) was rougher in every sense. I think he was a great coward."

Wheeler Theodore, probably the least known of the brothers, fled to Canada in 1863 after being indicted by a Madison County grand jury for the rape of a fourteen-year-old girl. He lived under the name of Theodore L. Wheeler in Alexandria, Ontario, where he died on March 20, 1911.

"Hiram Denio, the youngest son, was named after an eminent judge of the old Court of Appeals." "No blame can be put on him," Mulligan wrote. "He did as his elders told him." Neighbors in Bardeen's Corners, where he spent his later years, described him as "a tall, fair-haired man with a mustache, who always rode horseback."

Rhoda's four daughters had inherited some of her beauty. Their strict training showed in the erectness of their carriage and the way they held their heads. At dances and other socials they ignored comments caused by their low-cut dresses. They climbed stairways without glancing to see if their ankles were covered from sight of the town rabble. They enjoyed the furor they aroused, but were clever enough to pretend unconcern.

Rhoda sent them to Whitestown Seminary, where Lucia, Charlotte and Calista showed considerable musical talent. While attending the Seminary, Calista met a young attorney named William O. Merrill, whom she married. She died at their home in Whitestown in 1853 at the age of 37, leaving two children, William and Maria. Lucia married Charles Edwards, a Waterville farmer. She died in 1858 and her only son, Charles, passed away the following year. Mary Charlotte married Asa Collins and spent most of her life in Pittsford, Vermont. She had two children, Grove and Grace.

Maria Cornelia, who never married, possessed the same domineering qualities of her mother and Wash, but lacked their initiative. Mrs. Anna Collins, her niece, described her as a "tall, raw-boned woman, with a voice like a man," who "often dressed in men's clothing at night when she went out." Cornelia detested housework. Nicknamed the "Outlaw Queen," she did her best to live up to the title. She had her hair cut short, rode horses astride and liked the out-of-doors. She also possessed good taste in clothing, but the dresses, hats and shawls did not become her.

Life must have been pleasant for the Loomis family when all the children lived at home. While neighboring farmers and their wives labored from sunrise to sunset and found time only for church and its activities and an occasional singing or spelling bee, the Loomis children rode their fine horses about the countryside, gaining friends and making mental notes of farmers and merchants who seemed to be prospering.

The homestead literally overflowed with guests. It was not unusual for twelve or more young people to arrive early and stay for both dinner and supper. Rhoda served good, hearty meals. Noonday dinner usually consisted of a plentiful variety, according to Hall. There were "potatoes, turnips, baked squash, corned beef, boiled ham, sweet apples, white pot (custard), black applesauce, maple sugar for sweetin', a porringer of maple syrup, eight or nine mince pies piled on top the other, hasty pudding, nutcakes and cheese — all washed down with steaming cups of tea, barley coffee, or milk."

The family, particularly Rhoda, must have enjoyed entertaining the young people. According to Cummings she used the gatherings as a classroom for corrupting the morals of the guests. "One of her sons-in-law says that she has set her face against all wrong doing," he wrote, "but this does not agree with accounts given by neighbors. They accuse her of inciting young visitors to petty peculations and crime.

They were led to them by Walsh, who invited them to ride behind his fast horses and studied their characters. If they were licentious, the attraction was blooming girls, who had been brought to the mansion as servants on the promise of good wages and started upon an infamous career. If they were given to drink, the best liquors were set before them. When they were about to leave the house, the old lady would place a hand on their arm and say: Now don't come back without stealing something, if it's nothing but a jackknife.'

"The first time they might return with the carcass of a sheep or lamb or a tub of butter. Their dexterity was praised and the fruits of the marauding were placed upon the table.

"Sometimes they served as pickets and gave timely warning of the approach of the law. The most of the thieving and barn burning is done by these young rascals, the Loomises acting as receivers and disposers of the stolen goods. They do the planning and their young pals carry out the work."

Wash Loomis was only twenty-one when he and a friend, Riley Ramsdell of North Brookfield or Nigger City, as it was more widely known, were arrested for stealing a receipt for seven dollars from Joseph Shepard of Marshall. A jury found both youths guilty, but the Loomises, by using obstructive tactics and forfeiting fourteen hundred dollars in bail, carried the case to the Supreme Court, which reversed the decision of the lower courts and the young men went free.

In building up their gang the Loomises drew no color line. Like the majority of residents of the Valley, they opposed slavery, and permitted escaped slaves to live in their old home on the hill. Two of these colored members of the gang, Salem and Dick Loucks, gained considerable notoriety as horse thieves.

Salem Loucks was in his teens when Constable Henry Keith of Brookfield and a posse eluded the pickets on the pinnacle and surrounded the homestead at dead of night. Keith went up on the front porch and rapped loudly on the locked door. After an interval a glow from a lamp appeared inside. The door opened slightly to reveal Mrs. Loomis and Cornelia in their night clothes.

The constable identified himself and said he had a warrant for Salem Loucks' arrest. The women denied that the young horse thief was in the house and refused Keith permission to search the building. Cornelia came out and sat down on the step, apparently thinking nothing of her modesty.

"You're not going to search our house," she declared.

Keith, certain that the Negro was in the house, cautioned his men to guard every window and door. One of the officers shouted that Loucks was escaping. Two of the Loomis girls, with a Negro between them, were headed towards the Swamp. When Keith made a grab for him, one of the girls blew out his lantern. The posse hemmed in the trio, only to discover that the Negro the girls were escorting was a stranger. In the meantime Salem Loucks had escaped.

Keith, a conscientious little man with a purposeful chin and a red wig several sizes too large, returned to his hotel in Brookfield and bided his time.

His opportunity came sooner than he expected. The Valley was feeling the first flush of prosperity that came with hop growing. An Englishman, Benjamin Wimble, had set out the first hop yard on the land of Jotham Tower of Sangerfield in 1821. After several years local hops caught on in the international trade. Raising hops was like sitting in on a big poker game. Fortunes were made or lost on the turn of the market. As might be expected the Loomises grew hops. Their chief competitors were the Terrys, Risleys and Abbeys.

Good harvests were celebrated by barn dances known as hop digs, which drew the young people from all over the Valley. In October, 1847 Allen, Edwin and Ira Abbey held a big hop dig in Ira's big barn, which stood along the Swamp Road some two miles south of the Loomis farm. The Loomis boys and some of their young friends drove over to take part in the festivities. They found the Abbey barn crowded with young and old, most of them dancing to the lively tunes of a fiddler. A good time was being enjoyed by all until Grove Loomis started dancing with Sarah Avery, thus stirring the jealousy of Allen Abbey.

Wash Loomis later said he "didn't think there would have been any difficulty that night if he (Allen Abbey) had not struck Grove Loomis first."

The fight soon became a free-for-all. David Loomis, a kin of the family but no friend, went after Wheeler Loomis with his fists swinging. Wheeler knocked him down and as he tried to get up, knocked him down again. Chairs and clubs were swung with telling effect. One of the Loomis gang hit Allen Abbey on the head with a club and he fell at Grove's feet, whereupon that dandy stomped on him with his boots, leaving him bloody and unconscious.

David Loomis and Allen Abbey swore out warrants against Wheeler and Grove, charging them with assault and battery with intent to kill.

Constable Keith had no trouble arresting Grove, but Wheeler could not be found. On a hunch Keith went to the Loomis farm one night with a small posse.

"The pickets on the hill watched our approach and warned the family," Keith related. "When we arrived the doors of the house were bolted. I knocked on the door and when it was opened I saw Mrs. Loomis and Cornelia. They assured me Wheeler was not in the house and would not allow me to search. I had no authority to break open the doors, and had I done so without finding my man, I would have been punished, through the family's influence with the law. I decided to resort to strategy. I rubbed some mud on the shoulder of one of my posse, who knocked on the door and asked for help. The old lady Loomis took a light and surveyed the newcomer through the window. My man said he was a traveler who had been thrown from his wagon and hurt badly. The mud on his shoulder bore out this story. The kind-hearted old lady told him if he would come in she would rub some camphor on his bruises and give him some whiskey. The door was opened and my party and I rushed into the house. We searched from garret to the cellar without finding a trace of Wheeler. As we were descending the stairs near the sitting room, Cornelia told me to watch out for the paint. The stairs were boarded up and the boards covered with fresh blue paint. I detected an uneven crack at the bottom of one of the boards. My curiosity was aroused, so I pulled off the boards. There stood Wheeler, confused and sheepish. I served the warrant and bundled him off to the office of the justice."

Grove and Wheeler were arraigned in Morrisville, the county seat of Madison County, on charges of assault and battery with intent to kill. The Loomis lawyers, taking advantage of loop holes in the law, succeeded in gaining continuous postponements, while the family's activities kept them busy.

As villages and cities in Central New York were being linked more closely by the new corduroy roads, a wave of burglaries brought terror to the Valley. Tollgates were burglarized, homes and stores were entered and ransacked. Under cover of night, sheep, cattle and horses were driven from their owners' barns and pastures. A housewife who left her washing out on the line would find it missing in the morning.

Only the property of the Loomis family and their close associates seemed to be immune. As the law officers remained inactive the farmers decided to take matters into their own hands. Late one afternoon in the latter part of December, 1848 several sleigh-loads of armed men surrounded the Loomis homestead and forced an entrance. Ignoring threats they began a systematic search of the premises while the family was held under guard.

Concealed trapdoors were found in several of the rooms. Large stores of dress goods, umbrellas, furs, buffalo robes, shovels and other merchandise were taken from closets. Similar hiding places in the barns uncovered whiffle trees, neck yokes, harnesses, saddles and log chains. A bobsleigh filled with loot was taken to Waterville for identification.

At the Court of Oyer and Terminer in Rome the Loomises were charged with stealing over one hundred dollars worth of dress goods, fringes and silk from Jacob Loak of Sangerfield Center. Wash was indicted for burglary on charges that he had entered the carriage house of Daniel C. Douglas of the Center and stolen two buffalo robes and a saddle.

These cases, together with those of Wheeler and Grove, dragged along for over two years, while lawyers wrangled and witnesses failed to appear. Indictment after indictment was dropped until only one remained, a charge against Wash for riot. The final straw was broken when the Loomis attorney claimed he could not produce Wash, for that individual had left the state. Judge Mason ordered the indictment dropped in Madison County, while the Oneida County case was filed away in Utica with the pencilled notation, "Absconded."

CHAPTER III

WASH LOOMIS GOES WEST

Wash Loomis and his friend, Riley Ramsdell were among the eighteen men who left the Chenango Valley at various times during 1849 to seek their fortunes in the California gold fields.

Gold was discovered at Sutter's Fort on the Sacramento River on January 24, 1848 by James Marshall and the news spread like the wind around the world.

Among the first to leave the Valley were Alfred, Charles C. and Leander Terry, neighbors of the Loomis family. They were three of the seven sons of Mr. and Mrs. Horace Terry. The brothers booked passage on a sailing vessel and went around Cape Horn to reach California. Later they went north to Washington Territory and settled on Alki Point, which was later a part of Seattle. They became prominent businessmen, and Charles Terry was a member of the first territorial legislature in 1854.

Descendants of the Loomis family as well as many of their neighbors claim that before Wash Loomis started for California, he was engaged to Anna Mason, the daughter of Edward Mason, a neighbor and gave her several thousand dollars. This money was hidden in a jar in the orchard on the hill. Later, Anna dug up the money and her family used it. She and Wash never married.

Loomis and Ramsdell walked a greater part of the way to California, according to John Mulligan, who heard a few meagre details from Ramsdell many years after he returned to the valley. Mulligan was driving his team along a valley road one day and picked him up.

"I gave him a ride on my outfit one morning," Mulligan recalled. "He talked all the way and I did not ask questions."

"At St. Joseph, Missouri, Loomis and Mr. Ramsdell hired out as drivers on an overland bull train, and it was necessary to walk. Mr. Ramsdell told me that in a short time their feet became so sore that the foreman of the train shod them in Indian moccasins. Their feet became calloused and gave them no further trouble," he said.

The trip west was undoubtedly similar to that of other gold seekers. The wagon train made its way through the land of the hostile Pawnees, was ferried across the Kansas River by ropes and huge logs attached to the wagons and headed for Fort Kearney. Sometimes they passed other caravans, many of which contained a number of women. Graves with grim guideposts of boards adorned with buffalo skulls marked the edge of the trail.

When the overloaded wagons began to tell on the oxen and mules, furniture and other unessential goods were abandoned beside the trail.

In a few weeks the train pulled into the recently established military post, Fort Kearney. The post with its ten adobe houses was a welcome sight. Here the wagons were repaired and supplies were replenished before the journey continued.

The wagon train passed unmolested through the lands of the Sioux and Cheyennes as these tribes were not on the warpath. Huge herds of buffalo were seen as the train moved slowly from the lowlands to the high tablelands and then across the snow-tipped Rockies.

Evidently when the train on which Wash Loomis and Ramsdell worked reached Sacramento, the two men went their separate ways. Mulligan said he failed to ask Ramsdell what had occurred in the gold fields.

"I do not know how long Wash stayed there, but the story was that he became involved in horse stealing which hastened his return. It was claimed the authorities trailed him all the way back to the Nine-Mile Swamp where his powerful legal backing would allow them to do nothing," Mulligan remarked.

"Wash remained in California several years," Amos Cummings wrote for his Weekly Sun history of the Loomis family, thirty years after the California trip. "At one time it was reported that he had been hanged by a Vigilante Committee. He returned from California before the death of his father. His return is said to have been accelerated by a dispute with one Burns over some pastureland. There were high words.

" 'Are you fixed?' asked Burns.

" 'I am,' Wash replied.

" 'All set,' said Burns, 'let's go out and settle it.'

"They drew their revolvers and went out. On the way Wash tried to settle the dispute by shooting Burns in the side. The wound was a slight one, but Wash's treachery told upon the community. They gave chase with a rope. He escaped into a canyon road and was followed by a friend on horseback. Wash rode the pony over two hundred miles pursued by Burns' comrades. It was even asserted that they tracked him to New York."

Older friends of the Loomis family claim it was Delos McIntyre, who came from Coontown, a small hamlet near Leonardsville, who was the "friend" mentioned by Cummings.

According to the stories, McIntyre wrote home that he was returning with a miner who had struck it rich. Delos did return, but alone. He had two bags of gold and a rope burn around his neck which he always tried to hide with high collars.

Edward Lee Terry of Manlius, a nephew of the Terry brothers, disclosed that Wash had told his father, Everett Terry, a neighbor and friend, as well as his Uncle Carl Terry, that he was at Lake Washington at a mill selling whiskey to Indians in trade for furs, which was against the law.

"Another fellow came butting in," Terry said and "Wash said, 'Get the hell out of here.' "

"One word led to another and finally it came to a showdown, and Wash shot the man," Terry recalled. "Wash had to leave that area in a hurry."

Wash's nephew, Grove Loomis Collins, and some of the family's neighbors, claim Loomis and Leander Terry went into business together in Seattle. Wash is supposed to have given his share of the firm to Terry when he returned east. Lee Terry also returned to Sangerfield and remained there.

The date Wash returned is not known. Mrs. Julia Benton Mason, a neighbor, who remembered his returning, "He rode a beautiful mare which he called the California Mare, and had a bag of gold. Wash claimed he rode the mare all the way from California."

Fitch recorded in his journal shortly after the event, "In 1849 he went to California. That was the time gold was discovered there. Quite a large number went there at that time. I don't think Wash dug much gold while he was there. I have been told he had to leave there for stealing horses and cattle. They done so much such work stealing, the boys hunted them and drove them from the country. Several got hanged to some tree, but Wash was smart to get away with a whole hide and came back home where he lived until he was murdered," he said.

Wash Loomis brought a touch of the western cowboy back with him in addition to his gold, according to Fitch. "One day I had been over in the swamp and I met Wash riding a mule. He had on a Mexican saddle and bridle with a lariat on the mule's back.

"He was coming down a hill and the crupper had broken and the mule tried to buck with him and got the saddle up on his neck. That left Wash off over his head and down went the mule all in a heap. Wash says 'that mule makes me think of my brother, Plumb. He is always getting into trouble and does not know how to get out.' "

Many years later while in the Madison County Jail at Morrisville awaiting trial, Wash told Deputy John E. Clark of Erieville that when he went west, he traveled north to Oregon and had been a member of the Territorial Legislature when it was first organized. He told others he was a member of the Washington Territorial Legislature.

Wash was doing some wishful thinking, for his name does not appear on the records of either legislature.

CHAPTER IV

CORNELIA LIKED MUFFS

The family carried on nobly during Wash's absence. The girls kept themselves in the spotlight through escapades which lent spice to stories men told in the taverns and caused the women to gossip over their teacups.

Cornelia, in particular, seemed to enjoy flouting the mores of the community. She stole things here and there and tried to bask in the notoriety gained by her parents and brothers. A major part of her escapades were recorded by early newspaper historians. A consensus of opinion of her victims' descendants, as well as older residents who knew her, indicate that the stories are true.

Cornelia often discarded the men's clothes she wore for frills and furbelows and accompanied her brothers to dances and other social gatherings. Old timers remembered having seen her at dances in various communities.

While attending a dance in Clarkville (Brookfield) one evening she became enraged when rudely snubbed by most of the young ladies who were present, and decided to get even with them. She confided her plan to Grove and a moment later they were on the floor dancing. After making certain that no one was watching, Cornelia and Grove danced up to the door of the cloakroom. She slipped from her brother's arms and went inside. While Grove watched to give warning she selected two expensive muffs from a pile on a table. Raising her skirts waist high she quickly pulled a muff up over each leg. After re-arranging her clothes she returned to Grove and continued their dance.

A group of men were discussing the mystery of the stolen muffs a few days later in a Deansboro tavern. One of them, a hostler, chanced to glance out the window. He called the others to look at Cornelia Loomis being driven past by one of her brothers. The hem of her dress had become caught and a good portion of her leg was exposed.

A low whistle of admiration issued from the hostler's lips. "Speaking of those muffs," he said, "I don't think the searchers looked in the right place. If they had looked on that girl's legs, they might have found them."

Encouraged by the ease in which she had taken the muffs, Cornelia repeated the trick at the Central Square House in Central Square and the Madison Hotel in Madison and at several other parties.

R. E. Van Dyke of Stratford, Vermont, who once lived in the Valley, wrote: "Before my mother was married she, with eighteen or twenty girls and as many fellows, were out to a country party one night. The lady of the house gave the girls a large bedroom upstairs in which to take off their things and pile them on the bed, dresser and chairs. In those days every girl or woman carried a muff. If you didn't have a muff you weren't in style. When the party broke up around two in the morning, a number of the girls couldn't find their muffs. They hunted high and low. Finally one girl, a little older and bolder than the rest, went around and pulled up the dress and petticoat of one of the Loomis girls and beheld that she had four or five muffs on each leg. She shoved her over backwards on the bed and called two girls to hold her hands and other girls held her feet so she couldn't kick. They disrobed her of the muffs and then led her to the door and shoved her out. That ended the Loomis girl going to any more parties."

At a dance in Hubbardsville that Cornelia and Charlotte attended, four muffs were found missing from the cloakroom. A search was demanded. When the time came for the Loomis girls to disrobe, they revealed where they had hidden the muffs.

According to Thomas L. Hall, Cornelia walked into a Waterville dry goods emporium one afternoon and asked the clerk if she might see the latest muffs and boas. Unaware of the identity of his customer, the clerk displayed several fur pieces.

"They are the latest we have," he said. "We got them from New York this week."

"They are nice," Cornelia admitted, "but they are not exactly what I have been looking for. I guess I will have to think it over. Noticing some bolts of cloth on the shelves at the rear of the store she said, "My mother asked me to bring home some samples of gingham. Would you give me a few snatches of your latest?"

While the clerk obliged, Cornelia picked up the best-looking muff, bent over, and pulled it up on her leg. When the clerk returned she smiled at him and said, "I'm sorry I caused you so much trouble."

After Cornelia departed with the samples of gingham, the clerk discovered that a muff was missing, so he rushed to see Constable Aurelius (Bill) Benedict.

"That was Cornelia Loomis up to her old tricks," the constable said with a laugh. "If she hasn't left town, I'll try to get your muff back."

Cornelia, indignant when Benedict took her into custody, loudly protested her innocence. "Where are you taking me?" she asked.

"To the lock-up."

"I won't go."

"Yes, you will, even if I have to drag you."

"My brothers will kill you when they hear of this," Cornelia cried.

Ignoring the threats the constable took her to the lock-up, where two women searched her and found the muff. The clerk failed to press charges, so she was released.

Wash came back to face the old charge of stealing Douglas' robe and saddle. The case staggered along, for over a year and was finally ended by the death of Douglas and Wash went free.

Bill was not so fortunate. Accused of grand larceny, he was tried in the new courthouse on John Street in Utica, where the Loomises encountered an opponent who was to prove a thorn in their sides for years. Roscoe Conkling, the newly appointed district attorney, was a tall, handsome, blond, curly-haired youth of twenty-one. He argued his case so successfully that the Court sentenced Bill "to be confined in the county jail two months and to pay a fine of seventy-five dollars and to stand committed to the county jail until paid not exceeding six months after the expiration of the first two months."

Old George Loomis, who had added several parcels of land to his farm during the intervening years and had also purchased 129½ acres at Bardeen's Corners, Oswego County, did not live long enough to see his family reach their destiny. He died on February 26, 1851 at the age of seventy-one and was buried at Sangerfield Center. No headstone was ever erected to mark his grave. Wash supplied the only vocal epitaph, according to Hall: "Our father was a good Christian man. I think he was glad when his time came for many reasons. Mother ruled us and ruled him. There was no peace. When he tried to have his way as any man should, it brought on an argument. Towards the end he grew very tired." As the father died without a will, the property went to his ten children.

The operations of the family were apparently expanding rapidly. Bill Loomis, after his release from jail, spent considerable time traveling about the countryside on business. Residents were suspicious of the friendly "visits," according to numerous stories collected by Mrs. Charles Ruggles of Oneida from older residents of that area. "Despite his pleasing personality and the good prices he paid for the horses and cattle he wanted, the farmers and tradespeople at whose homes he would stop to eat or stay at night spoke guardedly in his presence. It probably was more than coincidence that after one of his trips J. J. Knox's general store at Knoxboro was entered and hundreds of pounds of flour were taken. On Stockbridge East Hill a thief entered through an unlocked window of a farmer's home, shortly after Bill departed, and took a wolf skin robe. The robe, with fourteen others, was later found in the Loomis home. Bill was often accused, but never arrested for actually participating in these crimes. 'I never take things,' he said a number of times, 'but I can hide them where God himself couldn't find them.' "

During the autumn of 1852, while Bill was on one of his trips through the Oneida Lake section buying cattle, he had supper at the Burdick farm and spent the night there. He and his host's daughter, Martha Ann, were attracted to each other. He returned to court her, and they were married on February 11, 1853. They went to live on a farm on the Pine Plains, on the west bank of the Oneida Lake Canal, a wild and lonely area a few miles north of Higginsville. Property deeds reveal that Martha Ann paid Peter and Catherine Gerber $200 for five acres on May 20, 1856. Subsequent purchases until 1865 gave the farm 236 acres.

The Loomises remembered that Bill had served two months in jail and apparently blamed Reuben Wygart, the Verona farmer whose testimony had sent him there. When a brown mare valued at $100 was stolen from Wygart, Bill and Grove were indicted for grand larceny. Spriggs, their lawyer, gained a postponement of the trial and acted as surety on $1,000 bail. Court records from Oneida County show no conviction.

Cummings wrote: "The evidence against William seemed conclusive. He was seen with the mare, and the animal was found on the Loomis farm. Wygart and the best judges of horses in the country fully identified her. The Loomises pretended and proved by respectable witness that they bought her of one Bush. The people, however, were confident that there could be no mistake . . . For once one of the gang was caught 'dead to rights.' Dr. Preston (his cousin) said: "Bill I've often told you there'd be an end to your halter. They've got you this time.' "

" 'You wait,' William answered. 'I've got the books at home to tell exactly where the Wygart mare is.' "

The ending of the story has been supplied by Hall: "On the day of the trial the real Wygart mare ran up the lane leading to the Wygart barnyard. She was brought to Morrisville, where court was in session, and resembled the mare taken from the Loomis farm so closely that her owner could not detect the difference. She really had been stolen by some of the gang and run down into Pennsylvania. Grove Loomis recovered her in time to prevent his brother's conviction."

The Loomises, to revenge the arrest of Bill and Grove, brought a series of damage suits against Wygart, who lost everything in the long court sessions that followed. Reduced to penury, he loaded his family and remaining possessions on a train and went west, hoping to make a start where there was no Loomis gang.

Bill's youngest daughter, Helen Louisa, who became Mrs. Kelly Hyland said her father liked nothing better than to hold his children on his lap and let them read to him. She said he was particularly fond of "The Indian's Lament" from, "The Third Reader." According to her the children knew nothing of the doings of the gang. She also denied her father had ever resided in Bardeen's Corners, though Mr. and Mrs. Arthur Dunn said the Loomises once resided on their farm and Mrs. Loomis gave birth to one of her children there. Mrs. Dunn recalled her mother acted as mid-wife and like most expectant fathers, Bill "just disappeared" and did not return until the ordeal was over.

Confirmation of these statements came later, when Bill was arrested for passing counterfeit money. Several of his friends from Bardeen's Corner's came to testify as character witnesses at the trial. Miss Minnie E. Ladd of Oneida said: "My father Joseph Ladd, who was only seventeen, was one of those who went. They had to tell that Bill had behaved himself while in their neighborhood and was a good citizen."

CHAPTER V

ALBANY MONEY

The panic of 1857 led to a wave of counterfeit money during the following year. Taking advantage of the fact that there was no national currency, the Loomises began to deal in counterfeit bills issued by Albany counterfeiters. "Albany money became a by-word for counterfeit," Mulligan stated.

Grove Loomis spent a few days in Utica early in January and apparently had no difficulty in disposing of some counterfeit bills which were bad imitations of Onondaga Bank and Housatonic Bank issues, so he pursuaded Jane Barber, a notorious acquaintance, to aid him in their distribution. During the next few weeks they separately worked various sections of the city. Each night they would meet to count their profits.

All was moving smoothly until February 25th, when Jane gave a grocer one of Grove's bills in payment for a half pound of tea. The grocer sent the bill to the Oneida Bank, where it was pronounced counterfeit. He also gave the police a good description of Jane. Deputy George Klinck arrested her. At her examination several shopkeepers identified her as the woman who had given them similar counterfeit bills. The Recorder cajoled her into revealing the name of her accomplice.

Klinck, armed with a search warrant, drove down to the Loomis farm. The family received him courteously and allowed him to search the house and premises. He recovered several articles Grove had purchasd with the counterfeit bills and appropriated a few documents which he believed could be used as evidence. He found no trace of Grove.

Several weeks elapsed before Klinck learned that Grove was staying in Oriskany Falls at the Sargent House, a rambling frame structure on the corner of Main Street and Schoolhouse Hill. He sent a process to Officer Benjamin H. Peebles of that village to serve. Grove tried to escape over the enclosed runway connecting the hotel with the Opera House, but Peebles grappled with him and slipped handcuffs over his wrists. An excited crowd gathered and some of Grove's friends threatened to attempt a rescue, whereupon Peebles said he would shoot anyone who tried to interfere while he escorted his prisoner to the lock-up in the Engine House. Grove was relieved of a Colt revolver, a counterfeit bill and several good bills. Peebles notified Klinck of the capture and sat down to await his arrival.

Julius Glazier, a friend of the Loomises who resided in the village, rode swiftly to Sangerfield to inform the family. Historian Hall offered this version of a folk tale which has been repeated in the Valley for over three quarters of a century:

"When Wash was told of Grove's arrest he flew into a rage. 'He's a damn fool,' he cried. 'I wonder if he had sense enough to get rid of the long green he was carrying in his boots?"

"The informer said he didn't think so.

" 'Saddle the California mare, Plumb,' Wash ordered. 'I'm going over and see if they've found that money on Grove.'

"Upon arriving at Oriskany Falls, Wash went immediately to the lock-up where Grove was held. The officer in charge refused at first to let him in. Wash was so persistent he was finally admitted.

" 'What the hell do you mean stealing my boots and leaving your old cowhide ones?' he demanded, advancing upon the cell. The officer who was watching went out.

"It took only a minute for the brothers to exchange their footwear. On his way home Wash turned the mare into a concealing clump of bushes. Dismounting, he pulled the boots from his feet. The double tops were packed with counterfeit bills."

Klinck took Grove to Utica, where he was brought before the Recorder on charges of passing counterfeit bills. A clerk from the Oneida Bank testified that the bills were counterfeit. "I am well-acquainted with the genuine bills of the bank," he said. "The characteristics of these bills that stamp them as counterfeit are the paper on which they are printed, as well as their general appearance. The engraving is poor, but a good imitation of the genuine. The signatures are also very good imitations and if signed to a draft of the genuine plate would not attract any attention of being forgery."

After William Holden, a clerk and William Smith, drygoods merchant, identified Grove, the Recorder set bail at $3,500 on the two counts. Grove, unable to post that amount, was locked up in the Mohawk Street jail. Two more complaints against him boosted the bail to $5,500. As the Loomises could raise only $3,500, they could not get him out of jail.

The prisoner, unhappy over his confinement, sought means of escape. A loose stone in the wall caught his eye. He found it easily removable. He confided this information to other prisoners, who agreed to help him tunnel through the wall. Using plates and spoons for tools, they made rapid headway until the jailer became suspicious. He entered the basement with drawn pistol and ordered the men back to their cells. He put fetters on Grove. Loomis later wrote a letter of protest to Sheriff Hall, pleading for sympathy.

The Loomises heard of this new development from The Utica Morning Herald and decided to make a move. They knew that the counterfeit bills were to be presented in court by District Attorney Jairus Munger. If the damaging evidence could be removed George stood a chance of being acquitted. In some way they learned that Munger was carrying the bills on his person.

They also knew that Munger, who resided in Camden, spent evenings in unlicensed saloons, playing cards with friends. Wash and Bill went to Camden "on business" on April 8. That evening Munger and his friends were playing cards in the back room of an illicit saloon. The game broke up about midnight and Munger started for home. When he was some distance from the business section, two shadowy figures emerged from the darkness and leaped on him. A noose was tossed over his head. As he struggled, the rope tightened until he lost consciousness.

When he regained his senses his attackers had fled. He reached instinctively for the pocketbook which contained the evidence against Grove Loomis. It was gone! He awakened a deputy sheriff and reported all that had happened to him, stating that although he had failed to see his assailants, he was positive they were Loomises, for nothing but the counterfeit money and eleven dollars of his own had been taken. Warrants were issued for the arrest of Wash and Bill Loomis.

Klinck found Bill loitering around the Utica depot and took him into custody. After arraignment he was remanded to jail to await the action of the grand jury in Rome on a charge of highway robbery. The grand jury failed to find the indictment and Bill was released. Wash managed to elude the authorities.

The Loomises, concerned over Grove's fate, sent Spriggs and Pomeroy, their lawyers, to make another application to have Grove admitted to bail. By this time the amount had gone up to $8,500, but Spriggs produced it and the judge let Grove out.

His arraignment on eight indictments came up on June 19 but, much to the disappointment of curiosity seekers, Grove failed to appear. Jane Barber was also arraigned, but the Court considered the evidence against her to be insufficient and she was released.

The Herald, sure that the Loomises would not forfeit their money, confidently expected Grove to appear at their next session, but he stayed away.

In the meantime Bill was carrying on for the family. The Herald, after reporting that a man named Charles Robbins had appeared to swear out an affidavit accusing Bill and Jesse

Hitchings of Higginsville of passing counterfeit money, said: "While at the latter place, according to his statement, Loomis and Hitchings made overtures to him to go into the counterfeiting business, the twain representing that they were manufacturing bogus coin in the North Woods beyond Redfield and were also dealing in counterfeit bills. Robbins made other statements which will appear when his affidavit is read upon the examination revealing his knowledge that Loomis and Hitchings were engaged in the manufacture and disposal of counterfeit coin."

Deputy Sheriff Klinck and Officer Donaldson drove to Hitchings' store near the Erie Canal between New London and Higginsville. Keeping their identities and purpose secret, Klinck ordered beer from Hitchings and invited Donaldson to have a drink with him. In order to gather evidence Klinck paid for the drinks with a two-dollar bill. Hitchings gave him as change a counterfeit gold dollar and the balance in silver. The officer thought the fifty-cent piece was also counterfeit.

Klinck pocketed the change and left with Donaldson without serving a warrant on Hitchings. They proceeded to the Loomis home and arrested Bill. With one prisoner in custody they drove back to the store to find that Hitchings had left for Rome. Whipping up their horse they took up the pursuit and caught up with Hitchings and placed him under arrest, though he protested that he knew nothing about the counterfeit money he had given them. Both prisoners were lodged in the Utica jail.

Robbins failed to show up at the trial and a county-wide search failed to produce him. Though Klinck had gone back to search Bill's house, he had found no counterfeit money, so Bill was released. Hitchings was released on $500 bail and court records do not show the disposition of his case.

The Loomis girls also entered into the counterfeiting game. A farmer named Russell Crumb in West Brookfield had a yoke of oxen for sale, but no one would pay the exorbitant price he asked.

On an April day, when the Valley was digging out from under an unexpected eighteen-inch snowfall, Cornelia, dressed in men's clothes, appeared at Crumb's place and said that "he" wished to buy the oxen for cash.

"How much are you asking for them?" she asked in her best mannish tones.

"Two hundred and sixty dollars," replied the farmer. "And I'll not take a cent less for them."

"Your price is mighty high," Cornelia argued. "I'll give you two hundred."

The offer was the best anyone had made, but Crumb refused. "Ill get my price or I don't sell them."

The "youth" started to walk way, then stopped and considered for a moment, and turned back to Crumb.

"If they are worth two hundred and sixty dollars to you," "he" stated, "they are worth that much to me." Cornelia pulled a well-filled wallet from her pants pocket and took out several crisp banknotes. "I suppose you will give me a yoke so I can drive them home?"

Crumb shook his head. "I'll throw in a yoke when you throw in two dollars for it," he said.

Cornelia grinned and counted out two one-dollar bills and handed them to the farmer. She said impishly, "I hope you won't charge me for writing out a bill of sale."

Crumb watched the "youth" drive the oxen away before he went into the house to brag to his wife how he had managed to sell the oxen at his own price.

Crumb drove to Waterville the next morning to deposit the money in the bank. The cashier counted the money, frowned, then counted it again.

"Is there something wrong?" Crumb asked.

"Where did you get this money?"

Crumb told him.

"You've been cheated," the cashier said. He placed the two one-dollar notes in front of the farmer. "These are good. The rest are counterfeit."

Crumb thoroughly aroused, drove to the Loomis farm and found his oxen in the pasture. He demanded of Grove that the oxen be returned.

"I don't know what you are talking about," Grove said. "We bought those oxen last week and paid two hundred and fifty-five dollars for them." He produced a bill of sale.

The farmer went to a justice of the peace and swore out a writ of replevin that was given to Constable Keith to serve. The oxen were returned to Crumb. Grove Loomis went to North Brookfield, pleaded innocent to a charge of unlawful possession and posted bail. At the hearing the justice dismissed the charges and ordered the oxen returned to the Loomises.

CHAPTER VI

WANDERING SHEEP

Sheep raising had always been a major occupation on the Loomis farm. Flocks usually ranged a few hundred head, but at their peak were known to have run as high as fifteen hundred animals. The family not only washed, carded and spun the cloth for their own and their laborers' clothes, but sold wool and mutton. The brothers often traveled as far west as Illinois and Wisconsin, buying sheep.

Grove Collins, who spent his youth in the Loomis household, related this sidelight on these expeditions: "My uncles told me they would go west and buy a few sheep and then start them on the long drive east. On their way they would gradually build up their original flock by adding many hundreds stolen from farmers along the way. By the time they arrived in Sangerfield they would have a thousand or more head.

"I cannot tell you now the exact routes they used in their drives, but they did go by way of Pennsylvania. On one such drive homeward they put up for the night in a drover's tavern in that state, pasturing their sheep in the tavern's corral. The next morning, when they went out to round up their flock, they found almost all of them lying dead. It seems during the night some one had poisoned the animals' drinking water.

"I think this drive discouraged further western trips, for my uncles said they seldom ever went that way again."

By 1858 the Loomis flock had been increasing miraculously in numbers each week, while farmers in the Valley complained bitterly of midnight raiders of their pens.

One fine spring night a farmer residing in South Hamilton was awakened by the barking of his dog. He quickly roused his son, a lad of nine or ten years, and they went out to investigate. At the command of his master, the dog led them to the back part of the farm. As they were passing a wood road a man stepped out from behind some bushes and seized the farmer by his shirt collar.

"What the hell are you doing here?" he demanded.

The farmer recognized his accoster in the moonlight. "What are you doing here, Grove?" he retorted.

The outlaw released his hold and stepped aside.

"That's all right, Deacon," he said, "you just go back to bed and forget that you got up."

The farmer thought Loomis' words sufficient warning; after calling his dog, he and his son went to bed. The following day a neighbor reported the loss of twenty-eight sheep.

A few days later the owner recognized his property on the Loomis farm, all nicely sheared, branded with a big L, with their ears cut squarely across the tips, thus obliterating the owner's earmark. Needless to say the farmer never recovered his property and did not dare to prosecute.

As these raids continued unchecked some of the farmers talked of organizing a posse to raid the Loomis farm. They knew Wash had been selling a lot of mutton during the past few months. In fact he had been indicted on April 5th for delivering fifteen pounds of spoiled meat to Levi Schoonmaker, a butcher, and charging him for good meat. He was tried and found guilty on December 1, and was fined forty dollars.

When news that the farmers were organizing reached the Loomises, they became alarmed. The night raids ceased and Wash planned desperately to avert a raid on the farm.

Sangerfield Township boasted several families of Terrys, three of which contained a male member named Horace. To distinguish these Horaces in conversation, one had been nicknamed Dancing Hod, one Laughing Hod, and the other, who resided on the Swamp Road between the Loomises and Edward Mason's farm, Swearing Hod.

Swearing Hod Terry was a big, red-faced, likeable man who managed to get along with everyone. He had a son named

Ham and it was known "he set a right store by that boy." When Ham "took sick and died it was a severe blow to old Swearing Hod, but he tried to make the best of it."

For years it had been the custom in Sangerfield when anyone died to pay the sexton fifty cents to toll the bell in the church steeple. Swearing Hod drove down to Sangerfield and handed the sexton a dollar bill. "Give it a hell of a jingling," he said, as he wiped a tear from his eye. "Ham was a good boy."

When the minister came to preach the funeral sermon, Swearing Hod said to his hired man, "Put the parson's horse in the shed and give it a damn good feed. The minister is a damn good man."

This blunt profanity of Swearing Hod's made Wash Loomis consider him a perfect decoy in his scheme to cast suspicion on his neighbors.

When Edward Mason went to inspect his sheep a few mornings later, he found that their number had been increased by fifty full-grown rams and ewes. Sensing something wrong he called on Swearing Hod and learned that he had lost a similar amount the previous night.

"I think I know who did this," Mason said. "Don't say anything to anyone, but you'll have your sheep back by tomorrow."

Mason returned home and called his small son, Morris. The boy gazed with questioning eyes while his brawny father picked up a large cudgel near the woodpile. "This isn't for you, son," Mason said. "We're going on a little hike over to the ravine and it might be useful."

Young Morris took his father's hand and walked with him over the hill that stretched upwards from the rear of their home. He noticed that his father was leading him across the lots towards the ravine which separated his father's farm from that of the Loomises. As they neared the ravine they heard the murmur of men's voices. Suddenly they stood on the steep sloping edge of the ravine, gazing down at a dozen or more men seated in the half-circle below. Some had pistols strapped at their waists, while others had rifles lying within reach.

"You wait here, son." The husky farmer half-slid, half-walked down the slope to face the men who had been unaware of his presence until the rattling stones falling into the ravine warned them. They sat grim and tense, hands clutching their weapons.

Wash Loomis arose and greeted Mason. "Howdy, Ed," he said. "What brings you over here?"

"You know damn well why I'm here, Wash," Mason roared. "Last night you put fifty of Terry's sheep with mine. I don't know why you did it, but I want you to get them out of there or I'll lick hell out of you."

Wash smiled and nodded in agreement. "We've never had trouble, Ed, and we won't now. I give you my word those sheep won't bother you after today."

"Thanks, Wash," Mason said gruffly, "I believe you." Feeling as if he were leaving a hornets' nest, he climbed the steep side of the ravine to join his son.

When he retired that night he listened carefully for any sounds that might come from his pasture. He drifted off to sleep without hearing anything but the chirping of the crickets in the fields. Early the next morning he walked out to his sheep pasture to find that Wash had not broken his word. Terry's sheep had been separated from Mason's and were back in their owner's pasture.

Though Wash was chagrined over his failure to sweep the Terrys and Masons into his cauldron of hate, he did not entirely abandon his plans.

In June he suddenly announced that his family had been losing sheep for several months. As proof he stated that on October 29th of that previous year twenty-five of his sheep were found on the farm of Jeremiah Clark at Thompson's Mills in the town of Hamilton. Clark denied stealing the sheep, saying they had strayed to his farm. He had readily returned them to the Loomises. Now fifty more sheep were trailed some fifteen or sixteen miles across lots to the Clark farm.

Jed wasn't much at keeping up a farm; he preferred to work out. In Earlville, Sherburne and Brookfield he would "take a stint" on some farm for a lump sum in cash and then, by working day and night, finish the job in the least possible time.

On Sunday mornings, dressed in his best clothes, he would arrive at the church earlier than anyone else. Standing on the church steps he would greet the congregation as they arrived and when any unattended ladies drove up he would help them from the carriages with a low bow. After hitching their horses in the church shed he would enter the church in time for the sermon. He always occupied a front pew, assisted the minister with prayers, led the psalm singing and passed the collection plate. If the minister was absent Jed often conducted a lay service.

Church over he would drive home, change his clothes and go out on sheep stealing forays. He carred no lures with him, but was able to rope a sheep and coax a whole flock to follow him like dogs. In this way he raided the sheep pens of Ed Lamb, Byron Jenks, Irving Hill and other Sherburne farmers. He was arrested and sentenced so many times for sheep stealing that he would often jokingly give Auburn Prison as his home address.

On Monday morning the 21st of June, Wash, Grove, Plumb, and Denio, accompanied by Asa Collins and Long Sile Clark, drove to the Clark farm for their sheep. Jeremiah and William Clark defied the Loomises. Jed told Wash they were the fifty he bought from them a few days earlier and drove home in the daytime. Wash flatly denied having sold him any sheep and ordered his brothers and their two henchmen to drive the animals out of the Clark pasture. When the two Clark brothers attempted to resist the Loomises, a fight started. Jed was severely beaten by the gang and Bill fled as Wash whipped out a pistol and fired several shots over his head to frighten him. The Loomises drove the sheep back to their farm.

When Jeremiah had sufficiently recovered from his bruises, he went before Justice Livermore and swore out warrants against Wash, Grove, Plumb and Denio, charging them with highway robbery.

The day before the warrants were served, Wash learned of Clark's action. There was one course to take; he must strike first.

That evening, as Jed was driving his cows home, Plumb and Grove Loomis leaped out from behind a nearby thicket and flourished pistols in his face. Threatening to blow his brains out if he made a false move, they tied him hand and foot, drove him to the Loomis home and locked him up.

He was awakened at dawn by the wild barking of the Loomis hounds mingled with the hoarse shouts and curses of men and women. Doors slammed violently in the house as the sounds of a brawl rose from the yard. When the commotion had subsided, Grove and Plumb escorted him into the middle kitchen, where he came face to face with Deputy Sheriff Fitch Hewitt. Thinking the deputy had effected his rescue, Clark blurted out the story of his kidnapping. Hewitt produced a warrant for his arrest. Jed glanced at the document and saw that the Loomises had charged him with stealing sheep. He cried out in protest, but became silent when they threatened to gag him. Hewitt and the Loomis brothers drove him to Justice Livermore's farm to answer the charges. Clark managed to procure Attorney E. H. Lamb as his counsel. The Loomises were represented by Daniel Ball, the Waterville lawyer.

Lamb opened the trial by announcing that the warrant was defective. "It is not worth a snap," he charged. "It was improperly made out and my client is therefore at liberty to return to the scenes of his youth at any moment."

Ball challenged Lamb's statement. While the two attorneys argued over certain points of the law Justice Livermore started to prepare a new warrant. Clark, seizing the opportunity, slid quietly from the chamber and ran towards the Swamp. The Loomis brothers started in pursuit, but Clark "was not overtaken and thus the affair (temporarily, at least) ended."

At ten o'clock that same Sunday night, while Clark was a prisoner in the Loomis home, Deputy Sheriff George Klinck and Officer Charles Latham left Utica for Sangerfield Center to arrest Wash on a warrant for robbing District Attorney Munger that previous April. The officers went by way of Clinton, where they procured Deputy Sheriff Wood and Silas T. Ives to assist them. At three o'clock Monday morning the officers arrived at the Loomis farm. Here the quartet separated, each man arranging himself on one side of the house in order to cut off any attemtped escape. At daybreak Klinck knocked on the front door and demanded admittance.

A woman pulled the curtain back and glanced out. "Who is it?" she asked.

"Open the door," Klinck ordered, "or I will break it down."

A man's voice answered the deputy's threat, "If you do so, you will be killed." When the officer continued to pound on the door, the same voice asked, "Who do you want?"

"Wash Loomis," shouted Klinck.

He heard the occupants of the household rushing about. A rear door slammed violently. The hoarse cries of men and the shrieking voices of women were intermingled with the loud barking of Grove's dogs in the back yard, where Deputy Wood was stationed. Klinck and the other officers ran to his aid.

Four women, seven men and six vicious dogs rushed from the house and attacked Wood. While the dogs tore at his clothes, the men and women pelted him with rocks and stones. Grove and Wash broke from the attacking party as Wood's brother officers came to his rescue. Grove fled towards the Swamp pursued by Wood, but Wash overtook the officer and flashed a pistol in his face.

"I'll blow your brains out if you don't get out of here," he threatened.

Silas Ives ran up behind Wash and grappled with him. After a brief struggle Wash broke away and ran towards the house, still clutching his pistol. He was overtaken by Deputy Klinck, who managed to grasp his coat collar. Wash struck at the officer with his pistol but made no attempt to fire it. As Officer Latham hurried to Klinck's aid Wash heaved his pistol over the back fence to Long Sile Clark, one of the gang. "Shoot them, Si," he urged. "Shoot!"

As Long Sile raised the weapon and cocked the trigger, Klinck drew his own revolver. "Shoot, damn you," he shouted, "but I'll blast a hole through you first."

Long Sile dropped the pistol, while the assembled women denounced him for his cowardice. The officers handcuffed Wash, forced him into their carriage and started for Utica.

The case carried on for over a month, while lawyers wrangled over technicalities, judges evaded the issue, and The Utica Morning Herald complained of the inefficiency of the courts. One judge declined to hear the case, another could not sit because his daughter had died, and a third refused to see the prisoner because he might be called upon to preside at the trial.

Justice Wilcox of Whitesboro, the last judge to hear the case, told the newspapers, "After waiting about two hours for the witnesses on the part of the people to arrive or at least some of them and none of them appearing and no bail being offered in view of all circumstances, affidavits, and statements in the case, I became satisfied that it was my duty to discharge the defendant and I did discharge him."

His decision served as a bombshell to the law's efforts to end the Loomis reign, for his discharging of Wash killed the last warrant against them. They were free to perpetrate new deviltry.

CHAPTER VII

GROVE THE HORSEMAN

Grove Loomis inherited his father's love of fast, blooded horses and also kept a large kennel of fox hounds. Every year he organized the younger bloods of the Valley for periodic fox hunts. Although these hunts were conducted without scarlet coats or blasts from a huntsman's horn, certain well-regulated rules were followed.

Long before the hunters gathered at the Loomis farm, the fox's runways would be located and marked. When the hunt began Grove turned loose one of the oldest and best trailers from his kennel. As soon as the hound found the scent the huntsmen, some on horseback, others on foot, would start in pursuit. "If Grove and the men failed to get the fox the first time around, another and faster dog was turned loose," Hall explained. "If this failed, Grove brought forward the part greyhound known as Hathaway's Old Slut, which he had purchased from his friend, Bill Hathaway of Deansville (Deansboro). Old Slut would whimper and tug at her leash, waiting for Grove to slip the collar from her neck.

" 'Just a minute,' Grove would whisper as he stroked the dog's head. 'Just a minute.'

"As soon as he slipped the collar Old Slut would bound away to pick up the fox's scent. Once it was found she would trail the fox until she had killed it, usually far ahead of the hunters."

Grove began to buy and breed horses while he was still in his teens. He owned several of Kentucky-Hunter stock. In later years he changed to Blackhawk and Morgan breeds. As a breeder in 1844, when he was nineteen, he made a decision that changed the annals of the trotting world. During that year Samuel Welch of Waterville sent his hired man, Jotham Chase, to the Loomis farm with a four-year-old work mare named Madame Temple to breed her to a stallion named Bogus that George W. Loomis owned. Madame Temple had been foaled on the Elisha Peck farm near Waterville. Her sire was a spotted Arabian stallion which his owner, Horace Terry, had brought from Dutchess County. Terry sold Madame Temple as a four month old colt to William Johnson, who later sold her as a three year old to Welch.

When Chase arrived at the Loomis farm he learned that Bogus was not in condition. At the suggestion of Grove it was decided to use a registered but untried stud Wash owned, a one-eyed Kentucky-Hunter. Madame Temple gave birth to a filly the next year, a disjointed, gangling little bay. Welch named her Flora Temple. He did not think she was worth keeping, so he sold her for thirteen dollars to Nathan Tracy of Hamilton. Eventually she became a livery stable horse at Richardson and Kellog's Livery in Eaton. A cattle buyer purchased Flora and sold her for $175 to Jonathan A. Vielee of Washington Hollow, Dutchess County.

Under the guidance of Vielee and several subsequent owners, Flora Temple made trotting history, defeating Highland Maid, Lancet, Rose of Washington and the great George W. Patchen. At the Kalamazoo Horse Fair in Michigan in October, 1859 she established a world's record of $2:19\frac{3}{4}$ for a mile, defeating Honest Once and Princess. Flora Temple became a national idol; babies were named after her, as were steamboats and cigars. Liquor bottles and special coins carried her image and she was a favorite subject of the famous lithographers, Currier & Ives. Grove was always extremely proud of the part he played in her career, although history has ignored him.

Grove's passion for fine horses eventually led to the creation of a syndicate for dealing in stolen stock. Horses were farmers' most prized possessions and stealing them constituted a serious crime. The early harness horses were mostly descended from Orange County sites. The blackhawk and Morgan breeds that were later introduced from Vermont quickly gained popularity. A farmer would pay from $100 to $1,000 for a horse which, if stolen, was resold to the Loomises for $25, Mulligan pointed out. "If these animals were disposed of without any trouble, the thieves received a bonus of $15. Grove knew where every horse stolen in the Sangerfield area was located. Sometimes he would help the owners locate their missing horses for a fee of $50. Whether the horses were returned or sold elsewhere, the Loomises always profited by the transaction. Grove spent much of his time traveling in various counties and Eastern states creating markets for the horses."

A large percentage of these stolen horses were disguised so cleverly that their owners failed to recognize them. Various materials were used to color white markings, sometimes paints, dyes and chemicals, but usually nitrate of silver. To create a white star on a horse's forehead, sometimes a hot baked potato would be tightly bound on the desired spot. This process was repeated until the bleach removed the color. Experts like Grove, Wash and Plumb could change a horse's appearance in ten minutes.

Black Abe Lovitt, one of several Negroes who worked with the Loomises, once stole a team of blacks from Thomas Jones of Mohawk. Three months later Jones received word that he would be able to find them in Redfield. On arriving in that village he found the team of which he had heard. They resembled the stolen team but he was unable to make a positive identification, as the horses were both chestnuts with white stockings and one had a star on its forehead. Jones liked the team well enough to purchase them. Black Abe laughed when he heard the story. "Yessir, dat sure am funny," he chortled. "Mister Jones done bought his own team back. I stole 'em myself an' had their markin's changed. Mister Jones bought his own team an' never know'd it."

The Loomis farm, straddling the boundry line between Oneida and Madison Counties and with the wild stretch of the Nine-Mile Swamp at its feet, made an ideal center for hiding stolen stock. The Pinnacle, rising like a great dome in the center of the hilly acres, was the highest spot in the Valley. Along the southern edge of the farm lay Tinker Hollow, a scattering of farms perched along the banks of the widemouthed gulley. The western part of the farm, covered with a dense woods, sloped down into Pleasant Valley. A partially disguised wagon road led up from Pleasant Valley through the woods, skirted the Pinnacle and led down to the buildings on the eastern slope. A deep gulley separated the Loomis farm from the adjoining Terry and Mason farms on the north. From the Swamp Road the appearance of the mouth of the gulley was deceptive. A thousand feet westerly of the road it widened and the slate walls rose thirty feet on both sides. Harold Mason stated that the Loomises sometimes pastured from twenty to thirty horses in the gully all winter without ill effects. There was water in the creek and two haystacks provided food.

The gulley may have been the foundation for the numerous "hidden cave" stories that have become a part of the Loomis legend. Harold Mason and his family, who owned the farm for many years, denounced all stories of secret caves as fictitious. Thomas L. Hall, John Mulligan, Phinett Carter and others who were acquainted with the Loomises also insisted there were no caves. D. Francis Searle of the law firm of Searle & Searle of Rome stated that Bill Loomis spoke of a cave once in his presence. "In 1888 I formed a partnership with Joseph I. Sayles and his nephew A. F. (Del) Sayles," he disclosed. "J. I. Sayles for a number of years had been the legal adviser of the Loomis gang in Verona and Sangerfield, but their activities in the horse business had ceased some years before 1888. Occasionally William Sr. and Jr. came to consult Sayles after my partnership. Senior occasionally drank and became talkative. On one such occasion he complained to Mr. Sayles that Plumb was dishonest; that he had not properly divided the proceeds of some horses that had been at the Sangerfield cave. His son tried to stop his talking but the old man insisted that Plumb was dishonest and could not be trusted."

More closely associated with the Loomises was the Nine-Mile Swamp, filling the floor of the Valley from Sangerfield Center to Hubbardsville, a distance over nine miles. A wild, forbidding area of cedar and pine trees and brush, it provided a sanctuary for members of the family and members of their gang when they were hunted, and a hiding place for stolen stock. The eastern branch of the Chenango River, pursuing a winding course southward, failed to drain it, but the Loomises knew every foot of its paths and every bog-hole. From the earliest settlement in the Valley the Swamp provided lumber for cabins and frame buildings, for fences and hop yards. Wild orchids bloomed in the depths of the Swamp. There was also the carrion smell of natural gas.

The Loomises found natural "swamp meadows" and on the largest one, a few thousand feet east of the homestead, they erected a small frame barn and used the cut and dried swamp grass to build haystacks to feed the stock kept there.

Constable James L. Filkins discovered the meadow during his relentless campaign against the gang.

"I spent hours in there," he related to a cousin, "sitting, watching and listening while trying to locate stolen horses. The hay from the meadow was kept piled on a big hay stack. One time I found horse manure on the ground but there were no signs of horses about. Once I was rewarded for my patience. I heard a horse's whinny. That whinny seemed to come from that big haystack. On closer examination of the stack I discovered a door neatly covered with hay. Opening the door I found myself looking into a small horse barn filled with horses. I looked the animals over but could not find any that resembled the descriptions I had from owners of horses that had been stolen."

The frequent raids on the Loomis farm by officers and posses proved annoying to the family, but did not stop their depredations. The brothers had simplified horse stealing long before expanding it into a large scale business. Armed with a blindfold and pieces of burlap or blankets to tie around a horse's hoofs to deaden the sound, they rode forth on moonless nights to prey on farmers.

"There was a Mr. Wadsworth living in Washington Mills who had a fine team of horses that the Loomises were determinded to get," Herbert Tyler of Utica recalled. "When they saw some team they wanted they usually got it in time. One fine morning Mr. Wadsworth went to his barn and discovered that his team was gone. A search was held but he never found his team.

"A neighbor and his wife had got up about four that morning the team was stolen, so they could catch the train to Utica. On the road the Loomises passed them driving the Wadsworth team. The neighbor thought it strange that the team moved along without making any noise.

" 'That's funny,' he said to his wife. 'Those horses' feet don't make any noise.'

"The horses' feet had been muffled.

"Another man named McGraw who lived in Utica across the tracks also had his team stolen by the gang. 'Darnest set around here,' he is said to have remarked. He also searched a long time, but his team was never traced."

Aunt Neva Watson of Brookfield remembered that Mrs. Henry Davis had an uncle named L. Hall who lived on Ayres Hill. "He had a fine black horse," she said. "I think it belonged to his brother-in-law. One night he led the horse up from the barn and put it in the woodhouse attached to the house when the Loomises were seen around the neighborhood. He heard the dog bark in the night, got up, but saw no one. In the morning his horse was gone.

"He got word to his brother-in-law and they went into a livery stable run by friends of the Loomises and found his horse in a box stall. He spoke its name and the horse answered and came and laid its head on his shoulder. He bought an old second-hand harness, built a two-wheeled cart out of two old wheels that were lying around and drove back to Brookfield."

Young Herbert Throop of the Center boasted an intelligent horse he had trained to dance, kneel, roll over and play dead. One night the horse was stolen. Herbert and his father, Erastus Throop, drove to the Loomis farm and demanded that Grove return the animal. While Grove registered indignation a horse whickered loudly from the nearby pasture. In stride and build the animal resembled Herbert's horse, but its markings and coloring were different. Grove insisted he had recently purchased it from outside the state. Walking to the fence Herbert voiced a command. To Grove's consternation the horse obeyed. At the boy's insistence the animal went through its entire repertoire of tricks. When the elder Throop led the horse from the pasture and started homeward, Grove did not interfere.

One September Grove visited the Clarkville Fair in Clarkville, now Brookfield. He considered the winner of the blue ribbon one of the finest horses he had ever seen. The magnificent animal had white markings on its forehead and four white stockings. Arrayed in a glistening new harness, it was hitched to the finest carriage its owner could afford.

After the exhibition the horses were tethered around the inside of the fairground fence. In the afternoon, while other events were taking place, the section where the horses were tethered was deserted, except for a nine-year old boy named Orson B. Clark. The youngster stopped his play when he saw Grove Loomis approaching. He quickly hid, as he had heard fearsome stories of the Loomises from his parents. The boy saw Grove carefully glance around to see if anyone was watching. Grove then took a bottle from his pocket and began swabbing the horse with its contents. When he completed his work there were no markings on the horse. Grove removed the prize ribbon from its bridle, unhitched the animal from its post, backed the carriage from its place in line and slowly drove out of the entrance gate of the fairground. The few people who were standing near the gate paid no attention to either the horse or its driver as Grove drove away.

The owner of the horse and buggy never saw them afterward, nor did he ever find out who had stolen them. The little Clark boy, who grew up to become a photographer and businessman, told friends in later years of what he had seen. He said he was too afraid he would be killed to say anything at the time.

There is another story of a farmer who saw Grove and a member of the gang driving slowly past his farm in a buggy. They stopped their horse for a moment to admire a handsome pair of horses that were grazing in the pasture on the opposite side of the road. The owner thought nothing more of the incident until late that night, when he was awakened by the frightened whickering and pounding hoofbeats of his horses. Leaping from his bed he threw open the window. Muffled voices and the protesting screech of the rails of the pasture fence came to his ears. Pulling his jeans over his underwear and thrusting his feet into his boots, he shouted to his hired man, "The Loomises are stealing Frank."

The farmer seized a pistol from his bureau and ran from the house in time to see a buggy with the horse named Frank tied behind, departing rapidly down the road. Furiously the owner fired two shots in the direction of the vehicle, then went to the barn for a bridle. He caught his other horse and, riding bareback, started in pursuit.

On down the long dark road the farmer rode until he approached the slower moving buggy. Raising his pistol he fired two more shots. The thieves became frightened and cut loose the stolen horse. When the farmer stopped to recapture the animal, the buggy disappeared into the darkness.

CHAPTER VIII

FILKINS TAKES THE TRAIL

The escapades of the Loomis brothers dominated the news so completely that the appointment of James L. Filkins, a North Brookfield blacksmith, as constable of the Town of Brookfield in March 1858 went unnoticed. Filkins, then thirty-four years old, had a pasty, pock-marked face set off by a sandy goatee and hair of the same color. Though he stood five feet, eight inches in height, his heavily-muscled body and shuffling gait made him appear shorter. An introvert, "The Little Constable" was known to have an uncontrollable temper.

Filkins told Cummings that he first heard of the Loomis gang when he came to Nigger City in 1846 to work in Joel Avery's blacksmith shop and shod horses for old George Loomis. Actually he had become acquainted with them several years earlier, according to Roy W. Cary of the Mile-Strip, custodian of the Champlain-Oneida Indian Battle Park.

"Filkins was a cousin of my father, John Cary, and he told him that the Loomises had him sent to prison," Cary related. "When Jim was about eighteen his parents, Isaac and Margaret Filkins, lived at Stockwell, across the Swamp from the Loomis farm. Jim's father was a blacksmith and forced his son to follow the trade.

"One night young Filkins wanted to go sliding with the boys on the crusty snow, but his father wouldn't let him. Jim tied sheets together and let himself out of the second story window. The youth had his fun, but on the way home he saw Plumb Loomis leading a cow along the road.

"Next morning Isaac Filkins found his cow had been stolen. He and Jim found it hidden in a hollowed-out haystack on the Loomis farm. The Loomises refused to give the cow up, saying Jim had sold it to them for forty dollars.

Isaac had Plumb arrested for stealing the cow, and the Loomises retaliated by having Jim Filkins arrested. The Loomises and their perjured witnesses helped free Plumb, but Jim was sent to prison. Isaac Filkins would do nothing to help his son. Neighbors who liked the boy took up a petition and he was freed."

Several older residents of the Sangerfield area have related a story, as Hall did, that Filkins went to jail for stealing money from Uncle Isaac Marsh's store in Nigger City and came out reformed. A search of court records of both Oneida and Madison Counties failed to disclose any mention of the case.

Filkins had his first opportunity for revenge on the Loomises when he was summoned before Justice of the Peace Green in Clarkville, before whom Jeremiah Clark had sworn out a warrant against Plumb Loomis for interfering with his personal liberty. Filkins and Deputy Sheriff Henry Keith were ordered to serve it.

After swearing in a few assistants the officers proceeded to the Loomis farm. At three o'clock Thursday morning the 8th of July Deputy Keith rapped on the back door.

A woman's voice responded from within, "What do you want?"

"I have a warrant for Plumb Loomis," Keith replied. "Tell him to come out."

"He isn't here," the same feminine voice replied.

At that moment Plumb and Long Sile Clark, a leading member of the gang, leaped out of a window and dashed towards the Swamp, closely pursued by Filkins and one of the posse. Long Sile escaped, but Filkins overtook Plumb and threw him. Though Loomis struggled desperately he was quickly handcuffed.

"Help! Murder!" he cried. "Filkins is trying to kill me."

The constable struck him savagely across the face. "Shut up or I'll brain you."

Filkins took his prisoner to Justice Green in Clarkville, who postponed the examination until two o'clock the following afternoon. As the village had no lock-up Deputy Keith took Plumb to his hotel. While Keith and his family were at supper the officer saw a horseman talking earnestly to the prisoner. He dashed into the yard to face Grove Loomis, who sat astride the California mare, armed with two revolvers, a bowie knife and a short club.

"Release Plumb," Grove demanded, "or suffer the consequences."

The unarmed deputy, uncertain of Grove's next move, retreated to the hotel.

"Good evening, Mr. Keith," Grove called back mockingly, as he spurred his horse into a sweeping gallop.

Keith took every precaution to prevent any attempt to rescue Plumb, who was handcuffed to a trusted man in a front bedroom overlooking the porch roof. Two other assistants, fully-armed, were stationed in an adjoining room.

At sunrise Keith walked into Plumb's room to find the window open and Loomis gone. He awoke the sleeping guard and demanded to know how Plumb had escaped.

"I don't know," the guard replied. "I awoke at two in the morning and Loomis was in bed then."

Investigation showed that Plumb had jumped twenty feet from the window to make his escape.

The Loomis brothers, annoyed because the Clarks were still at large, persuaded M. C. Marsh, a deputy sheriff from the Town of Verona and a close associate, to help them arrest the Clarks and take them before Justice Samuel P. Marsh of Higginsville. Wash, Plumb and the deputy proceeded to the Clark farm in the town of Hamilton and arrested Jed and his brother, William, after a severe battle in which Wash received a thorough beating. The prisoners were taken to the Loomis home, where Long Sile Clark was waiting. Shortly afterwards the company proceeded to Higginsville, where the prisoners were herded into the chambers of Justice Marsh.

At the insistence of the Loomises and Long Sile, the Clark brothers were ordered held for bail. As neither Jed nor his brother had friends in Oneida County to furnish bail for them, Justice Marsh ordered them held until they could be taken to the county jail in Rome the next morning.

In the meantime Deputy Sheriff George Klinck received information that the Loomis brothers would be in Higginsville that night. Enlisting the aid of City Marshall David Hess of Utica, Klinck immediately started for Higginsville. At one o'clock Friday morning the officers managed to awaken a clerk in the canal collector's office near the village. When they had identified themselves the clerk told the newest exploit of the Loomises.

"At this time Wash is keeping guard over the prisoners," he declared, "while Plumb and Long Sile Clark are spending the night at the residence of William Loomis a little way from Higginsville."

The officers decided to ambush the Loomises on their way to Rome. Leaving their horse and buggy at the collector's office they started on foot up the canal towpath towards Bill's farm. When they were a short distance from it Klinck hid himself in a dense thicket beside the road and Hess lay down on the opposite side.

They were aroused at break of dawn by the sound of an approaching wagon. Thinking it might be the Loomises the officers parted the bushes and peered out. As the team drew opposite they recognized the driver as Mrs. Martha Ann Loomis. They made no effort to stop her and withdrew into the concealment of the bushes.

About seven o'clock the rumbling of another wagon was heard coming down the road. Plumb Loomis and Long Sile Clark were riding on the seat. As the officers tensed their muscles for a leap into the road, one of a group of farmers working in a nearby field saw them. Evidently thinking they were about to attempt a holdup, he shouted a warning to the occupants of the wagon. Klinck and Hess leaped into the road and almost collided with Wash Loomis, who was walking up the road unnoticed towards his brother's farm. Long Sile, on seeing the officers, jumped from the wagon and sped for the cranberry swamp west of the canal with Deputy Klinck in pursuit.

Plumb Loomis swung the ends of the reins over the team's buttocks, causing them to leap forward as Marshall Hess caught their bridles. The momentum of the plunging horses threw Hess off his feet, but he did not loosen his grip. Plumb lifted the heavy whip from its socket and struck savagely at him. Realizing the danger Hess relaxed his grip on the bridles and exerted every ounce of strength to throw his body away from the team. He landed solidly in the road and rolled out of danger as the team and wagon swept over the spot where he had lain. Bruised and shaken, he climbed to his feet to see Wash Loomis catch the tailboard and pull himself into the wagon. While Hess stood cursing the Loomises he was joined by Klinck, who had failed to catch Long Sile Clark. The two men walked slowly down the dusty road to Higginsville.

At the canal collector's office they learned that Plumb and Wash had stopped only long enough to pick up their prisoners, the Clark brothers, before continuing towards Rome. They also learned that Deputy Sheriff Henry Keith of Clarkville had picked up Plumb's trail. They decided to spend the day in Higginsville and await further developments.

Plumb and Wash, driving their prisoners to the Rome jail, suddenly discovered that they were being pursued. Wash tried to lash the team into a gallop, but Jeremiah Clark struggled to his feet and tore the reins from his hands. Plumb tried to help his brother, but Clark hung doggedly to the reins until the team came to stop as Deputy Keith drew alongside in his carriage. Plumb leaped from the wagon and escaped across the fields. Keith placed Wash under arrest. As the officer had no warrants against the Clark brothers he allowed them to return to Higginsville with the Loomis wagon and team, while he started for Rome with Wash.

In Higginsville the Clarks were taken into custody by Constable Marsh, who had previously arrested them with the aid of the Loomises. Another brother of the Clarks, who had come to furnish bail, was arrested. At the insistence of Klinck the prisoners were taken before Justice Blair. The Clarks pleaded innocent to the charges of sheep stealing and were released on bail, Hess becoming one of their sureties.

Shortly after Deputy Keith arrived in Rome with his prisoner he allowed Wash to send word to J. Thomas Spriggs, his Utica attorney, to meet them in front of the office of The Roman Citizen. Wash was immediately recognized and "quite a crowd gathered around to take a look at one of the notorious family. Their character was fully discussed." A. Sanford, editor of The Roman Citizen, listened with interest to the remarks of the crowd. When Deputy Keith prepared to start with Wash for Clarkville in Madison County, the editor turned to an acquaintance near him and remarked, "Should a bolt of lightning extirpate the whole family at once it should be a blessing."

Spriggs, overhearing the remark, advanced on the editor with clenched fists. "Damn you," he said, "shut up or I'll knock you down."

"Any time you want to try, come ahead."

The lawyer took another step towards the editor, then halted. Evidently Sanford's formidable appearance caused him to change his mind. After a few more blustering words he turned and left.

Wash was taken before Justice Green of Clarkville for an examination on the charges of assault and battery filed by Jed Clark. The prisoner's counsels, Pomeroy and Spriggs, argued that the warrant on which he had been arrested was illegal. David J. Mitchell, representing the People, objected. Justice Greene, obstinately held that the warrant was good. Wash pleaded innocent to the charges and was released on bail, which was posted by his attorneys.

Klinck, Hess, and Officers Long and Latham returned to Utica after spending several days unsuccessfully trying to arrest Grove and Plumb Loomis and Long Sile Clark. It was like chasing a Will o' the Wisp, they admitted. The brothers returned to their home under the shadow of the pinnacle to plan new conquests and punish all people who had dared to oppose them.

On the thirteenth of August, Klinck and four assistants attempted to arrest Grove on the old charges of passing counterfeit money and jumping his bail bonds. The pickets on the pinnacle saw the officers approaching on the Swamp Road from Sangerfield Center and sent a warning to the occupants of the house below. When Klinck and his men reached the Loomis home Grove was safely hidden in the Swamp. Realizing the futility of searching for him the officers returned to Utica.

A few days later the Messrs. McKibben and Wilkinson, publishers of The Waterville Times, received a note from Grove titled "August Fools," which severely criticized Deputy Klinck.

"The story looks too much like a fabrication to obtain currency through our agency," the publishers commented in their weekly, "and we have only to say to Grove L. Loomis 'Be a good boy and you will, as usual, come out ahead.' "

Deputy Klinck and Deputy Fitch Hewitt raided the Loomis farm several more times in a determined effort to capture Grove, but he discreetly kept himself beyond their reach.

"Mr. Klinck was down to see me," Grove told a friend, "but I chanced to be out hunting squirrels with a double-barrelled shot gun. I tried to get near enough to the deputy to get a shot at him, but could not.

"I laughed quite heartily at the temerity of our amiable sheriff, Fitch Hewitt, Esquire, who looked cautiously into our stove oven the other day, expecting to find me there. I sent word to Fitch that I was baked some years ago, and that if my gun had been loaded I would have peppered him on the spot."

New indictments were handed down by the Madison County courts for the immediate arrest of Wash, Grove and Plumb Loomis. Bench warrants were sent to Constable James Filkins with letters from Sheriff Milton Barnett and the District Attorney urging him to capture the brothers and not to allow them to escape. The letters were hardly necessary, for Filkins itched to invade the Loomis territory and settle several outstandng scores. According to Thomas L. Hall, Filkins had no intention of risking his own neck by making the journey alone, so he asked two of his neighbors, James Humphrey and Frederick Hall (the historian's father) to accompany him.

These two men were a few years younger than Filkins and like him were married and had families. Here the resemblance ended. Humphrey, who was of Welsh extraction, stood five feet, seven or eight inches in height; he was fair-haired and wore his chin whiskers extremely long. On very cold days he buttoned his vest over them to protect his throat. He was a cobbler by trade, but often carried the mail to North Brookfield station. His friend and neighbor, Fred Hall, was a quiet, gentle-natured man, descendant of Quaker ministers noted for their fearless piety. He was a carriage-trimmer by trade, a tall, handsome fellow, fair complexioned, with brown hair and short, trim whiskers. Being a Quaker, he usually dressed in somber gray.

Filkins, Humphrey and Hall started for the Loomis farm about an hour before daybreak. A light snow was falling and a chilling wind swept down the Valley. By the time they reached their destination the darkness had lifted and the wind and snow had stopped. Lights were burning in the Loomis house and in their barn. Wash, Grove, and Plumb, in the barnyard, were throwing hay to a few horses. When they saw Filkins and his men they scurried like rats to escape. Wash and Plumb climbed the rail fence enclosing the yard and started towards the house. Grove leaped astride a horse and, guiding it by his voice and knees, as he had neither saddle nor bridle, rode at breakneck speed towards the fence.

While the officers held their breaths, expecting horse and rider to crash, the horse cleared the fence with its rider, crossed the road at a wild gallop and vanished up the wooded hillside.

Filkins and Hall ran after Wash, while Humphrey pursued Plumb. The cobbler threw Plumb and sat down on his struggling form to wait Filkins' arrival. The woodshed door burst open suddenly. Cornelia Loomis and Adeline Glazier, Plumb's sweetheart, pulled Humphrey backwards off him. The Glazier girl, who weighed one hundred and eighty pounds, threw her full weight on Humphrey's head and shoulders, knocking him unconscious. Seizing the opportunity, Plumb escaped.

As Filkins and Hall were escorting Wash back to the house the young Quaker noticed Humphrey's predicament and ran on ahead to help him.

"Come on you," he shouted at Adeline, "get off him."

The girl paid no attention. Hall suddenly bent over her, locked his arms about her waist and tried to lift her, but Adeline's fingernails tore at his arms and face and made him release his hold. Still retaining her seat on the prostrate Humphrey, she swung wildly with her fat arms in an effort to keep Hall away.

"I'll fix you," Hall panted.

Ignoring her threshing arms and clawing nails, he leaped forward and seized her by the breasts. She screeched shrilly in pain and raked his face with her fingernails, but the young Quaker retained his hold. She stood the unbearable agony for a moment, then struggled to her feet. Hall loosened his grip and pushed her roughly aside. Completely ignoring her swinging arms and curses, he bent over the cobbler and lifted him to his feet. Humphrey managed to catch his breath while Hall pawed some of the snow and mud from his eyes and mouth. As soon as Humphrey was able to travel, the officers took Wash to Morrisville for an examination before a justice. Much to Filkins' discomfiture Wash was freed on bail.

CHAPTER IX

SHOOT PLUMB!

While Fred Hall was casually discussing the affair with Squire H. D. Phitts in the latter's three-storied Exchange Hotel in Eaton, Wash Loomis entered. Seeing Hall, his face darkened with anger. "I'm going to knock hell out of you," he cried, as he advanced with clenched fists. "I'll teach you to come to our house with that damned Filkins."

The Quaker reached backward and clasped his chair by the rungs. He was determined to use it as a weapon if Wash came nearer.

Squire Phitts stepped forward. "I'll have no brawling in here," he announced.

"We'll see about that," Wash retorted, "but first I want to wash my hands."

After stripping off his coat and hanging it on a nail, he rolled up his sleeves, lifted a dipper of water from the full bucket on the stand and poured it into the wash basin. When he had rinsed his hands he dried them on the towel which hung nearby.

"Now," he said, advancing toward Hall, "I'll attend to you."

Before Hall was able to arise, Squire Phitts intervened. "I told you I'd have no brawling in here," he said to Wash. "Get out!"

Wash attempted to push him to one side, but he had failed to reckon with the Squire.

"You asked for it," said Phitts. His fist caught Wash squarely in the face. As Loomis staggered backwards the Squire leaped after him, caught him by the shirt collar and the seat of the pants and threw him out into the road, where he landed heavily on his buttocks.

"Don't come in here again," the Squire panted as he threw Wash's coat through the doorway.

Wash shook his fist at his tormentor before he went limping away.

"I think that calls for a drink," the Squire said to Hall.

Filkins raided the Loomis place again a few nights later, accompanied by Hall, Humphrey and a horse dealer named Ephraim Conger. Once within sight of the house he sent Hall up the hill to cut off any possible escape from the rear. Humphrey was stationed up the road past the house, while Conger stayed below. Having placed his men, Filkins searched the basement barn, but found no sign of the two Loomis boys.

While he was prowling about the yard Grove's hounds in the woodshed started howling. As the din grew louder lights appeared in the windows of the house. Filkins and Conger approached the woodshed door, which opened suddenly to disgorge several hounds. Baying and panting, they started up towards the spot where Hall was stationed. Seeing the dogs, he scattered them with a volley of stones, but they immediately reassembled and started towards him. Panic-stricken, he pried a big boulder loose and rolled it down the hill. The rock missed the dogs completely and bounded against the woodshed as Filkins and Conger were entering the kitchen. The impact caused a few dogs in the kitchen to rush for the doorway. They missed Filkins but tripped up Conger, who sprawled on his face in front of Wash Loomis.

"What's the matter with you, Eph?" Wash laughed heartily. "What have you and Jim been drinking?"

Filkins must have felt ridiculous. He had come to capture Grove and Plumb; instead, had made a fool of himself. Angrily he searched the house, but did not find the brothers. He called his posse and departed with Wash's laughter ringing in his ears.

While Filkins searched for Grove and Plumb these two had taken refuge in the home of E. M. Glazier, the father of

Plumb's girl, in Oriskany Falls. Officer Benjamin Peebles of the village, with two special officers, A. T. Tilley and T. T. Thompson, went there to arrest them.

Describing the event, The Utica Morning Herald reported: "As Peebles and Thompson neared the premises they met Grove and Plumb making for their team. Peebles made a grab for Grove and as he did so Plumb struck at him with a cudgel which the officer took on his arm and thus saved his head. Grove then turned to run but was met by Tilley who presented a revolver and told him to stand. Grove's only answer was a shot from his own revolver which just grazed Tilley's cheek. He then took aim and fired at Grove. Two or three shots were exchanged when Peebles got rid of Plumb and came up. Grove started to run up the road with Peebles and his assistant after him. Grove turned around and fired a shot which was returned by Peebles. Grove then threw off his overcoat which impeded his flight and the race kept on for forty or fifty rods and eight or ten shots were exchanged. Grove finally leapt a fence and in the darkness succeeded in effecting his escape though it is believed he was hit and slightly wounded."

The Loomis attorneys, Pomeroy and Spriggs, made an application before the courts of Oneida County to have all the indictments against their clients dropped. When the Court inquired the reason for the unusual request Pomeroy gave the explanation "that they had thus far resisted arrest." The Court failed to consider this plea sufficient to warrant quashing the numerous indictments.

A posse of fifty well-armed men headed by Constable Filkins surrounded the Loomis residence on Saturday, November 13th, in a desperate effort to take Wash, Grove and Plumb. The brothers, alarmed for fear that Filkins might fire the building in an effort to force them out, appeared in the yard. Filkins shouted for them to halt. Ignoring his command they broke into a run as the constable fired several wild shots after them. Grove reached the shed where his stallion was kept saddled. Crouching over the animal's neck he spurred it into a gallop. Though twenty men surrounded him he rode recklessly into them, bowling them over. He and his mount disappeared down the road in a flurry of churning snow.

Plumb, ducking and dodging like a hunted fox, reached the Swamp and safety. Wash, menaced by a ring of guns, was forced to surrender. Filkins took him to the jail in Morisville.

His failure to capture Grove and Plumb had hurt Filkins' egotism and goaded him to vow either to capture or kill them. He encountered difficulty in raising a posse, for some of the older men were disgusted with his sadistic thirst for revenge. Though fully aware of the legal laxity in bringing the Loomises to justice, they had no intention of staining their hands with Loomis blood. Filkins found only nine willing men, including Ephraim Conger, Fred Hall, John Garvey and George Southard.

At five o'clock Monday morning the posse started for the Loomis farm in two separate parties: Filkins, with Hall, Garvey and Southard, rode in from the north; Conger and the others advanced on foot from Sweet's Corners. As Filkins' men neared the farm, Fred Hall who, like all Quakers, hated bloodshed, thrust his rifle upright in a snowbank.

"What are you doing, Fred?" asked Filkins.

"I won't need this," Hall announced. "I'll do no shooting."

The Loomises were watching for the officers, for Grove had received a note from a prominent Madison County official, telling him of the proposed attack and urging him to leave the county if he valued his life. Grove, heeding the advice, had caught the stage at the Center for Albany.

As the posse came within sight Plumb Loomis, disguised as Grove and mounted on one of his brother's fastest horses, rode out from behind the barn. George Southard, who carried no gun, leaned from his saddle and retrieved Hall's rifle. He merely planned to frighten Plumb by shooting over his head, but Filkins clutched his arm and brought the rifle barrel down.

"Shoot lower!" re commanded.

The roar of the rifle broke the stillness. Plumb reeled in his saddle and clutched his wrist.

"You hit him!" the constable shouted excitedly. "Fire again!"

He fired his own rifle, but the bullet missed. Plumb returned the fire, whirled his horse and galloped down the road. Seeing Conger and his men, he pulled his mount up shortly, but a bullet from Conger's rifle broke the horse's leg and the animal stumbled. Plumb, cursing loudly, fired his revolver at the posse until the hammer clicked on the empty chambers. By this time Filkins, Southard, Hall, and Garvey were closing in on him. Southard recklessly rode close to Plumb's horse. Leaning from the saddle he clubbed his rifle and struck Loomis a heavy blow on the head which dazed him and brought the blood streaming down his face. As Southard raised his rifle for the finishing blow Plumb's horse crumbled in a heap, pinning its rider. Despite his wounds Plumb freed himself. Clutching his useless, bloody hand he ran towards the Swamp. Some of the officers fired at him; others labored through the snow after him. They were too slow. He disappeared in the Swamp.

The Utica Morning Herald reported: "Officers tracked him for five miles by the blood which he left on the snow showing he had been severely wounded but they did not come up with him."

Plumb made his way through the Swamp to the Center, where his cousin, Dr. Medina Preston, extracted the bullet, bandaged the wound and hid him that night. He caught the morning stage for Albany, where he went to a hospital.

Filkins' posse thought they had been shooting at Grove, and the newspapers named him as the hunted man. Said The Herald: "We hear that a chase is still going on after Grove Loomis. Numerous officials, a large delegation from Madison

County and a portion of the population of the town of Sanferfield armed with rifles, pistols, clubs and other dangerous weapons are scouring the swamps. The mischief of it is, however, that Grove has many accomplices scattered through the town who help secrete him. We hope the hunt may be successful but doubt that it will."

A rumor that the wounded man had his arm amputated was also reported by The Herald. This was cleared up by a statement published in The Waterville Times: "A medical gentleman states that it was Plumb, and not Grove who was pursued. That Plumb was hit by one of the fifteen discharges, aimed at him under the supposition that he was Grove; that Plumb has since received his professional advice and care; and that Plumb was shot in the wrist, and the ball was imbedded there when he was called to see him."

The end of November found Wash still lodged in the Madison County jail, awaiting trial for the highway robbery of Jeremiah Clark and the attempted murder of William Clark. His attorneys beseeched Justice Holmes to allow their client bail, but Holmes turned a deaf ear.

"Wash must be tried this time," he announced grimly. "There is not enough money in Madison or Oneida Counties to bail him."

Mrs. Rhoda Loomis was furious, and evidently decided she would try to help him escape. She baked a mince pie, a very special pie, for in it she placed several small files. The pie was delivered to the jail with instructions that it should be given to her son.

The pie's deep golden crust made the jailer's mouth water. He did not think Wash would mind if he cut himself a slice. When he started to cut the crust, the knife grated on steel. He lifted the flaky crust and found the files.

"Say, Wash," he asked the prisoner a short time later, does your mother put hardware in all the pies she bakes?"

The question surprised Wash, although he surmised the reason for it.

"What kind of pie?" he asked.

"Mince."

"Yes," Wash laughed, "she always puts in pieces of iron when she bakes mince pies."

The Herald carried the story, but almost immediately The Hamilton Union denied that Mrs. Loomis had sent him the pie.

The Circuit Court which opened its session in the Madison County Courthouse the following March was notoriously liberal with justice. Several murderers who expected to pay the death penalty were astonished to find thmselves sentenced to two-year prison terms. The Court also admitted Wash Loomis to bail. His freedom was cut short a few minutes later when an Oneida County officer arrested him and took him to Rome to answer several indictments, including resisting Deputy George Klinck and other officers with deadly weapons.

Wash evidently took his change of jails lightly. He had no fear of being brought to trial by county courts which too often had made a travesty of justice. The Utica Morning Herald predicted: "As this county enjoys a reputation for being remarkably facile in bailing criminals, it is probable that Wash will soon be out again, and that will be the end of the matter."

Late in April Wash was given his freedom. A nolle prosqui was entered in his case and the indictments were dropped. He returned home with one thought in mind, to take revenge on Officer Filkins. Wash made no immediate attempt to attack the officer, for the ruthlessness of Filkins' raid had frightened the family. The officer preferred to shoot first and argue afterwards.

CHAPTER X

THE GANG TAKES OVER

The Loomises managed to escape the attention of the newspapers for a few months, but their machinations were visible in the criminal activities which swept the countryside. A blooded horse was stolen from Ballard Upson's stable in Camden on Christmas night, 1858. Several residents of the village told Upson they had seen a horse resembling his, hitched to a sleigh carrying two men in the direction of Higginsville. Upson enlisted the aid of the law officers of Oneida, Madison and Chenango Counties. They were able to follow the trail of the thieves south into Chenango County, where they learned that one of the men was Julius Glazier of Oriskany Falls, the brother of Plumb's girl.

Deputy Sheriff Bryant of Sherburne arrested Glazier two weeks later and took him before a Camden justice. He denied knowing another youth, James L. Trowbridge of Camden, with whom he had been seen. Further questioning caused him to make a statement: "I was with Trowbridge last Christmas night, but I left him early and went to Bill Loomis' place to spend the night. About three o'clock the next morning Trowbridge arrived with the stolen horse. We then took the horse and drove through several places and at last arrived at Samuel Peckham's farm in the town of Hamilton, Madison County. It was there I parted company with Trowbridge, he preferring to remain there with the horse.

"I returned to Oriskany Falls and a few days later Trowbridge came there to see me. He told me the owner of the horse had come for him and that he, Trowbridge, had escaped by drawing his revolver and taking to his heels. His story frightened me, but some of the Loomises came to my house and took me to Hamilton. From there I went to Susquehanna for a visit, intending to return when it was safe to do so. I returned yesterday and shortly afterwards Deputy Bryant arrested me."

Glazier was committed to jail, while a posse was sent out to capture Trowbridge. Sidney Peckham, who had sheltered the thieves and the stolen horse, became frightened. He returnd the horse to Upson. "I found this horse of yours running loose in my barnyard last Tuesday morning," he explained.

Trowbridge was captured shortly afterwards and was sentenced with Glazier to a short term in prison. The Loomises, with all their powerful legal talent, made no move to defend them.

The village of Hamilton was terrorized with rowdyism. "Drunkeness has run rampant in our steets," reported a Hamilton correspondent in The Utica Morning Herald. "No one is safe to appear out alone after dark for fear of insult. After a lewd carousal on last Saturday night (Jan. 15, 1859) one of the gang, Sam Edson, was arrested and sentenced to jail but managed to escape the officer."

At Deansville (Deansboro) thieves broke into the store of Page & Mowrey on Tuesday night, August 23, knocked off the knob on the safe with a sledge hammer, drilled through the outer wall of the safe door and then blew it open with a charge of gunpowder. They left with eighty dollars in cash.

In October, while the venerable Chauncey Miller of Sangerfield lay dying, thieves entered his barn and stole his oats. Immediately after Mr. Miller's funeral the barn was again entered and several buffalo robes were taken. In November Edwin Abby's hired man named Green was shot down in cold blood while attempting to stop thieves from entering his employer's barn. In South Hamilton DeWitt Dennison, who was arrested while passing counterfeit money, nonchalantly posted $1,000 bail and was discharged by Justice Mason to continue his activities. In Waterville a valuable horse was stolen from Edmund Terry and never recovered. Jack Keenan picked up a wealthy young drunk with his sleigh while driving from Deansville to Utica. When the drunk went to sleep in the bottom of the sleigh Keenan emptied his pockets. He awoke in time to discover that fifty dollars had been taken from him. The youth accused Keenan, who denied the theft. The young man grabbed hold of Keenan's neck and threatened to kill him. Keenan returned twenty-five dollars. The young man had the thief arrested, but it was a year later before Keenan was brought to trial.

While the thieves took their toll from the Valley, Jeremiah and William Clark, long thorns in the sides of the Loomises, were brought to trial for stealing the Loomis sheep in April 1860. Failure of the jury to agree caused an uproar in court and the presiding judge discharged them. A new jury friendly to the Loomises was impaneled and in record time brought in a verdict of guilty. The Clarks' sentences to prison terms constituted a moral victory for the Loomises. They had accomplished the impossible in bringing the Clarks to justice for a doubtful crime, while they, guilty of nearly every conceivable offense, remained free.

One of the best accounts revealing the operations of the gang during this period was told to a reporter of The Oneida Democrat-Union by Charles Terrill of Eaton in October of 1932. Terrill and his mother, Sarepha Cone Terrill, came to Eaton from New Berlin, Chenango County. Charles was about ten years old at the time of which he related: "I came to Eaton in 1849 and later my mother, a widow, was married to Richard Waters, a man of considerable means. He owned three places, one east of the village, where Fred Fitzgibbons now lives, one on the back street that leads to the station in which he lived, and the other a farm between Eaton and West Eaton, now occupied by a Mr. Mulks.

"This latter farm he sold shortly after his marriage to my mother and received in payment $1,000 in gold, which he put in a tin box, fastened it with a padlock and put the box in a big chest used for packing bedquilts in our spare bedroom, and locked the chest. My stepfather waited until Ellis Morse should go to Waterville to deposit this money, as there were no nearer banks at that time.

"One day a man with a fine span of horses drove up, fastened the horses, and came to the door. Mother went to the door and he asked if Richard Waters lived there. Being told that he did, I was sent to call him and the gentlemen invited to sit. When my stepfather came in the man told him that he was buying gold, which was at a premium, and asked him how much he had. My stepfather asked him how much premium he was paying and the gentleman said that it depended on the size of the pieces. Stepfather opened the stair door, which was directly in front of the man, and went up after the box, which he brought down, unlocked it and, running his hand through the money, lifted some up. 'Quite a lot of small pieces,' said the man. 'And quite a lot of large ones,' said stepfather. The man then named the premium and stepfather objected to it as too small. Then the man said, 'Gold is going up every day and if I come over next week I may be able to pay you more.'

"That was satisfactory and my stepfather carried the gold back upstairs, the man staying until he came down, when he went away.

"The next day being Sunday we went to the Baptist Church, stepfather ahead, mother following, and I lagging along behind. A man passed stepfather, bowed and smiled and met mother, who recognized him as the man who had called about the gold. She called to stepfather and told him that probably the man was going to our home, so we all turned back and found the man near the house, but he walked on to the bridge and then came back and went away, not stopping.

"One day the next week, when I came home from school, Mother said, 'Son, I have cleaned your bedroom today and you will have to sleep up in the spare room.'

"Later I went up to bed and sleep. Some time in the night I was partially aroused by cattle lowing, but rolled over and went to sleep again. Then something hit my head and I roused up and saw a man pulling up the curtain. He had already raised the window and was partly in the room. I tried to call mother, but there was such a big lump in my throat I could hardly make a sound. However, mother thought she heard me call and told stepfather to go up with the lamp and she would grab a towel and come as she thought I had a spell of nose bleeding. They came up and mother said, 'What is the matter, son, is your nose bleeding?'

" 'No, no!' I said, shaking. 'Look! Burglars!' pointing to the window.

" 'We're robbed, we're robbed!' cried stepfather, and ran to the chest, which he found locked. When mother had quieted me we all went downstairs. There was not much sleep for us that night.

"Stepfather went across the road to the home of George Morgan, who was a constable, knocked on his door, and as Mr. Morgan came to the door his big watchdog, who was kept in the barn to protect a valuable horse owned by him, jumped on him. 'Why Jack,' said he, 'who let you out?'

" 'Burglars,' said stepfather. 'They have stolen Frank,' said Mr. Morgan, and ran for the barn. He found the horse all safe and then wondered why the barn was broken into.

"Later, on going over to our house, he found his 18-foot ladder up to our windows. 'Well,' said he, 'there was only one man that knew I kept that ladder up on the haymow.'

"Next day we saw where a path had been made past the windows where a sentry could see if anyone went upstairs and so warn the burglar.

"When I went to school the next day, a teacher, Miss Campbell, came down the walk to meet me. She threw both arms around my neck and gave me a resounding smack, which I remember to this day, and said, 'My brave little hero.'

"Stepfather went right after Ellis Morse and the $1,000 in gold was deposited at Waterville without delay.

"Later we learned that this man was one of the celebrated Loomis gang."

In October Albert Steele's residence in Bridgewater was burglarized on a Sunday night and $2,500 in notes and mortgages and sixteen dollars in cash were stolen. The two pocketbooks with the papers in them were found beside the road next day by P. B. Crandall.

In the hamlet of Willowvale in the Sauquoit Valley, the machine shop and pistol factory of Amos Rogers and Julius Spencer was entered on Wednesday night, October 30th.

"About fifty-two pistols (were) taken," said Charles D. Rogers, an employee. "I was the first person who discovered that the pistols had been taken and that the window was forced open. I found the tools that the window was opened with — a crowbar, an axe, a claw and other implements which appeared to have been used to affect the entrance. The cupboard containing them was forced open and the lock broken. We always number our pistols consecutively. We knew the number contained in the cupboard and what ones were taken by the list that was taken the night before the robbery. The fifty-two pistols were worth $16 apiece."

That same evening Edward Montgomery and Edward Eastman stopped at the American Hotel in Waterville for a few drinks. It was a cold night, so Montgomery drove his horse and buggy into the hotel shed where the animal would have protection against the chilling wind. When he returned a few hours later to unhitch the horse and start for home he noticed his skunk skin lap robe was missing from the seat of the buggy. He reported the theft to the proprietor, Aurelius "Bill" Benedict, who was also one of the town constables.

"I saw old man Beebe and several members of the gang hanging about the streets tonight," Benedict said. "It won't surprise me if some of them stole it."

"It wouldn't surprise me either. Something ought to be done about it."

"The Times says we ought to organize a Vigilance committee and clean out the gang."

The men agreed and considered how an organization could be started. Benedict admitted it was a problem as everyone was afraid of the Loomises.

Montgomery slapped his chest. "I'm not afraid of the gang. I'm going to see old Beebe and get my robe back. It's worth forty dollars."

Benedict shook his head. "I don't think you'll have much success."

"Maybe not. Remember, Bill, it's a dark night, but it might be lighter before I arrive home."

Old Ezra Beebe lived over the hill next to Asa Carter's farm, on the Old State Road. Shortly after one o'clock the following morning Beebe's barn caught fire mysteriously and burned to the ground. A span of horses valued at $150 belonging to Albertus Spencer was lost in the fire. While the building was ablaze, loosened clapboards fell from the side and several pistols fell out. These were later identified as part of the loot stolen from Rogers & Spencer's machine shop and from G. W. Tallman, a government contractor in Utica.

Beebe rode over to Montgomery's farm in the town of Marcy and accused the young man of incendiarism.

"I hear you told Bill Benedict the night was going to be lighter," he said. "You meant you were going to burn my place."

"You damned old thief," Montgomery roared. "You dare to accuse me. Get off my place."

"I'll have the law on you—" Beebe spat.

Montgomery seized the old man by his coat collar, whirled him around and propelled him to his horse with a well-directed kick at his posterior.

"Now get going and keep going," he directed. "If I ever catch you around my place again, I'll ring your damn neck."

Cursing, Beebe climbed into his buggy and departed. Whether Montgomery was responsible for starting the fire was never proven. Ezra Beebe did not bring any charges against him.

On the 21st Ezra and his son, La Vergue, visited the inn operated by J. P. Clark in Deansville. In answer to direct questions Clark revealed that he kept several watches in a desk and his money in the drawer. Two days later Clark discovered that the watches, about seventy-five dollars in money and some notes were missing. The Beebe's were arrested and indicted but after they had jumped bail several times, their cases were dropped.

Thieves also visited Clarkville and stole a silver-plated harness from a Mr. Jordon. The stores of a Mr. Brownell and a Mr. Mowry were entered and a buffalo robe and other merchandise were stolen from each. The robes were found later, each hidden beneath a village church. The harness was never recovered.

The Madison Observer commented sharply on the thieving in the village of Madison: "Horses, harnesses, leather boots, shoes, buffalo and wolf robes, cloth, clothing, etc. were taken. Not long ago ladies' underclothes were taken from the yard of Allen Curtis, the same night a small quantity was missed from the yard of John Dye. The next night an attempt was made to enter Mr. Dye's home. A few nights later an attempt was made to pick the lock of Curtis and Dye's carriage house. It failed. On Tuesday night of the fifth, two valuable robes and thirty chickens were taken from Henry Taylor and a piece of cotton cloth from D. Z. Brockett. On Sunday morning of the tenth, a robe was stolen from Rev. C. Swift's carriage while he conducted religious services at the Durfee School House."

Although it was well known that the Loomises were acting as receivers of these stolen goods, the law was unable to implicate them. Their associates could not be intimidated to reveal any of the family's secrets. A few of the Loomis' dissatisfied laborers had threatened to seek recourse through the courts, but this brought the wrath of the Loomises on them.

A popular folk-tale concerns a member of the gang who became restless over sixty dollars the Loomises owed him and threatened to take legal action. He obtained a day off to go to Clinton on business. Suspecting the man's intentions, Plumb granted permission. "Why waste money on fare to get to Clinton?" Loomis asked. "You can take one of our horses."

The worker accepted the offer and drove to Clinton. Upon his arrival in that village he was arrested on a charge of stealing the horse and buggy from the Loomises. It was useless to try to prove his innocence when he was brought to trial in Deansville.

John J. Bennet of Utica, who was present at the trial, said, "The fellow swore on the stand that the horse had been a loan, but he couldn't prove it. I heard Plumb tell his attorney where to find the answer to the knotty legal point. Plumb suggested to his hired man that if he would forget about the alleged debt of sixty dollars, he would drop the matter of the horse."

This solved the problem and the hired man gave no further trouble.

"There was also another employee who, during an argument over wages, threatened to have the whole gang arrested," Mr. Bennet disclosed, "and he set out for Utica with that intention. When he arrived he was immediately arrested and taken before a justice for stealing a watch . Although he denied the charge, the watch was found in his pocket, where it obviously had been planted."

CHAPTER XI

THE WAR YEARS

Affairs in the Chenango Valley were overshadowed during the first few months of 1861 by a national crisis. On April 12th the Confederate batteries opened fire on Fort Sumter. The North and the South were plunged into a long and bitter conflict. President Lincoln called for volunteers and almost overnight every city, village and hamlet in the North responded. On May 10th The Waterville Times stated: "The Company forming here is nearly full. They proceed to Utica on Friday and thence to Elmira on Saturday at 11:00 A. M. to join Christian's regiment. They feel as if they had enlisted for a good cause." One week later the same paper said: "Last Friday about 9:00 o'clock the portion of Captain Palmer's company from this place bade farewell and started for the war. The Company proceeded to Deansville (Deansboro) accompanied by the Waterville Brass Band where they were joined by the Oriskany Falls volunteers."

On July 22 Charles Tucker and Charles Underhill of Madison University were authorized to recruit volunteers for Company G, 114th Infantry at Hamilton and Brookfield. Meetings and torch light parades were held in Hamilton, Clarkville, Leonardsville, North Brookfield and Hubbardsville. The war was like a fever; the martial music of the small fife and drum corps and the rousing speeches by smartly-clad officers in army blue stirred the imagination of the younger men. From the farms, the factories and even from the schools they came to enlist, giving their names carefully to Henry Corbin and Albert Nichols of Hamilton, who wrote them down on the enrollment sheet.

Grove and Plumb Loomis had returned from their self-imposed exile. Plumb tried to enlist, but the army physicians turned him down because of a bad heart.

"Believing his reputation was against him, he had his cousin, Dr. Medina Preston, give him a thorough examination," his niece, Mrs. Collins, said. "Dr. Preston assured Uncle Plumb that the army doctors had diagnosed his ailment correctly."

There is no evidence to indicate that the Loomises took any further interest in the war, unless it was to turn its effect on the countryside to their profit. Before the war the Loomises were said to have taken Salem Loucks, one of their colored men and a noted thief, south and sold him. The Utica Morning Herald stated: "It is reported that a gang of thieves have taken the negro south several times and sold him and that he always invariably came back to Sangerfield and divided the spoils with his sellers."

During the war the Loomis farm became a rendezvous for deserters. Constable Filkins raided the property and arrested Grove Loomis and Ezra Beebe for enticing and harboring deserters. The Herald said: "Grove L. Loomis who was arrested by Officer Filkins on Friday last was indicted at the term of U. S. Court in session at Albany on a charge of harboring, concealing and employing deserters. He waived examination and was held to bail in the sum of $1,000."

Neither Grove nor Ezra Beebe ever were brought to trial.

A reporter for the Utica Telegraph made this observation after a raid on the homestead: ". . . on looking in the window, no less than a dozen deserters were discovered, with military clothes upon them, and Wash himself was afterwards seen with a soldier's overcoat on. The house is evidently a rendezvous for these scamps; it were well if the locality could be rummaged, and a lot of these worse than rebels, arrested."

Wash, impatient to settle accounts with Filkins, got Grove and Plumb to aid him in seeking a legal means of obtaining revenge. Early in May the three brothers drove to Higginsville and persuaded Justice Samuel Marsh to issue warrants for the arrest of Filkins and certain members of his posses on charges of assault with attempt to kill. Alfred Collins, a friend of the Loomises who resided in the Town of Verona, also swore out warrants against Filkins and his men for killing the horse Plumb had been riding during the last raid. Collins stated that he had loaned it to the Loomises.

Filkins was standing in the doorway of the paint and harness shop under his home when Denio Loomis, somberly attired in a black frock coat and hat and accompanied by Constable M. C. Marsh of Verona, drove up to serve the warrants. Filkins submitted to arrest, but refused to be handcuffed or to give up his revolver. Denio drove to the crossroads in North Brookfield, where Wash, Plumb and Grove Loomis were waiting with a wagon in which Fred Hall, Ephraim Conger, Kit Mason, George Southard, John Garvey and several other members of Filkins' posses were sitting handcuffed.

"We've got you dead to right this time!" Wash exclaimed. "We're taking you and your men to Higginsville for trial."

"You can't do that," Filkins protested. "I demand you take me before a magistrate of this county where I can be admitted to bail according to law."

"The law does not accord such privileges."

"I insist it does," Filkins reported angrily. He removed his coat and flumg it on the ground. "I refuse to go with this party unless you proceed according to law."

Wash decided to use a different strategy. "Suppose we compromise, Jim," he suggested. "I'll take you before a Madison County justice. If he says I'm right, will you go to Higginsville with me?"

"Why Higginsville?" Filkins squinted warily.

"That's where the warrants were issued."

"I calc'late that's fair enough. I'll go with you." He put his coat on and climbed into the wagon.

Plumb Loomis sprang into the wagon and cuffed him on the head.

"We've got you this time, you murdering bastard," Plumb shouted. "When we get through with you, you'll wish you were in hell."

Filkins whirled about and caught Plumb by the throat. As Loomis struggled to break the iron grip that slowly throttled him, Filkins turned to Constable Marsh, who had watched in silence. "Are you going to give me protection of the law or do I take matters in my own hands?"

Marsh looked helplessly at Wash.

"What do you say, Wash?" Filkins asked.

"Release my brother," Wash said. "I'll see he doesn't bother you any more. He can ride in the carriage with Denio."

Filkins shook Plumb, then shoved him roughly aside. Gasping for breath, Loomis fell against the sideboards.

The ex-blacksmith shook a horny fist in his face. "If I get any more abuse from you, I'll knock you clean out of this wagon," he shouted.

Plumb joined Denio in the carriage. Wash and Grove climbed to the driver's seat of the wagon and Marsh seated himself near Filkins. The party proceeded in silence until they approached the main plank road stretching between Hubbardsville and Waterville. Grove, driving the team, showed no inclination of turning left towards Hubbardsville; instead he drove onto the dirt road at Sweet's Corners that led through the Swamp towards the Loomis farm. Aware of Grove's intentions Filkins jumped to the ground, followed by several of the handcuffed prisoners.

Grove pulled his team up beside the road.

"What's the trouble?" Wash asked.

"We're getting off here," cried Fred Hall.

"You know damn well what the trouble is," Filkins shouted angrily. "You had no intention of taking any of us before a Madison County magistrate."

Wash grinned apologetically.

"It is poor faith on your part," Filkins bristled. "I thought you were a man of your word."

Before Wash was able to reply Grove flung down the horses' reins and picked up a cudgel from the pile under the wagon seat. "Why waste time arguing, Wash?" he asked, Raising the cudgel above his head he advanced towards Filkins, who stood watching him through narrowed eyes. A sudden warning from Fred Hall caused Filkins to turn to see Plumb Loomis coming towards him with a broken fence rail.

Filkins drew his revolver and warned them he would shoot to kill. Wash jumped down from the wagon to help his brothers. He shouted for Constable Marsh for aid. As they started to move upon Filkins the other prisoners picked up some of the clubs that lay near them in the wagon. Although they were handicapped by their handcuffs they swarmed over the Loomises and threatened to kill them. Wash gave up. Following a compromise he agreed to drive the prisoners to Waterville for a hearing before Justice Church. Filkins agreed, and the party started off.

Half an hour later they were assembled in Justice Church's office in Waterville. The Loomises displayed their warrants and the Justice heard statements of both sides of the case.

"I can see no reason why Mr. Filkins should not have an examination before a Madison County magistrate," the Justice remarked. "As for the other defendants, if they will agree to answer when notified, I'll release them immediately."

Wash chagrined at this unexpected decision, turned sorrowfully to Filkins. "Jim," he said, "I'd rather give you the best horse I've got than to have you go back home this way."

Filkins and his wife were preparing for bed that evening when they heard a loud knock on their kitchen door.

"Who's there?" The constable hurriedly pulled on his trousers. "Who is it?" he asked again.

"Kit. Open the door — quick! I want to see you."

Filkins recognized the voice of Christopher Mason, a neighbor who only that morning had been a handcuffed prisoner of the Loomises. He unbolted the door. Wash, Denio and Plumb Loomis, with Kit Mason, Byron Tubbs and William Fleming, burst into the room. Filkins fought savagely against overwhelming odds, but Wash knocked him down and Denio handcuffed him. Plumb and Denio helped Filkins to his feet with several kicks. At Wash's instructions they prodded the prisoner from the room. Mrs. Filkins screamed for help but one of the gang pushed her roughly back into the bedroom and slammed the door. The Loomises dumped the battered constable into a wagon and drove him to their farm.

Mrs. Filkins hurriedly aroused the villagers. A posse of grim, armed men under Ephraim Conger rode hard for the Loomis farm, only to learn that Filkins had been taken to Higginsville, forty miles away. Determinedly they headed their horses towards the north.

At eight o'clock the following morning the Loomises drove into Oneida, where Wash permitted Filkins to visit an attorney, Mathew J. Shoecraft, to whom the Loomises showed their warrant. After reading it and understanding the irregularities of the case, he consented to represent Filkins. He drove with them to Higginsville.

Filkins was ushered into Justice Marsh's chambers. The magistrate who had issued the warrant for Filkins opened court and began the hearing. Shoecraft, who was afraid of neither man nor devil, bluntly termed the case against his client a trumped-up farce. Justice Marsh angrily tried to silence the attorney as the posse from North Brookfield rushed into the room with drawn guns. Justice Marsh quickly granted Filkins bail and released him.

The trial of Hall, Southard, Garvey, Conger and the other men who had assisted Filkins in raids on the Loomises took place at the office of a Justice of the Peace in Oneida Castle a few months later, Thomas L. Hall revealed. "David Mitchell, the picturesque, long-haired Hamilton lawyer, appeared for the prosecution, while Roscoe Conkling of Utica handled the defense," Hall said. "Mitchell, long noted for his courtroom dramatics, pictured the Loomises as a noble people, incapable of crime who were continually being persecuted. For the first time in his life the long-haired attorney overplayed his part. The Loomises were too notorious and both the jury and spectators found Mitchell's reference to them humorous. The prisoners were acquitted, but not before Conkling had summed up the entire proceedure with these words: 'We have met the Lion of Madison County, the Honorable Mr. Mitchell. He has shaken his mane and threshed his tail, but all of his words were of no avail.' "

Filkins' case never came to trial. After the acquittal of his special officers Plumb endeavored, without success, to have the grand jury indict him for attempted murder. Shortly afterwards one of the men who had served on the jury met Filkins on a street in Waterville.

"Filkins," he said, "we came very near indicting you for not killing Plumb."

The constable grinned. "The only apology I can make," he said, "is that it was so early in the morning I could not see very well."

Filkins immediately had Wash, Plumb, Denio, Grove and William Loomis, Byron Tubbs and William Fleming arrested on charges of assault and battery with intent to kill and they were indicted at the September term of the Madison County Court of Sessions. The Loomis attorneys had the case postponed from term to term until it was finally brought to trial before Justice William Campbell at the June, 1864 term of the Madison County Supreme Court. The action against Grove, Tubbs and Fleming had been dropped, so only the Loomis brothers stood trial. After a lengthly deliberation the jury found William, Plumb and Denio not guilty of assault and battery. On the 17th the jury returned a verdict of guilty against Wash, based on the fact that he had kicked Filkins. Justice Campbell fined him $25 and gave him thirty days in which to pay.

CHAPTER XII

THE SYNDICATE OF THIEVES

Rising prices and the army's need for cavalry and artillery horses caused outbreaks of horse stealing all over the state. Unlike the Loomises most of the thieves had no regular channels for disposing of the stolen animals and only a few were adept at changing a horse's appearance. Wash Loomis, aware of the situation, sent Grove to contact horse thieves throughout southern and western New York, while he covered the northern and eastern parts of the state. By offering good prices and bonuses together with a steady market, the brothers persuaded the thieves to join them in a syndicate with the distributing point at the Loomis farm.

Like a general mapping a strategic campaign, Wash ascertained the best routes to follow, made relay stations and found definite markets in New York, Pennsylvania and Canada. Horses and other stolen merchandise either coming or going to Alexandria or Montreal usually followed the route through Kingston, Cape Vincent, Pulaski, Williamstown and Higginsville, where Bill Loomis lived. After Denio located at Bardeen's Corners in Oswego County, horses would come by way of Pulaski, Mexico and Parish. The Albany market was legitimate, but the Loomises sold droves of disguised animals there without detection. They disposed of most of the stock stolen from their home vicinity in Scranton, Pennsylvania. A fourth route, to Vermont, followed closely that taken by the father of the family when he had migrated to Central New York; from the Winooski Valley to Whitehall, thence southward by way of Saratoga Springs to the Mohawk River, crossing in the vicinity of Palatine Bridge or Canajoharie.

The Loomis brothers were almost constantly on the search for suitable horses. During the warm summer months they traveled on horseback or rode behind a spirited team in a high-slung carriage or Democrat wagon. In winter they invariably used a two-seated sleigh, silver-plated and decorated with gold leaf, with red plumes at the front of the dash. Their appearance in any community usually led to the disappearance of horses.

This was the fate of a horse owned by Dinny Ryan of Plattsburg. Like a true Irishman, Dinny was passionately devoted to his wife and his horse. One day a Loomis, driving past the Ryan farm, stopped long enough to admire Dinny's horse and to inquire if he would sell it. Dinny refused to part with the animal at any price, so Loomis departed. A few mornings later Dinny discovered that the horse was missing. Although he advertised widely and offered a substantial reward the animal was never recovered.

"When my husband lost his horse," Mrs. Ryan said, "his heart was broken."

Thomas Dawson Cooper of Sterling in Cayuga County was renowned throughout the state for breeding fine horses. Several of his stallions and brood mares came up missing one day. He followed their trail to a small clearing in the nearby woods, where their shoe marks vanished without a trace. A friend notified the horse breeder that the Loomises had been seen with the stallions and mares. Cooper went to Sangerfield, but was unable to find any trace of his property.

At Ames in the lower Mohawk Valley stock began to appear and disappear mysteriously whenever five Negroes, all associated with the Loomis gang, were around. The leader, Black Abe Lovitt, a six foot Adonis in ebony, worked as a hostler and sometimes as a "house nigger." He had an unfailing thirst for rum, but when sober was considered a good hand with horses. Farmers often hired him to break their unruly colts. Black Abe helped steal many of the best horses from the same farmers who gave him employment. After disguising them they were taken to the Loomises for a quick sale.

The outstanding thief associated with the Loomises was Bill Alvord, a tall, solidly built, handsome man with dark hair and carefully trimmed beard. In 1862, he together with John Maxwell and John Simms, began operating "thief boats" on the Erie Canal. Alvord's boat, the "Dan Hartwell," traveled the canal from Buffalo to Albany; its crew stole cattle, horses and merchandise from the farms, villages and cities along the route. All this plunder was not taken to Sangerfield. Some was left at Bill Loomis' farm on the Side Cut Canal, and some was taken to the Loomis farm at Bardeen's Corners. Frequently the stock was spread around on the farms of Loomis associates until their markings could be changed and then sold.

Other people associated with the Loomises were the Mains, Beebes, Kenyons, Robinsons, Spencers, Helmers, McIntyres, Crandalls, Johnsons, Eastmans, Lombards, Montgomerys and Peckhams. Many of them came from respectable families and were well-educated, but all helped make the Loomis name feared and hated in nearly every upstate community. Wherever the gang's depredations were known, every innocent person named Loomis, whether related by blood ties or not, felt the lash of criticism. Even today many Loomises resent any reference to the outlaw branch of their family.

The Loomis name offered no more protection from Wash and his brothers than any other victims. About two miles south of the Loomis farm on the Swamp Road resided Russell and Hiram Loomis. One night a member of the gang cleaned out Russell Loomis' grain bin. Upon discovering the loss Russell and his hired man drove to the Loomis farm. Wash received them politely, denied the theft and firmly refused their request to search the premises for the grain.

The gang had no fear of the law. On Sunday, July 14, 1861 the small office of District Attorney Hiram T. Jenkins that stood at the corner of his yard on the Genesee Turnpike at Oneida Castle was entered by burglars, who used the key that had hung conveniently nearby for twenty years, and stole nearly two bushels of valuable papers. They included notes made out to both the District Attorney and his wife, bonds and mortgages totaling $15,000, and papers in fifteen civil suits and a number of indictments, including some against the Loomises. The District Attorney offered a reward of $100 for the recovery of his property and another $100 for the detection of the thief. All the papers except the indictments were found a few months later mixed in with leaves in a neighboring yard, after it was reported that Jenkins had paid Wash Loomis $250 for their recovery.

The gang was particularly active that fall. The newspapers listed burglaries and robberies daily. The gun shop of Earl Loomis at South Hamilton was entered and eighteen rifles and $400 were taken. A team of bay mares owned by Luman L. Blakeman was stolen from the barn of Thomas Collins in Madison. Over $100 worth of clothing and dress goods were taken from James Brand's tailor shop in Leonardsville. The home of Dr. Medina Preston, first cousin of the Loomis brothers, at Sangerfield Center was entered in September and ladies' wearing apparel and the doctor's overcoat were stolen.

Three work horses and a colt owned by Harrison J. Sweet of Marcy, a member of the "Marcy Horse Thief Detectives" were taken from his pasture on Friday night, October fourth. Captain Charles Lawrence was notified on Sunday and twelve members of the Thief Detectives fanned out in every direction for clues. Before dark on Monday they found the horses at the Loomis farm and took the thieves, all members of the gang, to jail.

Mr. Waldo of the firm of Blackman & Waldo of Waterville, returning from a business trip to Bridgewater, was held up within two miles of his home and his purse taken. Burglars broke into the office and shoe shop of Justice of the Peace Ira B. Crandall at South Brookfield, and took his justice's docket containing records for the past six years, packages of justice's blanks, and public documents. The thieves also entered the Crandall home without disturbing the Crandalls or their watch dog and took a $15 watch from a nail hanging over the justice's head.

Documents and family stories disclosed the wide area the Loomis brothers and their gang covered on their travels into the south and west.

Walter Fox of Olean recalled the brothers trading and selling horses in Virginia, and Mrs. Loretta Church of Atlantic City and her sister, Mrs. Lorena Sturges of Whitesboro, granddaughters of Welcome Welch, who resided near the Loomises remembered hearing about Jesse James visiting the Loomis homestead above the Nine-Mile Swamp.

Mr. Fox, who spent his childhood in Washington, D. C. and nearby Virginia, remembered meeting an "old-timer" near New Market, Virginia. "When he learned I was a York Stater, he told me his home farm was at Woodstock, Virginia,' Mr. Fox remarked.

"He said when he was young a farm next to his was occupied by a gang of horse thieves from New York State," Fox remembered. 'They were members of the Loomis Gang,' the old timer said, and then queried, 'Did you ever hear of them?'

"When I replied I had, the oldster remarked, 'Well, the fellows we used to see were always gentlemen around us. They sold us lots of good horses at reasonable prices. We figured maybe they were stolen up North, but as long as they were stealing 'em from Yankees, it didn't worry us any.'

"This just proves that the Loomis Gang got around a bit, as well as being well-organized," Mr. Fox added.

As unusual as it may seem, there is always the possibility that Jesse James and his older brother, Alexander Franklin (Frank) James of Missouri might have visited the Loomis farms at Sangerfield, Higginsville, or Bardeen's Corners.

The two granddaughters of Welcome Welch claim their grandfather often spoke of it, as well as their parents, Charles and Lorinda Welch Lathrop, who owned the Cedar Valley House at North Brookfield Station.

On the other hand, Roy Cary of the Mile Strip, whose father, John Cary was a cousin of James Filkins, said if the crusty little constable had known it, he would have done something about it. George Bissell of Waterville, whose father, Henry Bissell, took part in one of the raids, said he did not believe the story.

However, Butch Cassidy's Wild Bunch from "The Hole In the Wall," Montana, came to New York City to hide, and ended up in South America, so there is every possibility that Jesse and Frank James did visit the Loomises twice a year to swap stolen horses and other merchandise, as Mrs. Church and Mrs. Sturges claimed.

This is the way the sisters told the story:

"Grandfather Welch lived the next farm to the Loomises, but never had anything to do with them," the sisters said, except to be agreeable and say, 'good morning.' He said as long as they left him alone, he would leave them alone.

"One year the hops sold for a pretty good price a pound," Mrs. Church said. "Grandfather had a big lot of hops, and I believe he sold them in September. He drove one horse hitched to a sulky to Waterville and got the money.

"He was coming back late at night, probably 10 or 11 o'clock. There was a spree going on at the Loomis farm, and grandmother later said it was one of the meetings with Jesse James and his gang.

"This was the original Jesse James. His gang used to meet with the Loomises twice a year to exchange property each wanted to get out of his district. They met on the big plateau on the high hill in back of the Loomis home. There was a place for dancing, tables on which to eat, and even a band to provide the music. However, you couldn't hear the band down on the Swamp Road.

"Grandfather said as he passed by the Loomis house, the wagons and rigs were all headed in toward the house, and the horses were tied there. They were just as thick as they could be. He was a little afraid at first since he thought they might hold him up for his money, but he kept his horse trotting right along as if to make them think he was not afraid. He related, every little ways men would say, 'Good evening, Mr. Welch, good evening, Mr. Welch.'

"It was so dark he couldn't see the men who hailed him or identify them by their voices. He got home safe with his money.

"The next day my mother's brother, who was about sixteen or seventeen at the time, took his gun and went up on the plateau. He liked to hunt. Nothing had been cleaned up. The remains of food were on the tables, and the trampled earth marked the site of the dancing. Looked like the Loomises and the James Brothers had a real spree," Mrs. Sturges related.

The sisters also told of meetings of the Loomises and the Jameses held in Oswego County, beyond "Central Squre."

Mrs. Church and Mrs. Sturges were emphatic that the meetings took place. They said Plumb Loomis told the details to their grandfather.

After Jesse James was shot and killed by Robert Ford on April 3, 1882 in Missouri, his brother, Frank surrendered. While talking with a reporter, Frank said, "You will be surprised when I tell you that I have lived in Texas, California, Arkansas, Louisiana, Mississippi, Tennessee, Virginia, Maryland, and New York."

The Utica Morning Herald reported on November 21; "Last evening between eight and nine o'clock Menzo W. Cole of Deansville was robbed of $1,900. He had been to Verona Station to deliver hops which he had sold and was on his way home with the money. About half way between Vernon and Vernon Castle he met two men on foot in the road conversing together. As they came opposite him, they seized him by the coat collar and dragged him from his wagon and knocked him unconscious and stole his money. On coming to he went to Mr. Bartholomew's, the nearest house, and told his story. Meanwhile the horse had gone on to Knox's Corners where it was found. Marks were found near the site of the robbery where a horse and wagon had been turned into the street and hitched to a fence. One of the robbers was short and thick, with a large full face, covered with whiskers and dark complexioned. Cole did not see the other man's face, although it was a bright moonlight evening. Cole had $500 in Bank of Vernon bills, $1,000 in this State's money (assorted) and $190 in an order on one of his neighbors."

Daniel Peckham stole a sorrel mare from Henry Babcock in the town of Brookfield and was traced to the Loomis farm. He was one of the few men arrested and sent to jail.

Wash always disclaimed knowledge of the men who made the Loomis farm their hangout. Richard Meyers of Brookfield, who drove to the Loomises on business, was surprised at dinner time to sit down at a huge table in the kitchen with some of the biggest criminals loose in the state. "They sat eating," he said. "First one would come in and eat and say nothing. When he finished he would get up and go out and someone else would take his place. It made me feel funny.

" 'You must run quite a boarding house,' I remarked to Wash.

" 'I don't know what they do,' Wash answered, 'but they come and go.' "

The Loomises had their own way of punishing members who threatened their existence. One of their Negroes, who had grown tired of ill-treatment by the Loomises, made no secret of his fear of the family and obtained work elsewhere. He tried to collect his wages from the Loomises, and when they refused to pay him, he threatened to tell all he knew to the law. On his last day at the Loomises he was sent with other men to the hayfield on the upper part of the farm. As the men walked up the dugway behind the house, a scythe gleamed in the sunlight, and the Negro fell almost disembowled. A few hours later Julius Watson and Luther Babcock of Clarkville, who were hunting in the Swamp, came upon the Negro kneeling by the creek trying to wash the blood from his intestines, which he was trying to hold in place with one hand. Watson testified later that he and Luther offered to help him, but the Negro was in agony and did not seem to know what they were saying. He never saw the Negro again or heard anything more about him.

Clayton Risley of Hamilton, widely known floriculturist and historian, said Wash Loomis called his grandfather, Perry Risley, who resided nearby, to look at the dead man lying beside a fence in the lot.

"He was helping us hay it," Risley quoted Wash as telling his grandfather, "and he fell on his scythe and cut himself."

There are no records of the case ever having been investigated. Harold Mason stated that the dead man was buried in the northwest corner of the nearby Terrytown Cemetery. "Several years ago a bush that bore red berries grew on the grave," Mason recalled. "No one could identify it. Now that too has disappeared."

Other undisciplined members of the gang were framed by the Loomises for crimes they had not committed and turned over to the law officers for punishment.

Countless similar authentic stories and folk tales of cruelty have been told about the Loomis family, but seldom outside their own vicinity does one hear of their kindly deeds.

"The Loomises stole a team of horses that I prized very highly," Robert Roberts, who resided north of Hubbard's Corners, told a friend. "I promptly hitched up another horse and drove to the Loomises. Wash was at home and acted as if he had been expecting me. I knew he wondered why I had come alone instead of bringing a deputy sheriff.

" 'I've lost my team, Wash,' I said, 'Will you help me find them?'

"He seemed surprised at my request, for I neither demanded or threatened him as his other victims had done.

" 'Certainly I will, Mr. Roberts,' he replied, 'but you will have to accompany me.'

"I agreed and later that day we started out together in one of Wash's carriages. We journeyed southward for four days, far into Pennsylvania. Whenever we were hungry or needed a place to spend the night, Wash would stop at some farm or wayside tavern. There was always a table set for us or beds ready for us to sleep in. No one asked either of us any questions and we did not pay a cent out for the hospitality shown us. I sensed it was all a part of the vast Loomis organization. When we inquired about my horses we were always told that they were a short distance beyond.

"Eventually we located them and brought them back with us to my farm at Hubbard's Corners. I was grateful to Wash for aiding me in getting the team back.

" 'How much do I owe you, Wash?' I asked after our return.

" 'Why, Mr. Roberts,' Wash answered, 'I wouldn't think of charging a neighbor anything.' "

Everett Terry, a deputy sheriff who was born and brought up on the farm adjoining the Loomis place on the north, related in later years, "I remember well enough seeing them drive off the stolen horses they had accumulated. After changing the appearance of these horses by dyeing and clipping, they would be hitched one after the other to the tail of a wagon. The boys would go over the turnpike to Albany to sell them. During the Civil War they did a big business.

"Some enterprising young thief made off with my favorite mare one night during hop picking time while I was attending a dance at Chet Buckley's. Another young fellow who was there told me my horse and buggy had disappeared. I ran from the barn in time to hear the drumming of hoofs and the creak of the carriage wheels going across the bridge in the hollow.

"I hurried home and harnessed up another horse and started out. I picked up Grove Loomis, who lived nearby, to help me in the chase. There was a light frost covering the ground and we could follow the thief's trail with ease. Through the night we went and finally found my stolen mare and carriage near Pitcher in Chenango County near the Cortland County line. The thief had disappeared. The mare had made the trip of fifty-five miles in five hours and was in a sorry state. I was mighty glad to have Grove with me that night."

Perry Risley, who lived up the road from the Loomises, missed his yoke of oxen from his barn one morning. He went to the Loomis home. "I think my oxen have strayed from my barn," he said to Wash. "If you should see them wandering around I wish you'd let me know."

"I'll have my men see if they can find them," Loomis said. The next morning the oxen were in Risley's yard.

Tim O'Connell had a yoke of oxen that the Loomises wanted to buy. Realizing that they might be stolen if he refused, Tim agreed to sell. The Loomises paid him $100 and drove the oxen away. When the Irishman went to the bank to deposit the money he discovered that forty dollars was good money and the rest counterfeit. Tim went to the Loomises and handed Wash the counterfeit money.

"I ain't the complainin' kind," remarked Tim, "but by jashus I don't want this kind of paper."

Wash took the bills and grinned. "I'm sorry, Tim," he said. "I didn't know my brothers gave you this."

He reached into his pocket and extracted a large roll of bills. He counted out sixty dollars and handed them to his neighbor. "Here's your money," he stated, "and take my word it is good."

Big Tom Brady, another Irishman, who lived on the eastern slope of the Chenango hills on a cross road between the turnpike and Stockwell, owned a spirited team which Grove wished him to sell.

"I'd like to, Grove," Tom said, "but my wife kinda sets a store by those horses and wouldn't let me."

"I'm sorry, too," replied Grove. "I'd like to own those horses."

"And, Grove—"

"What, Tom?"

"My wife would be mighty broken hearted if those horses were stolen."

"I wouldn't blame her. Have no fear, Tom. Your horses are safe."

"And they were," Tom Brady commented later, "although the Loomises were stealing horses all over the state."

On another occasion a Lowell farmer driving to Rome overtook a handsome, well dressed man walking along the road and offered him a ride. The stranger proved himself a good conversationalist; he spoke with authority on crops, horses and politics. Talk turned to the Loomis gang.

"What's your opinion of them?" the stranger asked.

The farmer's good humor vanished. "I think they're a damned pack of thieves," he said, "and the sooner they're exterminated, the better off we'll be."

The stranger's eyes twinkled. "I guess they are a bad lot. Did they ever bother you?" he asked.

"Nope, and I hope they don't. But if they're hung, I'd like to help string 'em up."

In Rome the farmer halted his team and watched the stranger alight. "Sorry I ain't goin' no further," he said, "but I turn here to go home."

"That's all right," the stranger said. "I'd appreciated the ride and our interesting conversation."

"By the way," the farmer called to him, "you didn't tell me your name."

"I'm Wash Loomis," the stranger said.

CHAPTER XIII

UNDERGROUND STABLES

The Loomises had man-made underground stables for the stolen horses and other stock, but evidently not in the Sangerfield area.

The stories of underground caves at the Sangerfield home farm have persisted for many years. One such story was related by Shirley Marion "Pop" Risley of Earlville to Carl Carmer, who used it in his book "Listen For a Lonesome Drum" (1936). Risley claims it was told to him by an Irish peddler, that Plumb Loomis stepped on a clod of dirt and the whole side hill behind the house opened up and showed a big stable.

Neighbors of the Loomises claim the story is false, and even Risley said he did not believe it.

However, stories of underground stables have persisted as being "back in the woods" on Bill Loomis' farm near Higginsville and the Loomis farm at Bardeen's Corners.

Walter Fox related the following incident concerning an underground stable:

"Around 1912 or 1913, probably, a large stockade, enclosing maybe five or ten acres with running water through them, was discovered buried deep in some woods either between Checkered House and Dugway, or Dugway and Maple View (once Union Square).

"As I recall now the high board fence which was in a dilapidated condition was discovered by some kids on a hike. Just about everyone but the elderly owner surmised that it too had once served the nefarious purposes of the Loomises. Again relying on human memory which may err, the owner, a man in his mid-seventies, then was reticent about discussing the 'find.' This again led to the surmising that possibly he had more knowledge of the gang's activities than he was

111

telling. He was a church member in good standing when I knew him, and an exceptionally law abiding citizen."

Fox said it was only fair to state that the Loomises he knew around that area were good citizens, trying their best to live down the bad name given them by the Loomises who weren't even related to them in some instances.

A somewhat similar story was told by Mrs. Church of Atlantic City. Mrs. Church claimed she visited the underground stable near Central Square (about 1930). She claimed that Jesse James often met with the Loomises there.

"One day my husband and I went out with a young man named Earl Selby and his wife from Utica, to the woods up there (beyond Central Square)," Mrs. Church recalled. "We took our lunch and planned to spend the entire day.

"Well, we got to Central Square and we took a left hand road from there. We drove up near Bardeen's Corners and left our car, and had to walk up a trail. He (the Utican) knew the way because he had been there with someone from Syracuse. He had a compass with him or I don't think we would have ever found our way back.

"We followed this trail and we eventually came out into the most beautiful glen you ever saw. It was a big area and covered with beautiful grass. There were several trees, but not close together. I thought it was lovely," she said.

"There was quite a rise in the ground there, and I said, 'Oh, there is a stream, I can hear the water lapping,' and he said, 'Oh yes, over there.'

" 'And they tell me this is where the Loomises and the Jameses used to meet and used to bring their stock in here and exchange it sometimes,' she said.

"Mr. Selby went up there on the slight knoll and picked out a spot where the markings were. He pulled on a piece of sod that you could never see in the world, and underneath that were doors, trap doors. They used to take that sod away and there were trap doors where they could drive their cattle right in.

"My, that was an awful big place under there," Mrs. Church stated. "We went and looked over the edge by this brook and you could see how far the underground stable extended. It was right on the brink with about enough room for a man to walk along the edge of the brook. They had a few windows on the brook side, but none on the knoll side.

"Someone lived there, in the old days, and took care of those cattle, whenever they got them, or horses. I bet if you could locate that farm, you could still find the underground stable.

"Mr. Selby who took us there said it was found by a man, whom I think was president of a bank in Syracuse, while he was on a hunting trip," Mrs. Church explained.

"Never heard of a cave or underground cavern near the Loomises Sangerfield farm," she said.

CHAPTER XIV

LOOT FROM THE LOOMIS ATTIC

Constable Filkins, having grown resentful of the farcial justice practiced in the courts of Madison County, began seriously to consider moving to Waterville in Oneida County, where Morris Terry, Reuben Tower and several other prominent hop growers and business men had promised to finance him in a campaign to break up the Loomis gang. His decision hinged on his campaign for re-election to office. Wheeler Loomis offered his support and Filkins accepted reluctantly. When the ballots were counted on election day in March, 1862 Filkins discovered that he had lost by three votes. The Loomises had helped to get him out of office.

Filkins moved to Waterville with his family and settled down in a big, roomy house on the corner of Stafford Avenue and Hooker Street. He found the village of 1,110 people thriving and prosperous. Unlike its earlier rival, Sangerfield Center, it had progressed steadily during the sixty-nine years of its existence. From the first few mills and dwellings along the banks of Winona Creek, the community had spread eastward and westward along Main Street, Front Street and Back Street. The hop yards on the outskirts had brought wealth and fame to the village. Fine dwellings of wood, brick and stone lined the wide streets. The village also boasted four churches, three schools, an academy, a bank, a fine weekly newspaper, The Waterville Times, mercantile, grocery and hardware stores.

The American Hotel was the scene of many spectacular exhibitions and its hotel barn and horse sheds housed many small traveling circuses. The collection of tinted horse-prints in the Park Hotel's barroom drew admirers from all over the county. Jap Easton's saloon served a frozen delicacy known as ice cream.

Filkins' efforts to break the power of the Loomis gang had established his reputation. When Constable Orlando Stetson failed to qualify for re-election Filkins was immediately nominated for constable by both political parties. Despite the efforts of the Loomises, who controlled some 500 to 800 votes in Oneida County, he was elected by a large majority.

"I accept the nomination," he told the men who were responsible for his victory, "on the promise of you people to stand by me in my efforts to uproot this hellish gang. At this time I can enumerate seventy persons in the town of Sangerfield alone who are either affiliated with the Loomises or stand ready to harbor or bail them. Many are land holders and nearly all are of fair standing in this community."

When Denio Loomis heard of Filkins' election he patted the revolver hidden under his coat. "By God," he swore, "if Filkins ever comes on our premises again, I'll shoot him."

Denio's threats became so troublesome that the newly-elected constable procured a peace warrant which was given to Officer Beardslee to serve. Beardslee went to the Loomis farm with one assistant, Albert Root, who later became a Hamilton dentist. Denio tried to escape, but was quickly handcuffed by Root. The officers brought him to Waterville for an examination before Justice Church, who released him on bail.

Thoroughly angered, Denio charged Root with drawing a revolver and threatening his life.

"Root did not even properly belong to the posse," he argued.

This point was debated at Root's trial. From the opening of the trial everything had been in Loomis' favor. Officer Beardslee, when called to testify, even refused to swear that Root had been a member of his posse. Denio had two trained witnesses in his behalf. Root had no defense, and for some unknown reason the Court would not permit him to take the stand. Denio was allowed that privilege but made one mistake. He was too positive that the revolver with which Root had threatened him and had been loaded because "he had seen the points of the bullets when it was pointed at him."

Justice Church called for the revolver. Without looking at its chambers he pointed it at Denio.

"Tell me, Mr. Loomis," he declared, "looking at this revolver, would you tell the Court whether it is loaded or not?"

Denio squinted at the weapon, then lifted his eyes until they met those of the Justice. "No," he stated, "it is not loaded."

Justice Church broke the revolver and, turning it upside down, allowed the bullets to fall on the bench. "Mr. Loomis," he said sternly, "you did not know whether this revolver was loaded or not, for you could not see the points of the bullets." He rapped with his gavel. "Case dismissed."

Early in April Filkins began planning his next move against the Loomises. There was no doubt that much of the merchandise stolen over a period of several months was secreted on the Loomis farm, but it was almost impossible to find a victim of the gang with enough courage to make a formal complaint. The reasons were obvious. In practically every case where someone had taken action against the family, revenge had been swift and thorough.

Towards the middle of the month Julius Corey of North Brookfield asked Constable Filkins if he would search the Loomis home for some goods stolen from his place a few months earlier. On Friday the 25th Filkins obtained a search warrant and went to the Loomis farm, accompanied by Corey, John C. Hall of Cherry Valley and John W. Marsh of North Brookfield.

They found Wash and Cornelia at the homestead. Filkins displayed his search warrant and was surprised when they courteously invited the men in and offered to assist them. The men started in the cellar and carefully searched each floor. They reached the garret without finding any of the loot they were certain was hidden in the house.

As the brother and sister watched, the officers carefully inspected the contents of several trunks, piles of cast off clothing and odd pieces of furniture without success. Filkins sank to his knees and started to drum on the floor with his fists. He suddenly shouted in triumph. Using a jackknife, he pried out a panel of perfectly matched flooring and found a large hole underneath. As the light was poor in the attic he had one of the officers go downstairs to find a candle. Wash sent Cornelia and one of the other men also to procure a light. While they were gone Wash told the other member of the posse to keep quiet, and then pulled several sacks from the cavity in the floor and hid them in a part of the room that had been searched.

Filkins returned and found the hole empty. The officer in whom Wash had placed his confidence feared the constable's wrath more and quickly told of the sacks being removed. Filkins found the sacks. One contained boots and shoes and the other a robe that had been stolen from Edward T. Montgomery of Marcy and six revolvers taken from a pistol factory in Willowvale. Wash insisted that the goods belonged to his family and that he had witnesses to prove it. Filkins ignored him and took the filled sacks away as possible evidence.

During the next few days victims of the gang from Utica, Marcy, Leonardsville, Willowvale, North Brookfield, Hamilton and other localities appeared in Waterville to inspect the exhibit. Almost everyone identified something that he had owned. Julius Corey's property was recovered, as well as several whips and blankets taken from Leonardsville. The revolvers belonged to a lot taken from Rogers and Spencer's Pistol Factory in Willowvile. Montgomery identified his robe.

Filkins arrested Wash Loomis on a charge of grand larceny. As Justice Church was about to open court, he glanced from Wash to the constable.

"Why do you bring this infernal scoundrel before me?" he asked. "Why don't you take him out and hang him?"

The property taken from the Loomis home was submitted as evidence and the claimants testified to their ownership. Filkins, Corey, Marsh and John C. Hall each took the stand to testify how the goods had been found. Wash waived examination to the charge against him and Justice Church held him to bail, setting the amount at $500. As soon as the money was posted Wash was rearrested by Filkins on a charge of receiving and possessing stolen property. Again he waived examination and Justice Church fixed $500 as the amount of bail on the charge. This was also paid by friends of the Loomises.

During the hearing James Brand, a Leonardsville tailor whom the gang had robbed a few months earlier, discovered a spectator wearing one of his stolen coats. He pointed the man out to Filkins, who identified him as a member of the gang. The constable arrested George Peckham at the tailor's insistence, but the prisoner denied the theft.

"I didn't steal it," he argued. "I bought it from John Hall."

The day following Wash's release a farmer named Brown, who had been missing sheep, swore out a search warrant against the Loomises. Filkins drove to the Loomis farm with Brown to look for the sheep. As they were entering the driveway Plumb and Denio, who were examining some horses, leaped on two of them.

"Wait a minute." Filkins jumped from his buggy and waved his hands. "You needn't run. I've no warrant for you."

Wash received the constable and Brown with almost exaggerated politeness. "I didn't expect you to call again so soon," he said to Filkins. "What's the charge this time?"

The constable grinned and produced a search warrant. "Mr. Brown has been missing some sheep and has asked me to look over your flock."

Wash told them they were welcome to look. "I'll have Plumb and Denio drive them up here into the front yard." He shouted brief orders to his brothers.

Brown pointed out his sheep to Filkins, who had them separated from the others.

"Well, Wash," Filkins stated, "we've found what we came after."

Loomis stroked his beard thoughtfully. "You know, Jim," he remarked, "there's a damn sight of iniquity in this county.

John Hall probably stole those sheep and put them in our flock to cast suspicion on us. Mr. Brown, you can ask any of your neighbors who have lost sheep to come up here and look our flock over."

When the Oneida County grand jury convened District Attorney Hiram T. Jenkins sought the indictment of George Washington W. Loomis on charges of grand larceny and receiving stolen goods. The merchandise found in the Loomis garret was presented as evidence. As soon as the evidence had been accepted the witnesses were called to testify. The first was Edward T. Montgomery, who gave Marcy as his address.

"About the 30th of October, 1861," he said, "I had a robe stole from under a shed of the American Hotel in the village of Waterville between the hours of six and ten. About the 18th of April, I next saw the robe in possession of Constable Filkins, who told me he found it secreted in the house of G. W. W. Loomis. The robe was worth thirty dollars."

Constable Filkins was called next.

"I am the officer who made the search of the Loomis' premises and found the robe referred to. (I) found no men at the house. (I) found the robe in the Loomis' garret in a bag with six revolvers of Rogers make. The robe was rolled up in an oil cloth very tightly. (I) think the robe was worth upwards of thirty dollars. I showed the pistols to Mr. Rogers who identified them by their number and otherwise as part of the lot that was stolen from his shop last October in Willowvale, about fifty in number."

After Filkins' testimony had been taken the remaining witnesses, Bradford Montgomery, John C. Hall, Julius Corey, John W. Marsh, Charles D. Rogers, George W. Tallman, Edward Eastman, Charlotte Beebe, Henry Stower and Lewis Rogers were heard.

"I am employed in the pistol factory at Willowvale," Rogers testified. "The firm of Rogers and Spencer. (I) was in the shop the morning on the 30th of October, 1861. (I) found that the cupboard had been broken open. My brothers told me that fifty-two revolvers had been taken. I identified the pistols shown me by Officer Filkins as those found in the house of Loomis. I know they were part of a lot stolen from our shop."

As soon as the last witness' testimony had been taken the District Attorney reminded the jurors that an indictment could be found in which a count for larceny and another for receiving stolen goods might be included. He cited a page from Wharton's Crime Law as his authority.

"The punishment for such crimes," Jenkins continued, "could not exceed five years imprisonment, or six months in the county jail or by a fine not exceeding $250, or both."

After a conference the grand jurors found the indictment against Wash Loomis for both charges as requested.

Wash's trial was scheduled for the latter part of the month but his attorney, Daniel C. Pomeroy, wanted to study the case. He sent a note to the District Attorney:

"Rome Aug. 25th
Friend Jenkins

Will you consent that the indictment against G. W. W. Loomis go over this next term of court? I don't believe he can get ready.

Please let me hear from you by return mail.
       Yours truly,
       D. C. Pomeroy"

Jenkins agreed to let the case go to the December term; and then, at Pomeroy's further insistence, it was postponed until the January, 1863 term. By this time the District Attorney had agreed to bring only a charge of larceny against Wash for stealing the revolvers from the Willowvale factory. The indictment for receiving stolen goods based on the finding of Montgomery's robe in the Loomis garret was filed away.

On the 13th Wash failed to appear and his surety, Calvin Bently, was forced to forfeit the bail he had posted for Loomis. The next day Wash appeared with his attorney. The trial was a travesty. Without leaving the courtroom the jury gave a unanimous verdict of "Not guilty."

CHAPTER XV

FIRES IN THE NIGHT

"You'll smoke for this," was an ominous threat the Loomises sometimes made in anger, older residents have related and across the countryside barns, hop kilns and other buildings blazed fiercely against the dark curtain of night. There was never any evidence that the Loomises were to blame. During the hundred years they resided in upstate New York only the father, George W. Loomis, had been indicted for arson in 1837, but even that case never came to trial.

Newspapers usually devoted a single paragraph to the area fires, as The Times reported in 1862: "Tues. Sept. 23. A barn filled with hay, grain, farming tools, etc. belonging to Joseph Deity in the town of Sullivan burned to the ground. Three men were seen prowling around but there is no evidence."

Henry Dennison Crandall and his wife, Phoebe, who resided at Coontown on the highway between Leonardsville and West Edmeston, learned that the Loomises' smoke threat could not be ignored. The Crandalls, an elderly couple who operated a large farm, kept five young milch cows in a pasture near their home and Mrs. Crandall made butter and cheese.

"My father made his money during the Civil War by making butter and cheese," Mrs. Marian Crandall Maxson of West Edmeston revealed. "My father used to get up at two and three o'clock in the morning and drive to Oneida Square in Utica to sell his dairy products. They brought high prices during the war days.

"When anything was stolen in those days it was generally taken to the Loomis farm, but the people were too afraid to go there after it, for the gang would be sure to get revenge.

My father had his young cows stolen and he went to the Loomis farm. He found the cows in the Loomis barn.

"Plumb was there and he said, 'What do you want, old man?'"

"Father said, "I want my cows you stole.'

"Plumb denied having them, but father opened up the stanchions and let out his cows. Plumb picked up a heavy stool and hit father, but father made him put it down. As father drove his cows from the barn Plumb said, "Well, old man, you've got your cattle, but you'll smoke for them one of these nights.' "

The argument over the stock occurred in the autumn of 1862, Mrs. Phoebe Baldwin Davis of Brookfield recalled. "I remember because my mother, Martha Coman, was Crandall's hired girl for twelve years," she said.

"After Mr. Crandall recovered his stock, Mother and her sister, Emily, were down in the orchard near Five Corners gathering apples. Wagons and carriages were continually passing on the roads, but the girls paid no attention until they heard the angry voices of two men. The girls crawled through the brush to spy. They saw two men, Mr. Crandall and Grove Loomis, arguing. Grove was cursing.

" 'Damn you,' Grove shouted, 'why didn't you act like a man instead of a sneak in coming over to our place and searching for your heifers? If you had come to me, I'd have got your heifers. Now, by God, you'll smoke for this.'

"Mother didn't know what Grove meant, but she learned. In April of 1863, Mother was in her bedroom off the woodshed getting dressed to attend a church social. It was nearly nightfall, and Mother said there was a hollow roaring sound in the air, as if a strong wind was blowing outside. Mother said she was afraid a storm was brewing and she wouldn't be able to go to the social. Then she heard a crackling of wood and smoke began to come into the bedroom. Mother opened her door and found the woodshed and rear of the house in flames. She got out of the building and found the

Crandalls were safe. They got out what furnishings they could, but the house burned down before their eyes.

"Mr. Crandall felt sure the Loomises were to blame for the fire, but there was no way to prove it. He built another house on the site and worked hard to regain his loss."

The Loomises were unable to escape the menace of fire. The year 1864 was extremely dry, and crops were stunted and failed to mature for lack of rain. By July fires had started in the dry timberlands all over the state. The woods north and west of Rome were burned over, and forest fires were reported simultaneously at Watertown, Syracuse, Jordan, Pulaski and Lowville.

On Saturday, July 23, The Utica Morning Herald reported: "Waterville—The woods on what is known as the 'Nine-Mile Swamp,' about four miles south of this village, are on fire. The fire started on Mr. Roswell Conger's land yesterday morning, and is supposed to have originated from the burning of a brush heap by Mr. C. . . ."

That same night the Loomis' big barn and several of their out-buildings went up in flames, consuming several horses, wagons and their recently-harvested hay. It was a blow to the family, who claimed everything "was destroyed before anyone knew there was any fire in the barns."

Wash Loomis ignored the theory that the raging swamp fire had reached out to swallow up their buildings. "It was that goddamn LaVern Beebe who fired our place," he insisted, but would offer no further explanation concerning that member of his gang.

The Loomises started immediately to replace their buildings. The Earlville-Waterville Plank Road Company, which was on the verge of bankruptcy, started to sell some of its tollgates after the public refused to pay toll for the bad roads. The Loomises purchased the tollhouse near North Brookfield and started to move it to their farm. Using oxen and heavy rollers, they had reached a point about three miles north of Sweet's Corners late one afternoon when they quit for the day. A few hours later seventeen-year-old Henry Bissell of Waterville and his friend, Julius Montgomery of Peck's Corners, drove past and saw the building.

"I had heard the Loomises had bought it and were moving it," Bissell related. "I began to think of all the people I knew whom the Loomises had burned out, and I thought I would help even the score. Julius and I climbed out of the carriage and looked around. Seeing no one, I took a gallon can of kerosene out of the buggy and threw it on the toll house. I lighted a match and touched it off. The flames shot up into the air as Julius and I drove away in a hurry. Later I heard that the Loomises thought the friction of the rollers had started the fire."

By September the continual drouth had taken its toll of the hop yards in the area. The destruction was so widespread, scarcely a single hop yard remained unharmed. The hops that reached the market sold for the low price of forty cents. Farmers who had mortgaged their farms, putting everything into hops, were ruined.

The Loomises had never forgotten that Deputy Sheriff Ephraim Conger of North Brookfield had helped Constable Filkins lead posses in raids on their farm. They were further incensed when considerable stolen property was found at homes of many of their friends. In May, 1863 a covered buggy, double harness and a pair of matched wolf robes were stolen at Midford, Schoharie County. The property, valued at $900, was traced to Sangerfield, but there it had completely vanished. Several advertisements were circulated.

On Friday, September 23, 1864 Deputy Conger, accompanied by the owner and several Milford officers, found the buggy in the barn of Dr. A. N. Griswold at Clarkville. The robes were discovered at S. O. Maine's home some three miles east of Sweet's Corners. The stolen property was taken to Conger's Exchange Hotel at the Corners and locked in the barn.

About one o'clock the following morning Tom Mott, who had been hired by the Loomises, set fire to the barn in the loft and nearby shed. The flames were discovered about two o'clock and an effort was made to save the buildings. Conger and his help managed to save two of his five horses, also the stolen buggy and wolf robes. The fire spread and the men, thinking the hotel would catch, worked frantically to remove all the furnishings. The hotel was saved, but the barns and sheds burned to the ground. Conger lost three horses, two harnesses, a buggy, tools and all his hay and grain. Although he carried $2,100 insurance on the propetry, he estimated it would cost about $6,000 to rebuild.

Conger was certain that the fires had been started by an arsonist, but there were no clues to connect it with the Loomises.

The weather was temporarily forgotten when the October term of the Madison County Circuit Court and Court of Oyer and Terminer convened in the courthouse in Morrisville with Justice Balcom presiding. Several indictments against Wash, Wheeler, Grove and Plumb Loomis and Ezra Beebe were scheduled to be tried. Indications were that the Loomises faced a crucial period in their lives.

Four civil cases were disposed of on Monday, the 10th, the opening day, and Judge Balcom then proceeded to dispose of a large share of the court calendar. He then adjourned court for the day and instructed Sheriff William F. Bonney to have the Loomis brothers in court on Tuesday for trial.

That night a light rain began to fall. The moon was overcast and the village shrouded in darkness. About two o'clock in the morning a man walked swiftly up deserted Main Street to the Engine House near the Tillinghast home. The silent figure slipped around to the rear of the small building, found a window that was unlocked and entered. He located an axe on the hose cart and methodically set to work cutting the hose. When finished he restored everything to its place and left.

At two-thirty a horse galloped wildly over North Street towards Pratt's Hollow. The noise brought several villagers to their windows. The horse and rider disappeared, but the street was unusually bright. A thin pall of smoke settled over the village.

"Fire!" The fear-stricken cry rose high and shrill. "Fire! The courthouse is on fire."

Lights appeared in the buildings along the streets and men and women in brief apparel poured out of doorways into the road. The flames of the burning structure rose high above the trees. The fire bell in the cupola of the Engine House clanged repeatedly. The first volunteers who arrived threw open the doors and began to drag out the cumbersome pumper. As others arrived the pumper started to roll and it was pulled across the road to the fountain in front of the burning building.

The cupola of the courthouse was shrouded in flames and the vestibule on the lower floor in the northwest corner of the structure was also ablaze. Smoke poured from the roof and the explosion of the windows and the crackling of the burning wood caused many of the spectators to fall back. A bucket-brigade had been started as the pumper was primed. Some of the firemen started to raise and lower the wide pump-handles. A broken stream of water from the chopped-up hose doused the spectators. A heavy-set man elbowed his way to the pumper as some of the firemen ran for the extra hose in the Engine House.

"Wash was in town when the fire broke out and took his turn at the brake of the engine," Cummings wrote. "He seemed to be utterly astonished when someone told him that the hose had been cut.

" 'It's a damn outrage and I would like to help hang the man who did it.' "

The hose was quickly replaced and a stream of water shot on the burning building. The fire was already out of control. As the villagers watched the flames ate rapidly through the dry timbers; two hours later the structure collapsed in a hollow roar that sent a shower of sparks and burning embers high into the air.

The firemen saw that it was useless to try to save the courthouse, so they turned their hose on the adjoining jail and county clerk's office. The jail was an old wooden structure and the clerk's office was constructed of stone and was fire-proof. The light rain had soaked the buildings and neither caught fire.

The villagers slowly drifted homeward as daylight came. Only a burning pile of blackened timbers marked where the courthouse had stood. The Madison Observer reported: "Most of the books and papers of any great value in the courthouse were rescued. Wm. W. Osgood, Esq. of Hornellsville, who was in attendance upon the court as a reporter, lost all his minutes, including those taken at several other circuits. The courthouse was erected some sixteen years ago, under the supervision of Messrs. Ellis Morse, Samuel White and the late Oliver Pool, and was a convenient, well-built edifice and justly considered as an ornament to our village. As to the origin of the fire, there is no question that it was the work of an incendiary, who went about his fiendish business in so thorough and systematic a manner to fail in accomplishing his detection. As to the motive of the deed, there is a difference of opinion. So far as we are informed, there was nothing in the business pending before the court, either civil or criminal, that would make the destruction of the courthouse or the interruption of the judicial business desirable. Some impute the act to revenge for former criminal proceedings; while others find the motive in something besides malice, but none the less disreputable and which, if true, time will ere long develop."

Court reassembled later that morning in the big hall of the Madison County Hotel, but the accommodations were too small and Justice Balcolm made a final adjournment early that afternoon.

Sheriff Bonney and his deputies immediately launched a search for clues to the arsonist. The village board met in special session and unanimously voted a $1,000 reward for information leading to the arrest and conviction of the incendiary. The sheriff found a horse that had been reported as stolen the night of the fire from the western part of the village running loose in a pasture between Pratt's Hollow and Munnsville. No clue was found to identify the thief.

One month later the hop house and barns owned by Allen Risley near North Brookfield were destroyed by fire, together with 6,000 pounds of hops, 200 bushels of corn, 40 tons of hay; three horses, a cow, three wagons and all the farming implements. The fire was also believed to have been started by an incendiary, but there was no proof. Allen estimated his loss between $4,000 and $5,000.

The Loomises also had their revenge on Morris Terry of Waterville, the wealthy father of Cort Terry, when they sent Tom Mott to "smoke him out." The Times reported: "Last Saturday night at a quarter to twelve (October 7, 1863) citizens were awakened by fire in the barn and hop kiln on Sanger Street belonging to Mr. Morris Terry. He succeeded in getting his horses out of the building, but all his bales of hops were destroyed. The buildings were insured for $2,400. The loss was about $2,600."

Site of Loomis Homestead as it appeared in 1950's

Drawing of Loomis Homestead — Burned in 1866
(Drawn by Lance T. Walter)

Plumb, Cornelia and Grove
The Loomises Pose for Tintypes

Wash Loomis — Some Said He Looked Like John Wilkes Booth who Killed President Lincoln

Top — Denio Loomis Home

Bottom — Home of Mr. & Mrs. Grove Loomis Collins in Tinker Hollow where Wash's ghost was seen

Fred Hall, Cort Terry, Henry Keith and Henry Bissell —
They Chased the Loomises.

Waterville in 1860's

Dennison and Phoebe Crandall and their Home at Leonardsville.

CHAPTER XVI

UNHAPPY LOOMIS WOMEN

During these years of hatred and violence the big Loomis homestead on the knoll overlooking Nine-Mile Swamp was avoided by most people as a plague spot. Gone forever were the gay, carefree days when the young bloods of the Valley gathered there nightly to eat, drink, dance and make merry with the plump servant girls. Though the Loomis hospitality remained unchanged, the few neighbors who called socially became aware of the growing discord in the family's life.

"I have often visited at the Loomis home," remarked Miss Lucinda Green of Hubbardsville, whose father was one of Madison County's largest hop merchants. "I went there one day with Eveann Risley, the wife of Gurd Risley. We knocked on the side door, but no one answered. We heard voices and a shuffling of feet inside, so we knocked again. When no one responded this time we bent over and looked through the curtained windows into the kitchen. The room seemed filled with young men and Mrs. Loomis was passing a large pan of doughnuts among them from which they filled their pockets. When the pan was empty the old lady spoke to them in an undertone, which we could not understand, and they silently filed out through the doorway into one of the front rooms. We rapped on the door again and this time Mrs. Loomis came and opened it and invited us in.

" 'I am so glad you came,' she smiled. 'Cornelia and I are all alone and we had no one to talk to.'

"She took us into the living room where we spent the afternoon talking. Although Eveann and I listened and watched the doors, we found nothing to indicate the presence of others in the house. As the afternoon passed we spoke of leaving.

" 'Oh, don't go,' Mrs. Loomis begged. 'Please stay. The boys are away so much, I get lonesome. We don't have the callers we used to.'

" 'We must go,' I insisted. 'It is getting so late.'

" 'Stay a moment longer,' the old lady said. 'I have something to show you. Did you ever see a cotton plant?'

"When Eveann and I agreed we hadn't, she went upstairs and returned a moment later with a small jar in which a small cotton plant was growing.

" 'I planted this from some seeds that were given me,' Mrs. Loomis said, 'and I was glad when they grew.'

"We remained a little while longer, but when we made our departure Mrs. Loomis accompanied us to the door.

" 'Do come again soon,' she said. 'I get so lonesome being alone.' "

Wash and Grove quarreled frequently with their strong-willed mother. Plumb and Denio, who had been loyally devoted to their brothers when they were younger, began to side with their mother. Cornelia also favored her. Most of the dissention in the household was over the money and property, and Mrs. Loomis' fear that her sons' attachments might take them from her.

Jane Alvord, the only daughter of William Alvord of Brookfield, was one of the first of many women who made their home with the Loomises. Alvord was a noted criminal who, using various aliases, operated "thief boats" on the Erie Canal. After his wife, Maria, ran away with one of his associates, he took his daughter to the Loomis home. A handsome woman, Jane in 1854 gave birth to a son whom she named Charles. Mrs. Loomis threatened her life, but would not allow the girl to leave. She went berrying one day down into the Swamp and fled. Late that afternoon she reached the home of Mr. and Mrs. Fred Hall in North Brookfield.

"Jane was a well-meaning woman," Tom Hall, one of the family's sons, related. "She told my mother she had been forced to flee in order to save her life. Jane worked for my parents at the time we children were born. She later married a respectable, well-to-do farmer, and often returned to visit us."

Hannah Wright, the first mistress of George Washington W. Loomis and the mother of his only son, was the daughter of a German farmer who resided near the Bill Loomis' farm in the Side Cut Canal region, near Higginsville. In 1859, while Wash was in that area on business, he met Hannah. After a few weeks of ardent wooing the girl succumbed to Wash's pleading and promise of marriage and went to live with him as his common-law wife in the Loomis home.

Hannah met the severe criticism of her family and friends as the months passed by insisting that she was legally married to the noted member of the Loomis family. Wash never disputed her claim. Mrs. Loomis and the rest of the family referred to her as a servant girl. Mrs. Loomis' fear of Hannah was based on the presumption that the girl's influence over Wash might eventually lead to marriage and deprive them of his share in the home farm.

Hannah found the dissention in the household unbearable, yet she courageously ignored the family's animosity and remained with her lover. She was a quiet, dignified woman.

"I saw Hannah Wright only once," Miss Green related. "I was only a child at the time and was visiting Mott Terry's home on Sanger Street in Waterville. It happened that Cornelia Loomis and Hannah Wright chose the same time to also pay a social visit.

"Mrs. Terry courteously invited the women into the parlor, although she was well aware of the enmity existing between her husband and son, Courtland, and the Loomises.

"Cornelia was very plain looking and very genteel in her manners. Hannah was a tall, thin woman of middle age, with a pleasant face. They stayed only a few minutes, but it was the last time I ever saw Hannah Wright alive."

The situation in the Loomis household became definitely more critical when the family learned that Hannah was expecting a child sometime early in 1861. Wash Loomis was away from home on business a great deal. During these long periods without his protection, Hannah was bedeviled by Mrs. Loomis, who threatened her life if she did not leave. When Hannah could stand the ordeal no longer, Wash took her to the home of Mr. and Mrs. George Belfield near South Brookfield.

Hannah's baby, a boy, was born in the Belfield home on February 10, 1861. Wash proudly named his son Grove after his brother. When Hannah was able to travel Wash took her and her son back to the Loomis home.

Mrs. Loomis faced the issue squarely. The baby would now inherit Wash's property, which she considered should belong to her and her family. Mrs. Loomis had argued with her stubborn son to break off the illicit relationship and he had refused. More drastic measures had to be taken. Shortly afterward Thomas Jones, alias Tom Mott, one of the most unscrupulous members of the gang, came to the Loomis home to stay. Mott was fully aware of what he had to do, and waited patiently for the opportunity. Late in November of 1861 his chance came.

Hannah Wright was working in the middle kitchen when Mott entered with a double-barreled rifle. He carefully loaded and capped both barrels, so the woman's suspicions would not be aroused. Hannah went about her work and paid no attention to Mott, who removed the stock of his rifle and shoved the capped barrel-head into the fireplace.

The gun suddenly exploded and Hannah screamed in agony and fell writhing to the floor as blood poured from a deep wound in her thigh. Dr. L. F. Barrows of Waterville was sent for, but there was little he could do.

"The bullet has severed an artery and is lodged in her limb," he told Wash.

It was thought Hannah had a slim chance but, as the days slipped by, gangrene set in and the poison swiftly flowed through her veins. She died on Saturday, December 8, 1861.

The Waterville Times, which waged the greatest fight against the Loomis gang of all the newspapers, failed to investigate the full details of the shooting. The Times dismissed Hannah's death, without mentioning her name, with a sentence on Friday, December 13th: "The girl which we spoke of as being shot about two weeks ago, died Saturday last, from the effects of the wound."

A coroner's inquest was reported to have been held, but none of the testimony exists today. The newspapers barely mentioned Hannah's murder until a decade later.

Filkins told Amos Cummings, reporter for The New York Weekly Sun, in 1879, that Mott enlisted in the army shortly after Hannah's murder. In a moment of drunkenness he boasted to a comrade that "Plumb and Denio promised me $50 to kill the girl, as they were jealous of her influence on Wash." Then, Mott complained, "They cheated me out of the money."

Although Plumb Loomis' girl, Adeline Glazier, the daughter of E. M. Glazier, a wealthy forwarding merchant, stayed in the Loomis home, Plumb was resentful whenever his brothers brought their women home. Grove, after many promiscuous affairs, brought home a seventeen-year old girl whom he had seduced by promise of marriage.

Ellen, or Nellie Smith, as she was more familiarly known, was a tall, well-formed girl with jet black hair and dark, flashing eyes. She had somewhat angular features, a Roman nose, and walked with a proud, erect carriage.

"I was born in England," she confessed. "(I) came to this country when six months old. My parents have lived in the town of Madison since I was seven years old. I was with the Loomises sixteen years. I went to live (there) when I was sixteen or seventeen years old (Wednesday, June 17, 1863).

"I met Grove when I was fourteen years old. I had been to church on Sunday and stepped into Mr. Peckham's to warm. Grove Loomis was there and I was introduced to him. I saw him again the next summer at Mr. Britcher's where I lived. I went there (to the Loomis home) because he wanted me to and because he promised to marry me if I would go. I made (the) Loomises my home after I was sixteen. I never was married to Grove. I lived as his mistress.

"My parents lived about nine miles from (the) Loomises. Father told me if I would give up Grove I might come home, otherwise I could not.

"(At the Loomises) I occupied the back part of the house, the kitchen and dining room, as a general thing. I did not have free access to the sitting room and front part of the house. This was occupied by Mrs. Loomis, Cornelia, Plumb and Denio. The whole family had free access to (all) the house. I never went into the parlor in my life until Wash was a corpse there. I (have) heard Grove say he had not been there since his father died.

"Girls used to come and see Wash and Plumb all the time when I was there. (I) can't swear that the girls the Loomises had were bad. Plumb had a girl whom he married afterward. Another girl stayed with Wash. (The Loomises) took Elizabeth Calkins out of a poorhouse and she waited on Cornelia as a drudge. Esther Crandall was a sister to Joe (Crandall).

"I never saw them steal nor did I help hide anything. Thieves used to come there, a great many of them strangers to me. I remember when Plumb, Grove and Denio were looking for a stolen horse. I used to listen and found out some things."

Nellie was by no means a stranger to the inhabitants of the Valley. Her parents and brothers were respected farmers. She had many friends among the younger generation, most of them having attended school with her.

"Nellie Smith was one of my best girl friends," remarked Miss Green. "I first met her when we went to school together in the Valley. She was the sweetest and most attractive girl in the school. Her father was Bob Smith, a farmer, and she had two brothers that I know of, Fred and Tom. I didn't see much of her when our school days were over, but when we met again she told me she was deeply in love with Grove Loomis and had gone to live with him. I must confess I was deeply shocked at her words. The Loomis brothers were notorious for thieving, horse stealing, and passing counterfeit money. I tried to remonstrate with Nellie, but she refused to listen to me. She said she was eighteen and knew the step she had taken and all the costs. I seldom saw her after this meeting, but other acquaintances who knew her said Grove had become a changed man through Nellie's influence."

Dr. George Cleveland, a former justice of the peace of Waterville, tried to defend Nellie by announcing that he had legally married her to Grove, but she courageously denied his statement. She lived in sin, yet she was not a so-called "bad woman." Those people first to scorn and brand her as immoral were later the first to praise her kindness and honest sympathy. She was deeply religious and attended church almost every Sunday. Poor families accepted her offerings of food and clothing; mothers welcomed her capable hands when they bore their children. In sickness and in death she was always the first to respond with help, bringing a cheerful personality and little gifts to bereaved ones. She spent long hours in unfamiliar kitchens, baking and cooking for an entire family and their relatives. Nellie was no longer "Grove's woman," but the "Swamp Angel."

One young woman who never had been a member of the household nearly brought disaster to the Loomis family. Esther Parks was fourteen years of age and a definite psychopathic case. She was little known outside of her town until she became the victim of a brutal attack.

On Wednesday, September 16, 1863, The Madison Observer reported: "On Sept. 4, Esther Parks a girl of 14 who was subject to fits of partial derangement left the residence of her father Mr. George W. Parks of Smithfield to pick hops. She wore a bloomer calico dress, black velvet cloak, and black jockey. Not finding employment she started home and becoming deranged is supposed she wandered off through Stockbridge Valley to Oneida then to Hamilton then brought to this village (Morrisville) on Sunday evening of the sixth remaining overnight. She left the village walked in a northeasterly direction. Monday noon to the next Wednesday morning her whereabouts were unknown.

"On Wed. forenoon a gentleman passing along the road in the southwest part of Stockbridge discovered her lying on the road. Her limbs were tightly bound with a rope and a gag in her mouth. She had been raped. She was released and taken to her home. She said she was seized the night previous by two men in a wagon who bound and gagged her and took her to a vacant building. Afterwards they carried her back where she was found. When she left home she had $35 in money belonging to her father taken from her by the men."

Statements that may have been taken by the Madison County sheriff's department from Esther concerning the assault no longer exist, but other evidence indicates that she named Wheeler Loomis as one of the men. Wheeler was arrested the following week on a charge of rape.

"Wheeler was taken before Justice Ira B. Crandall of South Brookfield," Cummings wrote, "and was bound over. Bail was given. On the following night the Justice's docket was stolen. The thieves did not find the bail bonds because the Justice had mailed them to the County Court. The girl was then kidnapped to prevent her from going before the grand jury, but testimony of her father, mother, and physician secured an indictment. After this some constable got upon the track of the girl and found her in the Loomis mansion. She was taken home, but her terror was so great that she preferred to stay in jail two years as an assistant in the sheriff's family than to remain at home. She believed that the Loomises meant to put her out of the way.

"Wheeler jumped his bail bonds."

Action on the forfeited recognizance of Wheeler Loomis was tried at the September term of the Madison County Circuit Court during its four day session that started on Monday, the 21st. Loomis was represented by Attorney E. H. Lamb, and District Attorney A. N. Sheldon appeared for the People. The jury found a verdict in favor of the People.

Justice Joseph Mason transferred Wheeler's case to the Court of Oyer and Terminer that was also in session, and Loomis was indicted for rape. Wheeler pleaded innocent when arraigned. D. C. Pomeroy, who appeared for him, had the trial put over to the next term of court. The Court refused to allow the prisoner bail and Wheeler was ordered remanded to the custody of Sheriff William F. Bonney. The Madison Observer commented: "It is hoped that Judge Bacon, and all other Judges, will now allow him to remain where he justly belongs."

The evidence against Wheeler was not too conclusive. Sheriff Bonney ran advertisements in several of the county's weekly papers, including The Democratic Republican of Hamilton, on Thursday, October first with an offer of $500 for information concerning the assault on Esther Parks, ". . . And whereas, all efforts on the part of the public officers to discover and arrest the perpetrators of this criminal outrage have as yet proved unavailing . . . for the purpose of bringing to justice the person or persons guilty of the commission of the above named criminal acts (and at the reqeust of several citizens of said county) I hereby offer a REWARD OF FIVE HUNDRED DOLLARS for the arrest of the perpetrators of the above crimes, or for such information as shall lead to their arrest and punishment . . ."

The advertisement was carried by the papers for several weeks, even after Wheeler Loomis was indicted. The countryside was thoroughly aroused over the epidemic of burglaries and robberies. Court actions were in progress against Wash, William, Plumb and Denio for various charges. The four brothers were tried for assault and battery at the September term, but the jury failed to agree. Only one member of the gang, William Ellis, pleaded guilty to a charge of petit larceny and was sent to jail for thirty days. The ease in which the Loomises escaped justice infuriated the people and the hate was fanned by the newspapers of Central New York. The indictment for rape against Wheeler Loomis added fuel to the flames.

On October 6 Edward C. Bulkley and Samuel Peckham posted $2,000 bail for Wheeler's release. Justice Mason granted the request only on the condition that Wheeler pay Sheriff Bonney $600 to cover the expenses he had caused the county. The Loomis family made a $500 payment and Justice Mason found it acceptable.

Attorney Pomeroy took his client before Judge LeRoy Morgan in Syracuse on a writ of habeas corpus. The judge took bail for Loomis' reappearance.

Wheeler did not appear at the next session of court in Madison County or Syracuse. A few nights after securing his release on bail he started for Canada, where his father, George W. Loomis, under the alias of George Wheeler, had purchased property in the Third Concession of the Township of Kenyon, Glengarry County, Province of Ontario. Wheeler Loomis settled down as a farmer under the name of Theodore L. Wheeler.

The case was again brought against Wheeler at the Madison County Oyer and Terminer in February, 1864. The Loomis' attorney made an application for the trial to go over, but Judge William Campbell denied it. As Wheeler failed to appear the bail posted by his sureties was foreited. Although he spent the remainder of his life in Canada his guilt was never proven.

On May 18, three months later, The Madison Observer reported: "Mr. George W. Parks of Smithfield gives notice that his daughter, Esther has again left home, on the 10th inst., in an insane condition, and requests information concerning her."

Cornelia Loomis, who had amused the Valley with her youthful escapades, got her name in the Utica court records in 1865, when she was indicted for receiving stolen goods. Two years before the home of Roswell Conger in Sangerfield had been entered; a gold watch and chain belonging to his daughter had been stolen.

"I first saw the watch in the hands of Cornelia Loomis while searching the Loomis house for stolen property," Filkins testified in an affidavit. "I wrenched it from her hand. It was done up in a piece of cotton batting. She was attempting to throw it out of a window. I found a portion of other property which I was in search of, in the room occupied by Cornelia Loomis."

Cornelia entered a plea of innocence and swore that the watch had belonged to her father, although Conger had identified it by its serial number. The charges were eventually dropped.

Cornelia, now a confirmed old maid, had no qualms about wearing stolen clothes. She even appeared in court one day wearing an old-fashioned velvet cloak and a bombasine dress, articles Filkins knew had been stolen from a woman in Marshall quite some time before. He drove to the Loomis farm to apprehend Cornelia, who had been seen in Waterville wearing the bombasine dress.

The first person he saw was Plumb, who was scurrying for the Swamp with a bundle under his arm. Filkins pushed open the door and "there stood the fair Cornelia with neither cape on her shoulders or dress on her back. We turned from this spectacle of beauty unadorned . . . and went after Plumb."

When Filkins returned with his prisoner in tow he found Cornelia waiting for him. She was wearing the bombasine dress. Filkins and his men loaded her into a sleigh and took her to Waterville. When Plumb tried to interfere, Filkins caught him by the collar and squelched him. Grove also chose to be obstructive. "He sighted for us," said Filkins, "but did not fire."

Filkins, curious about what Plumb had been carrying, searched the Swamp the next day. "I learned from one of the constables that while I was chasing Plumb he dodged behind a hill and behind a house and down near the brook and came immediately back again. We visited the spot and found a hole in the ice in which he had probably thrust the cloak and it was carried into the mill pond."

Cornelia, who had been left in an unlocked room in the American Hotel in Waterville, escaped about eleven o'clock the night of her capture. "A respectable gentleman of Sangerfield carried her part of the way home," said Filkins, "thinking she was one of the Indian squaws at work making baskets in the Swamp."

Cornelia liked to tell about her girlhood exploits, but there is one story she never told, because the laughter of the Valley still echoed in her ears. As she took her seat on a train in Utica, three personable young men brushed past her. She smiled prettily and the men grinned back at her as they continued down the aisle.

Much to her horror, she discovered that her purse, which contained fifty dollars and several valuable papers, was missing. She notified the Utica police, but her possessions were never recovered. All the upstate newspapers told the story with considerable glee. Cornelia's reputation suffered. She who had been a queen among outlaws had been rudely dethroned.

CHAPTER XVII

THE HORSE THIEF

Charles Champlin shivered beneath the heavy thickness of the buffalo robe and blanket wrapped about him in the skeleton sleigh as he drove up Genesee Street in Utica that Friday afternoon the last of January 1863. As he felt the bite of the 35 degree below zero cold he suddenly wished he was back in his warm saloon in Whitestown.

Only a few hours earlier, Griffith G. Williams, a tailor, had asked him to break his newly purchased young colt. As the wind whipped up the snow in the street, he was sorry he had taken the job. Champlin drove up to the Central Hotel on the corner of Elizabeth Street. With stiffened fingers he tied the colt to the hitching rack. After tossing the robes over the animal, Champlin entered the side door of the barroom and ordered a drink. As the genial bartender placed a bottle and empty glass on the bar, Champlin glanced at the clock over the bar mirror. It was just 5:30.

While the Whitestown saloon keeper was lingering over the warming liquor, the outside door of the barroom opened and a short, stockily built man swaggered into the room. With a quick glance about him, he went up to the bar and ordered a glass of whiskey. As soon as it was placed in front of him, he gulped it down and tossed a dime on the bar. Turning he surveyed Champlin for a moment, then went outdoors into the storm.

A few minutes later as Champlin was about to leave, he stopped in the doorway. The colt and sleigh were gone. The chain on the hitching post which he had used five minutes earlier was still intact. Footprints in the new fallen snow clearly indicated that someone had unhitched the colt and driven off with her.

In growing panic, Champlin ran up and down the streets, stumbling over drifts, hoping to catch sight of the animal. When he was unable to sight either the colt or sleigh, he made his way to the home of Griffith Williams at 51 Lansing Street and reported the theft. Williams procured another horse and cutter from John R. Evans, a wagon maker. The three men then started towards New Hartford where they hoped to find some trace of the horse thief.

At the New Hartford tollgate, they asked Mrs. Hubbard, the keeper, if anyone had recently passed through driving a young colt hitched up to a skeleton sleigh. Mrs. Hubbard was unable to place the rig until Williams mentioned that the thills of the cutter were set in straight.

"I remember now," the gatekeeper said. She went on to describe a heavy-set man who had paid toll half an hour earlier, and who was driving a colt. "I seldom notice who goes through, but the peculiar way the thills were set attracted my attention. If that's the man you're after he went towards Paris Hill."

Assured that they were now on the trail of the horse thief, the three men took the left fork of the road past Jedediah Sanger's old home towards Paris Hill. When they reached that settlement, they stopped at Alex Van Valkenburg's hotel. The hotel keeper instantly identified the horse thief they were after.

"His name's Alonzo Dennison," Van Valkenburg stated. "He was in here an hour ago drinking. Lon's about 30 years old and lived about seven miles from Waterville, near the Loomises. If he isn't one of the Loomis gang, then he is no better than members of it."

The hotel keeper then went on to describe Dennison's brutality to the colt, which he said appeared to be nearly exhausted from hard driving. Williams asked if Van Valkenburg would like to accompany them to Waterville where they hoped to capture the thief. The hotel keeper quickly accepted the invitation. As he donned a heavy coat, boots and cap, he gave instructions to John Evans to put his tired horse in the stable and drive one of his. Evans drove to the stable and returned a few minutes later with the fresh horse. The four men crowded into the cutter and the pursuit was resumed over the winding road leading southward towards Waterville.

It was well past 10 o'clock that night when the men drove down Stafford Avenue and drew up before the yellow, box-shaped home of Constable James L. Filkins. The pock-marked little officer was in bed but was quickly awakened. When Champlin and Williams explained their mission, Filkins dressed hurriedly to accompany them.

At Filkin's request, Evans drove the party about the village, stopping at the taverns and hotels to inquire about Dennison. The first information came from Thomas Garvin at the American Hotel, where he was employed.

"I know Alonzo Dennison," Garvin disclosed. "He came to my house between 9 and 10 with a horse and sleigh and proposed to trade the same for a watch and five dollars. He appeared to be in liquor."

Orrin Tucker, a resident of Hamilton, told the party that he had seen Dennison with the young colt and sleigh and criticized the man's inhuman treatment of the animal. William Lewis, a tavern keeper, was also queried.

"Dennison stopped here some time ago," Lewis said "and offered to trade the horse with me."

About 2 o'clock the following morning Filkins made ready to start for the Dennison farm which was located near Sweet's Corners on the east side of the swamp in the Town of Brookfield. By this time the peace officer had gathered a small posse to assist the party. Philip Cox and John Garvin started southward on the Hubbardsville Road, while Filkins, Champlin, Van Valkenburg and a man named Demsey struck out westward on the winding Swamp road towards the Loomis farm. Griffith Williams stayed behind in Waterville.

When Constable Filkins and his party reached the Loomis farm about 2:30 o'clock that morning the big house on the knoll was shrouded in darkness. The officer spread his men out on three sides of the building, while he went up on the front porch and knocked loudly on the door. In a few minutes one of the upper windows was raised and Wash Loomis leaned out.

"What the hell do you want?" he shouted angrily.

"Come down and open the door," Filkins yelled as loud as his squeaky voice permitted, "or we'll smash it in."

Wash withdrew his head without replying and slammed the window shut. The constable waited a few minutes for the front door to be opened. When it did not open he left the house and started for the big barn across the road. As he reached the building and started to open the door, the upper window of the house slid open again.

"What in damnation do you want there?" Wash Loomis bellowed. "I have a stallion in there worth $7,000 and he is all perspiring. I have just had him out exercising him. Don't open that door!"

Filkins whirled to face the house. Before his lips could frame a reply, a side door opened and Wash rushed out carrying a lantern in one hand and a club in the other. Two grim faced men followed. One carried a revolver and the other a rifle. Constable Filkins eased his pistol from its holster.

"What is the trouble?" Wash inquired, "awakening a man from his sleep. Get out of here or I'll kill you."

Filkins cocked his pistol, pointing it directly at Loomis.

"I'm warning you not to strike or fire a shot," he said tersely, "or I'll blow your brains out."

The intense hatred between the leader of the Loomis gang and the peace officer seemed to electrify the atmosphere. Charles Champlin hurried across the road to side with Filkins. Loomis saw the figure in the dim light and turned abruptly to meet him.

"Who are you, and what's your business?" he asked.

"I'm Charlie Champlin from Whitesboro. We're looking for a young colt and sleigh that were stolen from me in Utica yesterday."

He was immediately recognized by Wash.

"Do you suppose I would harbor anything of yours?" he asked. Why, we used to go to school together."

Champlin asked if Alonzo Dennison had been there.

Wash Loomis shook his head slowly. "No, he wasn't here, but I can tell you where your horse is. Lon's a miserable fellow who knows how to steal, but not to hide anything. He lives in the second house, away down the road."

While the two former schoolmates were discussing Dennison, Constable Filkins had remained discreetly silent. Now he shuffled into the circle of lantern light, his pistol still clutched in his hand.

"I 'spose you wouldn't want to join our little party, would you, Wash?" the officer asked. "You can show us the way to Dennison's."

Wash evidently knew the constable was trying not only to bait but also belittle him. He accepted the challenge with a smile.

"Yes, I'll go with you," he said, "just as soon as I get some warm clothes on."

He called to the two men who had accompanied him, and they returned to the house.

Van Valkenburg and Demsey came from around the rear of the building to join Filkins and Champlin. Van Valkenburg whispered to Filkins to take a look through one of the kitchen windows. They went around the house, where Filkins glued his eyes to a small hole in one of the frosted panes of the middle kitchen.

"No one in there," Filkins said shortly. "The room is empty."

"There was a minute ago," the man from Paris Hill whispered. "When you first knocked on the front door, I heard a great stamping and shuffling inside that room. I looked through the window and saw no less than a dozen known deserters with military clothes on them."

The constable nodded thoughtfully. "It's no wonder Wash is anxious to get us away from here."

When Loomis emerged from his home a few minutes later he was wearing a blue army overcoat. Filkins glanced at him sharply but kept silent. Champlin was waiting for the men with the sleigh in the road. Wash was the last to enter. He said he wanted to examine the sleigh tracks near the barn.

"I think these are the tracks of the cutter Dennison was driving," Wash called from where he knelt in the snow near his barn. He held his lantern to highlight the narrow marks of the runners. "You can see where the colt and sleigh swerved towards our barn, then went on down the road."

Apparently satisfied with his discovery, the gang leader climbed in the sleigh with the men. The driver clucked at the horse, starting it down the snowy highway.

In the meantime, Philip Cox and John Evans, who had taken the shorter route on the Hubbardsville road, reached the Dennison farm. Leaving their horse and cutter at the side of the road, the men drew their pistols and cautiously made their way to the barn in the rear of the house. Cox opened the barn door and they slipped inside.

When the door was pulled shut, Evans lighted the lantern he was carrying and turned the wick down low. It did not take long to find the stolen colt, with the harness still on, in one of the stalls. Despite Dennison's inhuman treatment of the young colt, he had thrown Champlin's robe over her. The sleigh was not in the barn. Cox and Evans left the barn and started prowling about the premises, hoping that the horse thief would not awaken. It was near the house that Cox found the sleigh, where Dennison had concealed it, beneath a snow pile.

The two men decided not to wait until the rest of the posse arrived to capture the thief. They moved around the darkened building trying the windows and doors. All appeared to be fastened securely on the inside. There was no other way to get in but to break in. Evans and Cox put their shoulders to the back door and pushed. The catch gave and the door swung open. They listened for a minute but heard nothing to indicate Dennison had been awakened by the noise.

The men tiptoed through the downstairs rooms and finally found the horse thief curled up under the bed covers. Evans examined Dennison's trousers which had been flung carelessly over the back of a chair. The legs were wet. Then he strode over to the bed and shook him. Dennison sat up, blinking in the light of the lantern. Evans pointed his pistol at him.

"You're under arrest," he said.

Dennison protested his innocence, but Cox prodded him into dressing. They then shoved him out of the house and into their sleigh.

Philip Cox picked up the reins after Dennison was secured and started the horse in the direction of the Loomis farm. They met up with Constable Filkins, Champlin, Wash Loomis and the other two members of the party about a quarter of a mile down the road.

Filkins immediately took charge of the prisoner, while Cox and Evans explained the details of the capture.

The constable decided to start for Utica at once with the prisoner. Cox, Demsey and Van Valkenburg decided to return to their own homes so rode with him. They could pick up Griffith Williams and take him to Utica. Champlin, Wash Loomis and Evans volunteered to drive to the Dennison farm and pick up the stolen colt and sleigh.

"I went and saw the place where the horse was," Champlin said later. "She was in the barn and in a very bad condition. I sent the sleigh back and brought the horse, harness and robe back myself."

It was almost noon when Constable Filkins and Griffith Williams arrived in Utica with the prisoner. Dennison was turned over to Chief of Police David Hess who took him to the Mohawk Street jail to await arraignment.

The following Monday afternoon Dennison was given a hearing on the horse thief charge before Justice of the Peace John R. Timian. He pleaded innocent. Eight witnesses, including Filkins, Champlin and Williams were called to testify.

At the conclusion of the examination, the court ordered Dennison held for action of the grand jury which was scheduled to sit the following week.

On February 3, the Utica Morning Herald gave the following erroneous story of the case:

"A Case For the Grand Jury. Mr. Charles Champlin of Yorkville left a young horse attached to a cutter standing at the door of the Central Hotel on Fri., while he stepped within. Returning in a few minutes his establishment had disappeared. Suspecting the direction it had been taken he went to the house of Wash Loomis where after some delay and almost a fight with Wash and two other fellows, they found the horse in the barn and secured the thief who stole him, in the house."

Wash Loomis immediately brought suit for malicious libel against the Herald. The Utica Morning Telegraph and the Utica Observer had also carried more complete versions of the some story but these were ignored in the suit. The Herald's editors could think of no definite reason for Wash's animosity towards their paper, but they prepared to fight the case. At the first hearing in court, the Herald's legal staff had the case put over until February of 1864. On that date, Wash Loomis failed to press his charge against the paper, and the suit was dismissed.

Meanwhile, the Oneida County Circuit Court and Special Term of the Supreme Court opened its sessions in the Courthouse on February 9. Judge Bacon presided. Dennison's case was one of the 153 listed on the court calendar.

District Attorney Jenkins presented the witnesses against him. When all the evidence had been taken, the district attorney asked for an indictment against the prisoner for grand larceny. He placed the value of the colt at $300; the sleigh at $20 and the harness at $30.

The grand jury found the indictment for grand larceny and Judge Bacon set April 14 as the date of Dennison's trial.

Dennison was found guilty in April and sentenced to five years at hard labor in State prison.

CHAPTER XVIII
DEATH COMES CALLING

Filkins was also having trouble with a woman named Frances Van Dee, the sister of Jack Van Dee, whom he arrested with old Ezra Beebe on charges of burglary and receiving stolen goods. The couple, both members of the Loomis gang, had broken into a store at Milford, a small village on the Susquehanna River in Otsego County, and had stolen between seven and eight hundred dollars worth of clothing and merchandise on Monday, July 13th, 1863. They were seen making their get-away, and Filkins received a telegram ordering him to arrest them. When they appeared in Waterville he escorted them to the village lockup. He did not call in a woman to search the Van Dee girl, but forced her to strip. He took no delight in the shapeliness of her young body, but methodically explored each garment as it was removed. As he expected several articles of merchandise taken at the Milford store were fastened to the hoops which she wore under her dress. When he found nothing more he commanded her to dress and locked her in a cell next to Beebe's.

The couple was indicted in September. Before the cases came to trial Frances Van Dee brought a damage suit against Filkins for the indecent exposure of her body and procured the services of Sewell S. Morgan of West Winfield to prosecute her case. The constable was surprised at the girl's charges, but he knew a conviction could ruin his career. Daniel Ball, an eminent lawyer who was boarding at the home of Edward Hall in Waterville, agreed to defend him. The trial was held at Oneida Castle.

Sewell Morgan began his appeal to the jury by affectionately referring to his client as "Franky" and closing with the indecency of the "exposure of Franky's body to Filkins' offending eyes." When he had finished he strutted to his seat to await Ball's defense. Ball approached the bench, let his eyes wander amusingly from Frances Van Dee to Lawyer Morgan, and turned to the jury.

"Gentlemen of the jury," he said, "my opponent has spoken familiarly of the plaintiff as 'Franky' and dastardly of Filkins. I agree that any man who would strip a woman naked and search her person breaks all laws of decency. Yet, gentlemen of the jury, before we are finished with this case of the exposure of this woman's person, we're going to prove to you that the private parts of this woman are the most public places in town!"

A ripple of amusement grew louder as the spectators began to shout and cheer Ball's words. The Justice, much perturbed, banged his gavel for silence. When the uproar subsided Sewell Morgan hastily rose to his feet, mopping his brow with a large bandanna.

"Your Honor," he said, "My client does not wish to press the suit against Mr. Filkins. She prefers to drop the case."

Filkins had not forgotten a threatening note he had received in May. Unsigned, it read:

"J. Filkins—Dear Sir: As a friend to you and all mankind I set down to write to forwarn you of danger. That gang has offered one of their associates a good sum of money to kill you at some convenient time, and he says he doubts whether they will pay him if he should do so. He is a daring and bold robber. I dare not sign my name."

The constable always kept his revolver at his side and loaded, for he was never certain when a bullet might strike him down. He went about his duties conscientiously as always, but night and day the fear of death hung over him. He instinctively reached for his revolver when a loud knock on the kitchen door jarred the heavy quiet of the house that Thursday night of July 23. Filkins glanced at the clock beside the bed. It was a few minutes past midnight.

The bedroom was situated on the same side of the house as the kitchen, and the window was but a few feet west of the kitchen door. There were two beds in the room, one where he and his wife slept and the other for their four children. The small lamp burning on the table near the bed was the only light in the house. Filkins arose and pulled on his pants. Taking his revolver he went to the kitchen window that was covered with a blind.

"I moved aside the curtain," he said. "I spoke and said, 'Hullo, who are you and what do you want?'

"A person on the outside answered and said he was Mr. Clark's hired man and Mr. Clark had come by Van Dee's after dark and saw Jackson Van Dee at home. 'Mr. Clark wanted to let you know that he was there so you could go and arrest him.'

"I knew by the voice that it was Plumb Loomis and not Clark's hired man and while I was up in my own house, three different shots being fired into the house the same night and one of the shots took affect in my arms."

The glass shattered as the roar of a double-barreled shotgun filled that night. Filkins felt sharp, searing pains tear through his right arm and left hand. He cried out in agony as his blood began to drip on the floor. He staggered into the bedroom and collapsed on the floor.

"James, are you hit?" Sarah Filkins cried.

The constable groaned, his face bloodless in the lamplight.

"Yes," he answered faintly, "I am wounded."

His words were almost lost in a second blast of gunfire. The window of the bedroom was blown out as shotgun slugs and rifle bullets poured into the room and buried themselves in the door, in the mantel, and in the wall above the children's bed. The blinds were riddled and the lower sash of the window was torn away. Mrs. Filkins' piercing screams rose above the din, but her husband lay quietly on the floor. The assassins poured a third and last volley into the room. The whole village was now awake. Voices sounded on the streets and footsteps pounded on the boardwalk. As help came the gang retreated.

Filkins rose painfully to his feet, still clutching his revolver. He staggered towards the hall doorway.

"Must call Tom Westnage," he muttered. Instinctively he passed through the rooms to the staircase leading to the upper floor where Thomas Westnage, a disabled veteran, lived. The door was closed and, as he tried vainly to lift the latch, he fell unconscious.

When he opened his eyes he was undressed and in bed. Both arms were tightly bandaged. Dr. William Cleveland and Dr. George Bailey were in the room.

"How bad am I?" Filkins asked.

"The pellets from the shotgun tore through your right arm between the wrist and elbow and penetrated into and through the thumb and wrist of your left hand," Dr. Cleveland said. "It could be worse."

In the daylight hundreds of sightseers came to visit the scene. They examined the shattered windows. A few more inquisitive persons counted fourteen holes in the mantel, seven buckshot and forty smaller shot that had pierced the window curtains. Several recoiled in horror at the blood on the floor. At the constable's request his wife showed the editor of The Waterville Times the threatening note he had received two months earlier.

"The shots that struck me were fired by the hand of Plumb Loomis," he said, "and those that went into the bedroom window were fired by Denio Loomis with the intent to kill."

He summoned Aurelius (Bill) Benedict, a village officer, to his room. "Bill," he ordered, "I want you to go up to Beebe's place and look for a double-barreled shotgun that might have been recently fired. You might also go over to the Loomises and see what you can find."

Benedict would not go. The village residents were so terrorized no one would leave town.

Filkins recovered rapidly. A week later the sympathetic citizens presented him with a purse containing $200 as a testimonial. As soon as he was able he began collecting every scrap of evidence possible. Filkins succeeded in having Plumb and Denio indicted for assault with intent to kill in September. The case was postponed several times until the District Attorney agreed to drop the charges in December of 1864.

CHAPTER XIX

THE LOOMISES DESTROY EVIDENCE

The Loomises were a little late in their celebration of New Year's 1865, waiting until Friday, January sixth to attend a dance in New Berlin, Chenango County. The highlights of the shindig were reported a few days later by The Norwich Chronicle:

"There was a dancing party being held at the new hall and everything went off in an orderly and pleasant way until about ten o'clock, when a delegation from Brookfield, containing two at least of the infamous 'Loomis tribe' arrived and undertook to force an entrance to the hall without paying the bill.

"James Roberts remonstrated with them gently on the mistake they were making, when one of them undertook to stop the talk by knocking James down. Unfortunately for Mr. Loomis, he had undertaken more than he was able to perform, and he himself fell at the first fire. The Loomis family and their supporters then 'went in' for a general 'plug muss,' during which Roberts was cut with a knife in several places. They were finally driven out of town."

In April, when the church bells in the villages and cities pealed out the news of victory and the war was over, there was great rejoicing in the Valley. A few days later the bell in the church at West Edmeston tolled fifty-six strokes and the sound echoed over the Brookfield hills. The next morning a telegram reached Leonardsville stating that President Abraham Lincoln had been murdered. The Waterville Times carried the story on the twentieth in an edition edged with black. While the churches planned public services and prayers for the martyred President, Constable Filkins carried on his relentless fight against the Loomis gang.

Filkins drove to the office of District Attorney Jenkins in May to find out what had happened to the indictment against Wash Loomis for stealing Montgomery's skunk skin robe.

"Why, a nolle prosqui has been entered," the District Attorney said, "and the indictment has been dropped."

The constable then inquired what had happened to the indictments against the Loomises for trying to kill him. Jenkins tried to avoid a direct answer. "Why, the same course has been taken with the indictments in your case," he stated.

Filkins cursed angrily. "What kind of law enforcement do we have around here?" he demanded. When the District Attorney did not answer, he went on, "What was the cause of action for dropping the indictments?"

"Well, Sheriff Crocker came to me at the December term of court," Jenkins replied, "saying he had made an agreement with the Loomises to see them clear of everything before he went out of office. He wanted me to make his word good and asked me to help him, and I did."

Freed from possible criminal action in Oneida County the Loomises immediately turned their attention to Madison County, where several indictments were pending, including one against Wheeler for rape. Officials firmly believed that the courthouse in Morrisville had been burned to destroy the criminal records, but there was no evidence against the Loomises. The indictments against the gang were safely locked in the fire-proof county clerk's office next door. The clerk's office was burglarized on May tenth. There was little worth stealing, but the burglar carefully ransacked the desks and cabinet drawers and stuffed indictments and other incriminating evidence against the Loomises into the wide-bellied stove and burned it. Among the papers destroyed were those dating from 1860 to that time.

"Every indictment against the brothers was destroyed and as the statute of limitations had expired, new indictments could not be procured," Cummings wrote. "Among the papers burned was an indictment against one of the Beebes. Wash afterward called upon him and told him his assessment for the work was $100. The man borrowed the money and gladly paid him. . . . Their success in destroying indictments emboldened the gang. Robberies were a nightly occurrence, and Filkins found the brothers operating far down in Delaware county."

The tollgate kept by Daniel King between Oriskany Falls and Waterville was entered one night in August and fifty dollars taken. A few days later the tollgate between Waterville and Sangerfield Center operated by Charles Look was broken into during the early morning hours. The burglars carried away the drawer to the change table in which the toll collections were kept. The drawer was found near E. S. Brown's barn. It was empty, as the burglars had taken the wrong one in their haste. A drawer containing over fifty dollars had been overlooked.

The newspapers kept up their steady barrage of criticism of the Loomises and their gang, often referring to them as "black vomit" and advocating that lynching would be the only solution. There was practically no individual criticism, due to the fear of reprisal. One of the few exceptions was John Talbot of Norwich, who apparently did not fear the gang, for his angry letter appeared in The Norwich Union.

"On Wednesday night (October) 27th, Peter Enders, living one mile east of Sloansville on the turnpike had a bay mare stolen, valued at $200 and a silver-plated harness taken with the mare. The thief then came on to this village and hitched on to my light buggy and left going west. Mr. Enders and myself tracked them to Rockville and there lost the trail. But we still pursued west to Cherry Valley and there made a halt and put our horses in a wagon house attached to the hotel known as the Trion House. We still pursued west keeping the western turnpike and within one mile of Springfield Four Corners (four miles west of Cherry Valley) Mr. Enders horse stopped very suddenly on the road and refused to go any further. And on examination the horse appeared to be very sick manifesting great pain while at the same time sweat poured off him like rain, but by severe urging we got the horse to Springfield. As the horse approached the hotel a man spoke to Mr. Enders and told him his horse was poisoned and such proved to be the fact for the horse died in less than forty minutes after arriving at Springfield.

"The horse was opened and poison was found in his stomach. The examination was made by a thorough horse doctor.

"Thus, through the hellish combination of thieves, Mr. Enders lost his second horse, for there is not the least doubt but what his horse was poisoned by one of the gang to check the pursuit.

"Mr. Ender's carriage and the thief were seen near Sangerfield Corners about daylight on the morning of the 28th making for the celebrated den of thieves known as the Loomis Family of Oneida County, where no one dare go to get his property without great risk of losing his life. You recollect that Judge Sanford's property was found there and that the informer's tavern, stand, and barns were burnt by these devils.

"Why these scoundrels are allowed to carry on their business of stealing is a mystery to me.

"I think we had better get up a jury of Sherman's Boys headed by 'Judge Lynch' and go out there and clean the Loomis ranch out. There is no other way that the country can get rid of this infamous gang.

"We returned home after finding out where the mare and buggy had gone as we were well aware that it was useless for two of us to attempt getting our property from this gang."

The long-suffering citizens of the Valley finally held a meeting in the Baptist Church in North Brookfield to devise some measures of protection against the gang. An organizational committee was formed and during the following week other inhabitants who were believed not in league with the Loomises were asked to join. By-laws were made at the next meeting and it was decided that each prospective member should pay one dollar towards the expenses. As the cashier collected the money the church door swung open and Wash and Grove Loomis strode into the room.

"We have heard that you are forming an organization to stop the thieving and horse stealing going on in our neighborhood," Wash gravely remarked. "Grove and I think it is a fine plan and we want to join."

He tossed two one-dollar notes on the table. "Here's our money," he said. The brothers walked from the room laughing.

After a few minutes the meeting broke up and the people went wearily home.

CHAPTER XX

"WASH IS KILLED!"

Filkins reached a decision to clean out the Loomis gang by force that day in 1865 when he shuffled down Waterville's Main Street to see Charles Green, president of the bank. All legal means to bring the gang to justice had failed. The refusal of the Oneida and Madison County courts to issue new indictments to replace those that had been dropped against members of the family had been a blow to Filkins.

Three years before The Waterville Times had said: "For years it has been attempted to bring the gang to justice through process of law, but without success. The law proving an utter failure as a means of stopping the depredations and outrages of this vile gang, and no man's life or property being safe while it is within their reach, what is to be done? We think there is but one way to do in order to put a stop to it, which is, to use the California remedy; give them so many hours in which to leave the state, and if not gone at the end of the time specified, a judicious lynching."

"Filkins discussed the situation with my great uncle, Charles Green, the Waterville banker, and asked what he should do, and who he should get to help him—men on whom he could rely, and whom he could trust," Seymour Dunbar of New York City, internationally-known historian, wrote. "He wasn't sure of some. My Uncle Charles told him to be sure to get the help of Alexis Seymour, his brother-in-law, and my grandfather, and anybody whom Seymour recommended. Filkins and Alexis talked it over and organized their posse."

This posse, the Sangerfield Vigilantes Committee, is not to be confused with the Waterville Thief Detective Society, the Madison Anti-Larceny Society, the Hamilton Anti-Larceny Society and other earlier groups that were formed to combat the growing lawlessness. The few existing records of these vigilante groups fail to show that they even attempted to bring any of the Loomises or their known associates to justice.

The Sangerfield Vigilantes Committee met in a room over Bissell's store in Waterville and in Hiram Loomis' barn at Conger's Corners. Henry Bissell said the password was "Hops."

Fred C. Hall, a member of the 157th Infantry who had a medical discharge from the army, was one of the first men Filkins asked to take part in the proposed raid on the Loomises. "Father had just moved to Gorton Hill a day or two before," his son, Thomas L. Hall, Madison County historian, recalled. The date was set for eight o'clock, November 1, 1865.

Fred Hall had no use for Filkins. "Father refused point blank to accompany Filkins on personal or official visits to the Loomis home," his son stated. "The reason, Father said, was that Filkins would not or could not hunt the Loomises honestly. Filkins got three young men to go that night, Cort Terry, red-headed son of Morris Terry, Henry Bissell and John Garvey. Father's orders were to be there early, but he overslept, like a lot of others."

The historian was extremely prejudiced against Filkins, but there is a ring of truth in his statement that Filkins was only able to obtain three men. Something must have been amiss, or the little deputy deliberately ignored the Sangerfield Vigilantes Committee. Bissell and Terry were about eighteen years old, and Hall described Garvey as "a big, black-haired, black-bearded ex-soldier, a killer by instinct, who was later to die on the scaffold in South Carolina for murder." Phinnett Carter named Will Locke as a member of Filkins' party. Bissell later admitted that he and Terry were with Filkins, but refused to name and give the exact number of persons. He said, "All of us that took part in the raid swore an oath not to reveal any of our identities as long as any of us lived."

Filkins made elaborate preparations for the raid. He buckled on the long-barreled, ivory-handled .44 revolver he had taken from LaVergue Beebe. A small piece of the hammer had been broken off, but this did not impair its firing. He stuck a pair of handcuffs in a rear pocket and, noticing that his lanterns needed oil, he took a glass bottle from his kitchen and filled it at the American Hotel barn, where George Carlisle, the stage driver, was greasing a wheel of the stagecoach. About eleven o'clock Tuesday night, October 31, 1865 the posse started for the Loomis home on foot. When they reached the Center, Filkins led them across the fields, keeping near the edge of the Swamp. As the men trudged across Isaac Terry's land a pair of handcuffs slipped from one of the party's pocket and dropped silently into the grass. If Filkins had known of this he would have searched until they were found, for he wanted no evidence to mark their trail.

The men reached the Loomis farm a few minutes past midnight. The homestead lay shrouded in darkness. Silently Filkins and his men made their way towards the woodshed. For some unknown reason, Grove's dogs did not bark. Filkins found the door unbolted, so he pushed it open and stepped inside, followed by Bissell, Garvey and Terry. Their heavy boots made little sound on the shavings littering the floor. Filkins then tried the door to the outer kitchen, but it was locked. He whispered a few words to Garvey, who went out through the woodshed door. The three men inside could hear him calling Wash's name from the yard.

In the bedroom off the middle kitchen which Wash and his new mistress, Louisa Gates, occupied, the gentle tapping on the windowpane and the utterance of Wash's name caused Louisa, in her fright, to clutch her lover's arm so savagely that Wash woke up with a start.

"What is it?" he demanded.

"Sh-h," Louisa whispered, "there's someone at our window."

He heard a quick thump on the pane. "Wash!" the voice outside called in a low tone.

Wash tossed off the covers and crawled out of bed. Clad only in his underwear, he shivered as he glanced out the window. Seeing no one he stepped back. "What do you want?" he asked.

Garvey continued in an undertone, "Come to the back door. I want to speak with you."

Wash, fully awake, strove to recognize the voice, which he knew he had heard before, but could not place it. Associates often awakened him in the night.

"All right," he answered, "I'll unlock the door for you."

Rhoda Loomis also heard the voice.

"About ten minutes after the clock struck one," she testified at the coroner's inquest, "I heard someone passing my window, at the south end of the house. They seemed to speak at Washington's window. His room is next to mine. I heard first a thump on his window and then the outside west door open. This door is under the woodshed and opens into the woodhouse kitchen. I next heard Washington open his door and walk along towards the back kitchen, through the middle kitchen. I knew it was him from his walk and his manner of spitting."

Wash loosened the bolt on the woodshed door, which was pushed open violently from the outside. Filkins and his three men rushed into the room. Wash recognized his enemy in the glow from the lanterns. The constable's face was grim, his eyes were narrowed to slits and his revolver was pointed directly at Wash. Filkins ignored him and with his men passed through the kitchens to Wash's bedroom. Wash sprang past him and barred the door with his body.

"I don't want you in there," he said. "Come out. There is nothing in there you want."

Filkins shoved aside and entered the room. Ignoring the terrified Louisa, he looked under the bed. Rising, he held his lantern so that its rays reflected the terror in her staring eyes. Apparently satisfied, he walked out of the bedroom.

"No, there is nothing here but a woman," he announced. Then, as if seeing Wash for the first time, he said sharply, "I want you."

"What for, Jim?"

"You'll see. Come out in the back kitchen."

Wash retraced his steps to the back kitchen. Cort Terry closed the middle kitchen door behind them.

"Well?" Wash turned to face his enemy.

"Out there." Filkins indicated the woodshed with his revolver. He emphasized his command with a quick push that propelled Wash into the woodshed.

Wash caught hold of the staircase to keep from falling. When he again faced Filkins his face was drained of color. Garvey and Terry arranged themselves beside Filkins, while Bissell mounted the stairs. Without speaking Filkins handed his lantern to Bissell.

"Boys—" Wash extended his hand pleadingly. As he stepped forward the ivory-handled, long-barreled .44 swept in a glittering arc and landed with a thud. The blood spurted from Wash's head and his eyes rolled until only the whites showed. He fell headlong on the shavings. The ivory-handled revolver rose and fell, rose and fell, until Wash's hair and skin peeled from his skull.

"It was sickening," Henry Bissell said later. "Terry and I stood there on the back stairs and saw Wash struck with the long-barreled .44. I'll never tell who wielded the gun."

Filkins motioned to his men to follow him. They climbed the kitchen stairs to the upper hallway, where Lorenzo Bixby, a mason by trade who had been employed as a man of all work, lay in bed with half-shut eyes, feigning sleep.

"I then saw a light at the head of the stairs," he testified. "I raised my head and saw three men standing at the head of the stairs. Two of them stopped and the other came directly to the bed where I slept and held the lantern down near my face. I said, 'What do you want?'

"He said, 'Ugh!' He then stepped in the door of the room adjoining and said, 'Grove.'

"I heard Grove's voice say, 'Yes.' He then turned around and held his light to the face of the man that lay next to the alley on the other bed. He then held the lantern by the face of the other man in bed, and changed what I took for a revolver from his right hand to his left hand and rapped on the door again and said, 'Grove.'

"The same voice within said, 'Yes.'

"In a moment I heard the door unbolted and Grove came into the room where we were. The man at the door said, 'Well, Grove, I have come to see you in the night.'

"I suppose I know who that man was. He is the man who has been represented to me as James Filkins. Grove said, 'Yes, all right.'

"Grove closed the door and walked right out of the room down the stairs. Filkins walked right by the side of Loomis. The other two men walked down with them."

Grove Loomis was in a sullen mood as he had not retired until eleven after a strenuous day traveling about the countryside on business.

"I opened the door and went out," he testified. "Filkins was standing close to the door. He did not say what he wanted. He took me by the collar.

"I said, 'I will go with you, Mr. Filkins.'

"He said, 'I know you will,' and handled me rather roughly.

"Three men were standing near the head of the chamber stairs. They stepped aside and let us go down first. They had guns in their hands. Filkins did not have a gun, but he had a lighted candle in a candle stick. One of the others, I think had a lantern. They followed us downstairs into the middle kitchen. He still held on to my collar.

"I said, 'Let me see Wash for a moment.'

"We went nearby his bedroom. I started to go towards the door but he pulled me back by the collar roughly and said to me, 'He is not there. Go with me and I will take care of you.'

"We then went into the back kitchen and the others followed and closed the door behind them. Filkins walked on along towards the northeast outside door of the kitchen. He stepped along to my overcoat, which was hanging up near the door and felt in the pockets.

" 'Men, where are my handcuffs?' he asked.

" 'Mr. Filkins, you don't need any handcuffs. I will go with you.'

"He said, 'I think you will.'

"He was feeling in his own pockets when he asked where the handcuffs were. Instantly he struck me six or eight times in the head as fast and as hard as he could. I staggered across the room.

"He said, 'Men, knock him down.'

"Then they struck me two or three times. I did not fall. He then struck me five or eight times with a slung shot. He had a revolver which he fired at me which missed me and I think the charge passed into the fireplace. He then struck me twice with the revolver and broke the revolver in two.

"I then fell and he jumped on me two or three times on the side and stomach and the others, I think, kicked me at the same time on the head and neck.

"Filkins then said, 'Men, he is dead. Let us burn him up!'

"At that, he and they pulled down two or three coats and put them on me and also a bag of oats and a fur collar and threw on some camphene or something out of a bottle over me and set fire to it. It burned very quickly. They then went out of the door into the woodshed. I saw nothing more of them. I cannot identify either of the other men with him. I was conscious all this time.

"Immediately after they went out, my sister and Nell Smith came into the room and pulled away the burning clothes."

Louisa Gates huddled in terror until she heard Grove and Filkins and the deputy's men come down the stairs and enter the back kitchen. When Grove started to scream in agony, she leaped from the bed and, not bothering to cover her nightdress, hurried across the room to the kitchen door and tried to open it.

". . . But it was tight, someone was holding it; there was no way to fasten it. Then I went back to my room and screamed and tried to put my clothes on. While I was putting them on, I heard someone go to the back kitchen door, and try to open it."

Nellie Smith stood on the stair landing when Louisa Gates fled back to her room. When Grove screamed again she flung herself at the outer room door, her fingers groping for the latch.

"I opened it a little ways and Filkins came to the door with his revolver in his hand, pointed at me and said, 'Come another step and I will shoot you; it is no place for you in this kitchen tonight,' and closed the door. Then I heard Grove cry, 'For God's sake, don't kill me.' I went to the door again, opened the door and saw Filkins have Grove bent forward and pounding his head with a revolver. The tall man came to the door, pushed me back and closed it.

"Cornelia was then coming out of the north room. I said to Cornelia, 'They are murdering Grove in the back kitchen.' We pushed the door open, she and I. Grove was lying on the floor and Filkins was jumping on him. I heard Filkins say that he was dead and they would burn him. I turned and ran to call the folks."

Plumb Loomis, who slept upstairs, was awakened by Grove's agonized cries and the girls' screams. He was just rising when his bedroom door opened and George Day, a burglar who professed he was a clock-fixer, entered.

"They are killing Grove down below," he cried in panic.

"I said to him, 'Who or what?' " Plumb testified. "He said, 'It is Filkins, haven't you heard him?' Denio was with me in bed; he had not got up at this time. I said to George, 'Run downstairs.'

"He said, 'No, I durst not.'

"About that time I was dressing. George had on his pants, his coat on his arm, and shoes in his hand. I went down into the middle kitchen, going down by the front stairs. Cornelia was then trying to open the door into the back kitchen. She had got it open a little way.

"She said, 'Run back. Don't come this way any further. They will kill you.'

"I started further that way when the Smith girl said, 'Go back,' and as I was going I looked around. Cornelia had got the door open about two feet. I heard someone of whom I had a glimpse, and whose voice sounded like Filkins, say, 'Its no place for a woman here. Keep back or I will shoot you.'

"Cornelia then said, 'Grove is dead. The house is on fire. Run as fast as you can.'

"I ran for the front door and met Denio coming downstairs with a pair of rubbers in his hand. He had his clothes on and we went into the front yard.

"Denio said, 'Let's go this way (north).'

"I ran directly to Mr. Edward Mason's house across lots."

While Plumb and Denio ran for help and Nellie tried to arouse the other occupants, Louisa finished dressing and re-entered the middle kitchen, where Cornelia was frantically motioning for Plumb to hurry.

"I met Cornelia Loomis about the middle of the middle kitchen," Louisa testified. "She said, 'They are killing Grove.'

"Then I said, 'Oh dear! They have taken Wash and I know they have killed him.'

'Then I went to the back kitchen door and opened it and saw Grove on the floor. His coat he had on was in a blaze and a black overcoat had been thrown on to him, which was in a blaze. I took the overcoat and ran to the northeast door with it.

"Cornelia followed and took it away from me, and said, 'Girl, you will set the house afire and yourself,' and threw it into the fireplace."

By this time Rhoda Loomis had entered the back kitchen and stood gazing in horror at the burning and battered body of her son, whom she thought dead.

"He had a bag of oats under his head which was on fire," Rhoda testified. "Cornelia took it away and we extinguished the fire. The next I discovered Louisa Gates had hold of a coat which was all on fire. She was going towards the door as if to throw it out, and Cornelia caught it from her and threw it into the fireplace. I went to the fireplace to take it, and she said, 'Mother, don't take it out. It is all kerosene.' I let it be on the fire a minute or two, and then took it out and threw water on it and put it out."

When Nellie Smith returned from awakening the men on the upper floor, she and Cornelia quickly extinguished the flames about Grove's body. The room was heavy with smoke and the stench of burning cloth. Nellie knelt beside Grove and lifted his bloody head in her arms. She scarcely was able to recognize her lover, for his face was battered and swollen, one eye was black, and his scalp was so torn that a length of it hung down over his forehead. The blood seeping from his wounds stained his mistress' clothing and dripped on the floor.

"Have they killed you?" Nellie sobbed.

Grove's eyelids flickered and his eyes opened. He had not lost consciousness, but was so beaten he could hardly move. He tried to speak, but unintelligible sounds issued from his throat. Someone in the room called for spirits. Nellie returned immediately to her lover's side, raised his head again and poured a small amount of the bottle's contents between his bleeding lips. The fierce sting of the spirits revived him slightly.

When Filkins, Bissell, Terry and Garvey left Grove for dead, with his body shrouded in flames, their one thought was to get away as rapidly as possible. As they left the house Filkins poured what was left of the kerosene into the woodbox and set fire to it.

A man was seen entering the new barn. Opening his lantern he quickly touched off a wad of hay with the flame and threw it in the mow. As the flames spread upward he ran from the barn and joined the others.

Eli Tilby, from his room in the garret, saw them go down the road.

"I did not see them have any light," he testified. "I did not know them and I can't say how they were dressed as it was considerable dark. It was a good deal darker than it usually is when the moon is not shining. I cannot tell which way they went when they got to the road. There was then no light in the barn. I dressed myself as soon as possible and went downstairs. As soon as I got down, I saw that the barn was on fire. I went to the barn."

At the barn Tilby met Lorenzo Bixby, Frank Kent, Mrs. Loomis, Cornelia and John Stoner, or Stower as he was sometimes called. Bixby had extinguished the fire in the woodbox and had been the first to reach the burning barn, where he found the doors opened slightly and the interior a mass of flames. Indifferent to the danger he went inside and cut the halters of two of the seven terror-stricken horses stabled within. He tried to reach the others, but the flames and terrific heat drove him back and he had to leave them to die.

Cornelia caught hold of the pole of a covered wagon standing near the door and drew it away from the flaming structure. Mrs. Loomis called to her to draw it further away and the girl hastened to comply. Her mother then turned to the hired men.

"I went in front of the barn and saw John Stoner there and Frank Kent and soon after, Mr. Bixby and Tilby," Rhoda testified. "I said to John, 'Why don't you get out the hampers?'

"He said, 'I can't.'

"I said, 'You can. They are close by the door.'

"He tried, but whether he got any out, I don't know.

"He said to Bixby, 'Why don't you get out the horses?'

"He said, 'I can't.'

"He said, 'You can. Take an axe and break in the side of the barn and get them out.'

"But he didn't do anything about it. The horses were at this time jumping and springing. There were seven horses in the barn and none of them were saved."

While Mrs. Loomis was issuing orders to the men, Cornelia asked Bixby if he had seen Washington, Plumb or Denio.

Bixby wiped his stinging eyes with the back of his hand. "No, I have not," he answered. He went back to look for the Loomis boys.

Louisa Gates had returned to her bedroom for a bottle of liquor to give Grove. Wash always kept a bottle on the stand near their bed.

"When I got in there," Louisa testified, "I looked out of the window and saw the barns were all on fire. I forgot the liquor and came back into the middle kitchen and told them the barns were all on fire and said, "Oh, Wash is killed! Wash is killed! Why don't you look for Wash?' Nobody gave me any answer and I went back of the woodhouse and looked on some boards to see if I could see him; I did not find him, and went back into the house and met Cornelia.

"She said, 'Why don't you go up to Mr. Welch's and tell him that they have killed the boys and the barn is on fire?'

"Then I went out into the road, and went by the barn, about halfway up to Mr. Welch's and turned around to come back and cried, 'Where is Wash?' Then I went back to the house and went and sat in my bedroom and cried."

Grove Loomis stumbled to his feet, half-conscious, with his face swollen and bruised and his head dripping blood; some of it had dried and was matted with hair. Nellie begged him to lie down, but he did not seem to hear her. He reached for his hat, placed it on his head and staggered out into the yard. With tortured steps he made his way to the shanty where his prized horse was kept and unlocked the door. There was no sign of fire about this building, although across the road the burning barn and haystacks lighted the darkness. Turning back towards the house he saw the shingles smoking where embers from the barn had fallen on them.

"If you see any signs of fire in the shanty," he called to Nellie, "run up and cut the halter and let my horse loose."

He called loudly for a ladder. When some men brought one he and Nellie raised it against the side of the house. Holding a pail of water from the well steadily with one hand, he painfully clmbed the ladder, put out the fire on the roof and returned to the ground, where he leaned against the ladder. His head seemed ready to burst and his eyesight was failing. Almost blindly he found the door to the house and went inside, only to come out again and stagger towards the fence enclosing the front yard. Suddenly the world went spinning. His knees buckled and he sprawled on the dead grass.

In the meantime Plumb Loomis had reached the Mason farm, where he drummed on Mason's bedroom window until a light flared and the farmer's face appeared.

"Who's there?" Mason asked.

"Plumb Loomis."

Mason raised the window a few inches. "What's the trouble, Plumb?"

"Our house is all on fire. Can you come over?"

"Soon's I dress and wake John."

"I got to go back now," Plumb said, "and find Denio."

Plumb met Denio in back of Terry's place coming towards him. He saw for the first time that the barn was on fire.

"I went on to the hill and called the Negro, whose name is Dick Loucks," Plumb testified. "Denio remained behind while I was gone. We remained here some time and heard the women cry murder and other cries. After a while we went back to Mason's."

Mason had finished dressing when Plumb and Denio drummed on his window again. When he raised it the two outlaws climbed over the sill into the bedroom and crawled under the bed.

"What do you want now?" Mason asked.

"They've killed Wash and Grove," Plumb whispered hoarsely, "and they're after us."

"You've got to get out of here." The farmer shut the window and pulled down the shade.

"You must let us hide," Plumb pleaded. "You must save us."

"But you can't stay here," Mason insisted stubbornly. "If they know you are here, they'll come and burn me out."

"Would you have us murdered?"

"No, I'll have to take a chance. I don't want to see anyone killed. You can stay here for awhile. John's getting dressed. We're going over to your house. We'll tell your folks where you are."

"Thanks," breathed the two grateful Loomises.

Mason found his son putting on his clothes. "I'm going on ahead to the Loomises, John," he said. "The Loomis buildings are on fire."

"Go ahead, I'll be over directly."

John found a lighted lantern his father had left for him. He had little use for it, for flames from the burning buildings lighted the sky for miles.

"When I got to the burning barn," he testified, "some of the Loomis family and others were there. Soon after I got there, Willie Smith came to the barn and said to me, 'We want you to come up to the house and see Grove. He is pounded most to death.' I went up to the house and found him at the northeast corner of the house, near the door-yard fence. I told him to go into the house and I would try and get a doctor. He turned and started to the northeast. I don't know whether he went into the house. He walked and I think Nellie had hold of his arm. I soon went into the house and saw Grove on a bed in the northeast room. Soon I heard someone call for a light in the woodshed and found Wash lying on a pile of shingles. Mr. Welch, Mr. Bixby, father and myself carried him into the same room with Grove."

Bixby had just discovered Wash lying in a pool of blood on the woodshed floor. He called Louisa Gates and ordered her to bring the straw tick from her bed. Wash's body was placed on it. Louisa hurriedly found quilts and put them over her lover's body while Nellie Smith covered Grove, who was lying on the floor nearby. Mrs. Loomis and Cornelia came into the room, followed by some of the men. Rhoda tried to force a little liquor between Wash's lips, but he was unable to swallow.

Although the night's ordeal had shaken the seventy-four year old mother, she managed to remain composed, for Dr. Preston had been called and she was sure he could save her sons.

About four o'clock Plumb came home, leaving Denio at Mason's place. He found his family gathered in the north room and took his place with them to wait.

CHAPTER XXI

FILKINS IS INDICTED

Dr. Medina Preston reached the Loomis farm at sunrise. He glanced at Grove, saw that he was conscious, and turned to Wash.

"I found him pulseless without power of swallowing," he reported. "His extremities were cold with no evidence of life. He kept breathing a little and occasionally moving one arm. His sensibility was entirely gone and he was completely unconscious."

Upon examination Dr. Preston discovered that Wash had suffered four head wounds, one of them fracturing the skull. Wash's eyes were much bruised and swollen.

"Even under ordinary circumstances he could not possibly recover," said the doctor, "although in my opinion only the skull wound was necessarily fatal. I was there three or four hours, dressed Grove's wounds and burns and left him about nine or ten in the morning. I saw him (Wash) again about noon; life was almost extinct. I remained but a short time, but when I left he was still alive. I did not see him again alive."

Dr. S. G. Wolcott of Utica arrived a few minutes after Wash died. He performed an emergency operation on Grove and informed Mrs. Loomis that her son's condition was critical, as inflammation of the brain might have set in.

Rumors of the raid reached Sangerfield Center and Waterville by daylight. By noon it was a topic of gossip on the streets of Utica.

A reporter from The Utica Morning Herald, sent on special assignment, found the murder the all-absorbing theme. Rumor had singled out this one and that one as the murderers. "It is not our province at this time to speak of the character which the Loomis family bore among their neighbors or in the county," he wrote. "Murder is seldom justifiable, and disregard of just laws, never. There can be no excuse for this horrible deed, although winked at possibly by popular sentiment."

Coroner E. A. Munger of Oneida County held an inquest that same Wednesday afternoon at the Loomis home. The special jury was composed of Horace Tower, Foreman, Ebenezer Newell, Horace Wakefield, Eli Ackley, George M. Burdick, Ransome Benedict, A. Jerome Hale, J. H. Hearsey, Robert J. Thatcher, John R. Hewitt, C. C. Risley and Orenzo Barnard.

Munger called Mrs. Rhoda Loomis. Her voice was slow and tired as she told her story: "This town and this place is my residence. I am the mother of George W. W. Loomis, deceased. His age is 40 or 41 years. He has made his home here for the last ten years. The last I saw of him alive was between twelve and one o'clock yesterday. He was at home the night before. He was then apparently well. He was sitting in the back kitchen of this house. It was about nine o'clock. There were in the house Mr. Bixby, Eli Tilby, Frank Kent, John Stower, Amos Plumb Loomis, my grandson Charles Loomis, Cornelia Loomis, Louisa Gates, Elizabeth Calkins and Nellie Smith. These are all I recollect. My son Grove was not at home at that time, but was at Madison or Bouckville or somewhere. The next I saw of Washington was about three o'clock that night, by our time. He was under the woodshed. Two men were fetching him into the house. He was covered all over with blood and insensible. He never spoke after I saw him."

The coroner excused her and Grove was called. He was too weak to stand alone, but his mind was clear and he told of the unmerciful beating he had received at the hands of Filkins and his men, whom he claimed he was unable to identify.

Munger adjourned the inquest to the American Hotel in Waterville, where Lorenzo Bixby testified of his activities on the night of the murder. He also admitted that two other men had occupied the other bed in the room where he slept.

Louisa Gates and Plumb Loomis testified on Thursday. Plumb had found what was apparently the murder weapon.

"I picked up the barrel of a revolver on the kitchen floor before daylight. It was said that another part had been found to it. I left it with Bixby. I think I have seen the pistol before. I thought I had seen Filkins have it at different times. He had shot at me with it the year before. I recognized it by the marks on the end of the barrel and hammer having a small piece off the side. I think LaVergue Beebe had it before Filkins had it. I noticed the mark on the end of the pistol at the time Mr. Beebe's boy had it. I think the hammer was not broken at that time. I think the piece was broken off the hammer when I saw it in Filkins' possession. I think I saw it was broken. I never saw a pistol with an ivory handle before. I heard men talking in front of the barn when Denio and I came out the front door. I saw no light at that time with them. The pistol I have spoken of was a five shooter. There were three shots in it. I found the cylinder of the pistol about half an hour after I found the barrel. The girl found the barrel."

Dr. Munger asked Loomis if he had shown him the handle and barrel of the pistol Tuesday morning, and Plumb said he thought he had.

"Did you at that time have the cylinder?"

Plumb considered the question. "I can't say. I don't remember."

"Do you remember my asking you to let me take it into my possession?"

Loomis admitted that he had.

The coroner asked about the men known as George and Frank. Plumb denied any knowledge of George Day and Frank Jones or where they had gone. When he was excused from the stand John C. Mason was sworn. He was followed by Eli Tilby and Frank Kent. Each gave his version of the fatal night. The last to be questioned were Nellie Smith, Cornelia Loomis and Elizabeth Calkins.

The inquest was adjourned and on Friday afternoon the funeral of George Washington Loomis was held in the Congregational Church at the Center. His family, friends, crowds of curious sightseers and even enemies filled the church and overflowed into the yard. The Rev. Mr. Marshall of Madison preached the funeral sermon. Afterwards the body of the head of the Loomis family, in its lead coffin, was taken to the cemetery on Sanger Street and interred in the family lot back of his cousin's home.

The coroner's jury reconvened the following day. Statements were taken from Dr. Preston and Dr. George W. Cleveland. Dr. Munger also called two surprise witnesses to the stand, George Carlisle, the stage driver, and Charles Hubbard. Carlisle described how Filkins had come to the hotel barn for oil before the raid, and Hubbard described finding the handcuffs.

"I was out traveling last Tuesday and found a pair of handcuffs. I found them between three and four o'clock. It was on the farm of Isaac Terry, in the lower part near the swamp within a few rods of the timber. I have them in my possession. This was about one-half mile from the Loomis' house. There was a haystack on the Loomis farm a quarter of a mile distant, which was then burning. They were north from the haystack."

It did not take the jury long to reach a verdict. Horace Tower of Waterville, the foreman, gave the unanimous decision: "According to the testimony given, George Washington W. Loomis came to his death by the hands of three or more persons, and one of them was James L. Filkins."

As soon as he heard of the verdict Filkins went to the coroner and said, "I am ready to deliver myself to the authorities, so I may have a hearing."

Munger was evidently in no hurry to press charges. "Go home," he said, "and I will let you know when I want you."

Bill Loomis drove to Waterville and swore out a warrant for Filkins, charging him with murder. Munger ordered Filkins' arrest. The constable appeared when arraigned, but Bill Loomis, who had obtained a subpoena for a witness, failed to appear to press charges. Justice George W. Cleveland, tired of such tactics, issued other subpoenas and ordered a constable to serve them.

When Plumb appeared to ask a postponement, Cleveland snapped, "The Court refuses any further delay and calls Amos Plumb Loomis to testify."

Plumb made no move to comply, but asked to be excused from the courtroom for a moment. When the request was granted he walked down the street and did not return.

William White of Brookfield, representing the People, asked for the floor.

"Telegrams have been received from the District Attorney and Mr. Pomeroy," he declared, "to the effect that they wish the proceedings to be abandoned."

Ball instantly protested. "The whole matter is now in the hands of the Court and neither the District Attorney nor Mr. Pomeroy has the authority to control its action or direct it to suspend its proceedings. An investigation should be had and every person who was present at the Loomis home at the time of the homicide should be brought forward to testify of their knowledge of the matter and be subject to cross-examination, so that the true offender might, if possible, be discovered. And further, the Court should forthwith issue attachments and compel the attendance of the defaulting witnesses."

Cleveland admitted it was his duty to proceed and issued the subpoenas for the missing witnesses.

Constable Sanford returned that evening with two of the Loomis' hired men, Lorenzo D. Bixby and Nathan Gates, brother of Wash's mistress. It was evident that both men had been brought against their wishes. Bixby, questioned first by White, related practically the same story of the murder of

Wash that he had given to the coroner's jury. On cross-examination by Ball, "his memory of his past life up to within a few months was almost entirely blank," reported The Times. "He stated that from six to ten years of age his parents moved to Cadysville, Clinton County, but whether they remained one to ten years, he had no idea. From there they moved to West Plattsburg and remained from one to ten years. (He) did not know his father's business or who his neighbors were. Similar testimony which reads of idiocy, but with keen, sagacious, and crafty appearance to stamp him as concealing his past history."

Gates, more belligerent, told a fantastic story of having been asked by Filkins to assist him in cleaning out the Loomises. "I refused," he stated, "on ground that I had not nerve enough."

White rested the case for the People. Ball immediately insisted that all the witnesses should be produced. He was sustained by the Court.

The Brookfield attorney announced his withdrawal from the case.

Early the next morning Constable Sanford, Constable Leland and two assistants went to the Loomis homestead to attach the missing witnesses. Only Mrs. Loomis and Elizabeth Calkins were at home. The girl took refuge in the outdoor toilet; when Sanford tried to enter, she darted by him and ran back into the house by way of the back door, as Mrs. Loomis was coming out. The constable tried to catch the girl, but Mrs. Loomis flung herself on him. When he freed himself of the old lady's clutching fingers, the girl had disappeared.

The other officers searched the premises and contented themselves by looking through the windows of the home. John Stoner, the Dutchman, was seen in the wood lot, and offered no resistance when taken into custody. Justice Cleveland adjourned the hearing until Friday morning after Constable Sanford made his report.

Denio Loomis appeared on Friday and on Saturday Louisa Gates testified. None of the other witnesses showed up, although the sheriff's department and town constables searched for them. Lamb, who had represented William Loomis in the action, withdrew from the case and was replaced by Pomeroy, who appeared that evening and informed Justice Cleveland that he rested the People's case. The Court refused the request.

"As the most important witnesses have been kept concealed, this Court refuses to allow the People to rest," Justice Cleveland stated. He then adjourned the hearing until Monday.

The Circuit Court of Oyer and Terminer opened its sessions in Utica on Monday with Judge William J. Bacon presiding. The Judge stressed the Sangerfield murder in his opening address to the grand jury.

"The case will probably be brought before you, and if so, it is the duty of the jurors to give the case a careful hearing and upon proof furnished you of the authors of the murder. It is your duty to make a presentation to this court by indictment. Mob law cannot be justified. A good citizen might be sacrificed by the same rule on another day. Such proceedings cannot be upheld in a law-abiding community. If the grand jurors do their duty, the law is adequate to meet all offenses."

Judge Bacon's predictive statement soon became a fact. The Loomises evidently held up the proceedings in Justice's Court and took their case to the grand jury. Filkins was not even summoned to testify. The grand jurors heard only the testimony of the family and their gang, including several who were not at the farm the night of the murder.

The Loomises must have been exceedingly confident of their case. On Saturday, the 18th three of their men, Tom Mott, George Day and Frank Jones, entered the Park Hotel in Waterville and ordered dinner. They bragged loudly that they had come to clean out the village, kill Filkins and take revenge on other enemies of the Loomises. One remained in the dining room while the others went into the barroom to act as guards. Shortly afterwards Filkins entered the barroom. The men drew their pistols and started to curse him. Filkins, who was unarmed, brushed past them, hurried to his home buckled on his revolver and went back to the hotel. The three avengers, having changed their minds, had left their dinners and started back to the Loomis farm.

That same day in Utica the grand jury found five indictments against Filkins; the murder of George Washington Loomis; assault and battery with intention to kill Grove Loomis; arson in the first degree for firing the Loomis homestead; arson, third degree, for firing the barn; and arson, fourth degree, for firing a haystack.

Filkins knew nothing of his indictment until he read The Utica Morning Herald on Monday. Furious because he had not been notified, he drove with Ball to Utica to call on the attorney who had consented to represent him, Senator Roscoe Conkling. Conkling, who was only thirty-six at that time, was a handsome man with blond curls and beard and a deep voice. He had already achieved a national reputation, and it was generally believed he was jeopardizing his own career in accepting Filkins' case.

Filkins was arraigned that afternoon and pleaded not guilty to the indictments.

"Now that you have pleaded," District Attorney Jenkins asked, "what are you and your counsel prepared to do?"

Before Filkins could answer, Roscoe Conkling arose and faced Jenkins, whom he knew was friendly with the Loomises.

"I am prepared to say at once what I will do upon knowing the course proposed by the prosecution," he said challengingly. "I find that for some reason the findings of the grand jury have been encumbered by an extraordinary number of indictments, and a statement has been put forth in the public prints as to the vote by which the indictments were found unanimously, which, even if it were true, was in violation of the law, and calculated to prejudice the accused; and if in addition to all this objection was to be made to allowing bail, the defendant had better submit to the disadvantage and inconvenience of a trial at once, without time for proper examination, rather than be committed to jail until a future term of court."

District Attorney Jenkins was on his feet, waving his arms. He was angry, for he now realized how cleverly Conkling had guessed his plans.

"I am not willing to be put in the position of asking for a delay so that the defendant can make that a ground for being let to bail," he said, "but I shall oppose bail being granted."

"Although the indictments could not suitably be tried at the present term," Judge Bacon ruled, "the statement of the District Attorney threw it upon the Court to dispose of the case in some way."

"Relieve the case of that predicament," cried Conkling, "and cut the matter short. I would move at once that the defendant be let to bail."

Daniel Ball, who had been Filkins' counsel before the Waterville magistrate, submitted a statement of what occurred previous to the finding of the indictments.

"Mr. Filkins has been ready from the first to respond to any summons," he stated sincerely. "He has asked for an examination and the magistrate has attempted to hold it, but the Loomises have baffled and thwarted it by concealing witnesses and preventing their attendance and by various other devices. Mr. Filkins has voluntarily appeared at all times and had started for Utica as soon as he heard that he was indicted."

"The coroner omitted to have the defendant arrested," Jenkins said sharply, "and the constable has omitted to take him into custody and the public feeling is on the side of Mr. Filkins. Upon the evidence for the prosecution—and by that the Court must be governed in their motion—a jury would convict a defendant and therefore bail should be refused." He paused to pound a fist into the palm of the other hand.

"In cases of murder, the Court can receive bail only when, upon the evidence before the grand jury, the guilt of the defendant was not probable." As if to drive home his point he read passages from certain law books to substantiate his claims.

Mr. Conkling again took the floor. His blue eyes flashed with the heat of battle and one of his golden curls dangled on his forehead, "Your Honor," he said, bowing to the Court, "I wish to close my argument for the motion I have presented by maintaining the following propositions: First, that the old rule disapproved the allowance of bail to any man apparently guilty of felony and that under this rule there was no distinction as to the power of the Court between murder and any other felony. (Here he cited several cases to illustrate his point.)

"Second, That in England and in this state previous to the Revised Statutes, a difficulty was found in allowing and fixing the amount of bail after indictment, for the reason that in England and here until the adoption of the Revised Statutes the Court was shut out from knowing the facts in the case. There was no clerk of the grand jury and no minutes of evidence before them, and the defendant could not, as he can now, be heard to present proofs of his innocence or ex-explanations of the case. This difficulty no longer exists so far as regards the proceedings before the grand jury. The Court will now look into the evidence where it is necessary to do so, and will bail or not as proper, whether after indictment or before. (To this many cases were cited.)

"Third, A defendant is never to be punished before trial, and bail is never refused or made greivous in amount, except the object to be to prevent escape of the accused. Whenever the Court is satisfied that the appearance of the defendant at his trial will be secured by his giving bail, it is the duty of the Court to accept it. (To this various authorities were cited.)

"Fourth, In a clear case of guilt, where the defendant has no chance of escape but flight, the Court would refuse bail for felony, without reference to its grade, but the present case is far from being an instance of this kind."

Mr. Conkling further reviewed the case and evidence, showing the glaring improbabilities involved. When he concluded he sat down, breathing hard. He had done his best. The case was in the hands of the Judge.

After a brief consultation by the Judges, Judge Bacon pounded with the gavel. "We have reached a decision," he stated. "The Jurisdiction of this Court as to bail for felonies extends to murder as well as to other crimes. The object of bail is to secure the attendance of the accused and, whenever this object can be obtained and insured by acceptance of bail, it should not be refused. In many cases the facts are such as to render it unsafe to release the defendant from custody. In a recent case ten thousand dollars had been fixed and, although the other members of the court think this amount rather large in the present case, we have agreed upon it."

He made no mention of the term of trial at which Filkins was to appear. Conkling thanked the Court and said that bail for his client would reach the Court within a day or so.

On Friday the 24th twenty-eight prominent citizens of Sangerfield, Marshall and Brookfield drove over the hard, rutty roads to Utica during a blinding snowstorm to become sureties for Jim Filkins. These men were George Putnam, H. F. Locke, William Conger, C. C. Risley, J. Schryver, M. C. Hotchkin, John B. Norton, P. B. Haven, Charles Haven, J. S. Crumb, Charles Curtis, D. S. Bennet, C. B. Terry, Freeman Terry, Oliver Bush, William V. Durfee, J. L. Bissell, Roswell Conger and B. A. Beardsley of Sangerfield and J. Corey, Hazen House, T. H. Peck, Charles Peck, George A. Peck, Joseph Marsh, Ephraim Conger, Fayette Peck and B. C. Montgomery of North Brookfield and Marshall.

Said The Waterville Times: "Almost any one of the gentlemen would alone have stood the bail, but for several reasons which we will state. In the first place, the people of this community have strong faith in Mr. Filkins' entire innocence and believe that there is a deep plot laid to get him out of the way so that depredations upon property may be carried on in greater safety. Secondly, his townsmen desired to make an expression of this faith and belief. Thirdly, it was understood that the gang of incendiaries and thieves who infest this locality had declared that any person who should become bail for Mr. Filkins must take the consequences, and his bailor, a Deputy U. S. Marshal, has had his barn and hop kiln burned to the ground since he signed the bail bond it was probably thought best to adopt the suggestion of the old saying, 'In Union There is Strength.' Fourthly, they desired to show that the sympathy of the town was with their fearless, guiltless, and law-abiding officer and citizen rather than with law-breakers and outlaws. Yet, notwithstanding the staunch belief of the people of this town in Mr. Filkins' innocence, they strongly condemn the murder of Wash Loomis, and desire the arrest and punishment of the perpetrator of that lawless and wicked act.

"Had not the roads been in a terrible condition, some twenty more gentlemen would have gone out to sign the bail bonds, making about fifty in all."

As soon as the $10,000 bail had been posted, Filkins was released on his own recognizance. He was still under the shadow of murder, but nothing had been said to hinder him from continuing his campaign to clean out the Loomises!

CHAPTER XXII

THE CRANDALL MURDER

The death of Wash Loomis failed to end the depredations of the Loomis gang. The outlaws who comprised the organization came and went as usual after dark. The only noticeable difference in the family's habits were the curtained windows and the arsenal of pistols, rifles, shotguns and ammunition distributed through the rooms of the house as a precaution against further raids.

"I would often see strangers there in the morning," Nellie Smith confessed. "I knew victuals were carried to persons whom they did not want me to see. They had them concealed. I supposed them to be members of the gang. I never saw signals given, but the officers used to come there often. LaVergue Beebe, Tommy Mott, Hugh Kenyon, Bill Alvord, a man named Jones, Joe Crandall, Belfield and Curtiss used to come there. Members of the gang usually went up the front way to their rooms."

"Wicked Joe" Crandall, Isaiah Belfield and Shadrack Curtiss were comparative newcomers to the Loomis gang, although Crandall's sister, Esther, had been living at the homestead for a number of years.

Crandall and Belfield were local boys, sons of law-abiding farmers who suffered unjustly for their sons' activities, but Curtiss, a Canadian, in appearance and dress would have been taken for a hoodlum in any country. His coppery skin, piercing black eyes and thick black hair cut square at his shoulders, hinted of Indian blood. He dressed shabbily in off-sized clothing and wore a broad-brimmed black hat. His only concessions to vanity were the small gold nubbins which decorated the lobes of his ears.

The three men met at the Loomis homestead on Tuesday evening, December 5, 1865. According to circumstantial evidence the purpose of their visit was to plan the robbery of Joe's uncle and aunt, Dennison and Phoebe Crandall, whose house at Coontown between Leonardsville and West Edmeston had been burned by arsonists in 1862 and rebuilt.

Dennison Crandall had worked hard from boyhood. At sixty-five he was tall, straight and muscular, though his hair and beard had turned gray. "I'm not afraid of anything," was his proudest boast.

He was careful of his hard-earned money, but often lent sums to his neighbors. A shrewd judge of character, he kept three pocket-books named "The World," "In the World," and "Dirt of the World." A large sum of money was kept in the first, a larger sum in government bonds in the second, while a trifling sum scarcely filled the third. A lazy man received loans from "Dirt of the World," and when the farmer spoke of all the money he had "In the World," his friends believed him.

The day before the gathering at the Loomis homestead, Crandall had withdrawn from the First National Bank of Leonardsville his entire savings of $300 in cash and $1,800 in treasury bonds. When he got home he stuffed his money and bonds in his three pocket-books and secreted them in the mattress of his bed.

On the night of the 6th Dennison was in the barn doing the chores while his wife, Phoebe, prepared supper on the kitchen stove. Suddenly the kitchen door was thrown open. Phoebe turned to face two masked men. A scream welled up in her throat, but one of the men silenced her with a movement of his drawn pistol.

"We want your money," he said. "You'd better get it quick if you know what's good for you."

Phoebe took a few bills from a jar on the mantel and threw them on the table. The men were stuffing the bills into their pockets when Crandall walked into the kitchen.

"What are you doing here and what do you want?" he asked.

One of the masked men pointed a finger at him. "I demand your government bonds and money for the benefit of Delos McIntyre," he said.

Crandall shook his fist. "I'll not get a single dollar!" he cried. "Before I give you my money, I'll die first."

One of the men struck Crandall with a chunk of wood, but missed. Crandall leaped forward and landed a stiff blow to the outlaw's stomach. While the robber clutched at his middle, Crandall seized him and tripped him, throwing him to the floor.

The other masked man drew his pistol, but Crandall hit him with a chunk of wood again and again until he dropped to the floor and grovelled like a beaten dog.

The first outlaw, having recovered from the blow to his stomach, leaped on Crandall, but the farmer threw him aside like a sack of wheat, got him on his back and beat at his face with his fists. The second outlaw joined the fray and Crandall rose to meet him. The two outlaws leaped on him and bore him to the floor.

"Let me go," he panted, "and I will get you some money."

He broke loose, ran into his bedroom and slammed the door behind him. Though the room was in darkness, his hands found what they were searching for, a long flail stick which he had nicknamed his "headache stick."

The door was pushed open slightly and a pistol was thrust into the room. Crandall struck the hand with his stick. He swung the door open to face the burning eyes of the first outlaw. He raised his stick to ward off an attack, but the stick caught on the door-casing. The outlaw raised his pistol and fired point-blank at Crandall. The bullet furrowed the farmer's skull. He staggered but did not fall, and advanced toward the outlaws.

Mrs. Crandall, who was seated in her Deal chair, clutched her hands.

"Dennison, you'd better get the money and give it to them," she whispered.

At that moment a third masked man appeared in the kitchen. Crandall thought he came from the cellar way. Coolly, he raised his pistol and shot the farmer in the face. The ball penetrated below Crandall's left eye and lodged in the roof of his mouth. As he staggered across the room and plunged headlong, his wife screamed. The outlaw shot her through the head. The ball entered just above the ear, killing her.

When Dennison Crandall regained consciousness, the outlaws had fled. He spoke to his wife, but she did not answer. He dragged himself to his feet, sensing only one thing, that he must get help.

No one will ever know how he managed to cover the half mile to George Van Rensselaer Crandall's place. The first George knew of the tragedy was when he answered a battering at his door and found the blood-matted figure of his brother hunched against the sill.

Without recognizing him George dragged Dennison into the kitchen, where Henry Hickling and John Clark had been helping him to make butter.

"My God," Clark cried in horror, "it's Uncle Dennison!"

"Yes, it is me," Crandall whispered. "Two men came into my house and have almost killed me and I fear killed Phoebe. I want you to go and see what has become of her." When they asked what had happened, all he could say was, "I could stand the clubs but not the bullets." He then lost consciousness.

It did not take long for Hickling and Clark to arouse the countryside. Men came on horseback, in sleighs and on foot from the farms and nearby villages. They chose as their leader Ira Ordway, a West Edmeston storekeeper. The party approached the Crandall house cautiously, fearing that the criminals were there.

Hickling called to Phoebe. Receiving no answer, he pushed open the kitchen door, holding his lantern aloft. He returned to the party and said, "She is dead, I guess." A man was sent after Dr. Uri Munger of Leonardsville, the coroner.

Martha Coman, the Crandall's hired girl, who had been visiting neighbors, arrived. She caused considerable trouble by insisting that Mrs. Crandall's body be moved, but finally gave in when she was made to understand that the coroner was coming to view it.

She took a candle and went into her employers' bedroom, where she tore open the straw tick and found the three "World" pocket-books. Fearing to trust anyone with them, she put one in the bosom of her dress and tucked one in each of her stockings. She turned the money over later to the cashier of the Leonardsville bank.

When word came that Dr. Munger would be unable to come, Luke Hoxie said enough people had examined the body to testify at the inquest, so he ordered the body removed.

In the meantime, Drs. King and Crandall were working to save Dennison Crandall's life. They patched up the furrow in his skull, but were unable to remove the bullet from the roof of his mouth. The aged farmer was made as comfortable as possible, while they waited for him to die.

The three outlaws had planned to spend the night at a home near Bridgewater. Joe Crandall felt like celebrating, so he got drunk and went home with his mistress. They were awakened, told that Mrs. Crandall had been murdered and that testimony of witnesses would be taken at the coroner's inquest.

Mention of witnesses threw a chill of fear over the outlaw. He sent his mistress to tell the Loomis family and to get their advice. Denio Loomis came for him about noon and took him away in his carriage, disguised in one of his mistress' dresses and shaker bonnet.

Isaiah Belfield and Shadrack Curtiss appeared at the Loomis homestead on the night of the 8th. Cornelia took them in and got supper for them.

"You have cut up a pretty caper," Nellie Smith heard her say, "to go over there and murder those old folks."

"We went to the Crandall home to steal the bonds and money," Belfield said. "Old Crandall fought so hard we were obliged to shoot him."

"It's a pretty big crime for so little money." Cornelia's voice was edged with scorn. "If I had committed so big a crime, I would have got more money."

The two men left the Loomis homestead the next morning, several hours before Dr. Munger and his jury settled down to the business of taking evidence at Edwards' Hotel in Leonardsville. Martha Coman and Crandall's neighbors readily answered all questions. The jury agreed that no solution to the crime was imminent, nor was any clue found as to the motive save robbery. It ruled that Mrs. Phoebe Crandall had come to her death at the hands of persons unknown.

Dennison Crandall hovered between life and death for two weeks. When he recovered consciousness, he learned for the first time of his wife's death. Unfortunately, he was unable to identify the men who had attacked him and his wife. He remembered their appearance, their clothes, and the burning eyes of the light-haired man who had shot him, but beyond this he knew nothing. The men were strangers, but he felt certain he could identify them if he ever met them again. He posted a $1,000 reward for their apprehension.

CHAPTER XXIII

THE LOOMISES SEEK REVENGE

The Loomises and other criminals throughout the state found themselves forgiven for their early crimes in 1866 after the Supreme Court ruled that all offenses committed more than three years previous to the finding of their last indictment were unauthorized and could not be sustained. The area newspapers reported the story without editorial comment.

The Loomises refused to let well enough alone. Late in February Filkins received word that they had received a large quantity of counterfeit greenbacks and postal currency with which they intended to flood the state. He drove to the Loomis farm, armed with search warrants and accompanied by a small posse. Much to his surprise, Mrs. Loomis received him courteously and ordered a small keg of beer brought up from the cellar.

Arthur J. Tuttle, a resident of the neighborhood, said "the men had several drinks and began to lose interest in the raid until one of them started to examine the keg.

" 'It looks as if it has a false bottom,' he informed Filkins.

"Filkins examined the keg and then carried it out into the yard. He found an axe and knocked the keg to pieces. The bottom was packed tight with counterfeit money."

A search of the house produced a few other kegs with false bottoms packed with counterfeit money. In the upstairs room of young Charles Loomis, Filkins discovered several packages of spurious currency which he piled up to carry away.

"Put that down!" Wheeler Loomis' twelve-year old son stood in the doorway with a rifle in his hands.

"Where did you get this money?" Filkins asked.

"I got it in different places." Charles raised the rifle and pointed it at the constable. "Damn you," he swore angrily, "I'll shoot you if you take my money."

Filkins wrenched the rifle from the boy's hands, seized him by the shirt collar and took him downstairs, where he warned Mrs. Loomis to take better care of her grandson.

Filkins made no arrests, but took as evidence greenbacks and postal currency valued at $1,100, which he turned over to U. S. Commissioner Boyce in Utica.

Two other raids took place that week. Filkins, accompanied by a Binghamton detective, two Oneida County officers, Sheriff Asahel C. Stone, Undersheriff Asa Stone and Deputies Henry Keith and Ephraim Conger of Madison County, recovered a silver-plated harness which had been stolen from Race & Co.'s Livery in Binghamton the previous September. An officer from Herkimer found a horse, wagon and harness that had been missing from a livery stable in Oswego for nearly a year.

Upon orders from Commissioner Boyce, Filkins arrested Mrs. Loomis, Cornelia and Charles after encountering considerable trouble. While searching for more evidence, he saw Cornelia hide something under her dress.

The Waterville Times said: ". . . she ran like a deer, up one pair of stairs and down another, and through several rooms, at the time of her arrest, giving the officer a smart race. If the watch 'found at the house' was formerly old Mr. Loomis's and was honestly come by, how came it to be found in a roll of rags hidden on Cornelia's person? When Mrs. Loomis's bed was searched, some silver spoons were found hidden therein, from which the name or initials they once bore had been carefully erased. If she comes honestly by them, why should they be thus concealed and the markings dug out?

"While en route for Utica, Monday afternoon, the party stopped for an hour or so at the American Hotel in this village where the old lady created much amusement for the bystanders by her tantrums and the inimitable 'chin music' with which she regaled Officer Filkins. She utterly refused to walk, and had to be carried to and from the carriage.

"Cornelia objected to being arrested by Officer Filkins, drawing herself up proudly and declaring that she was 'of high blood,' and intimating that the said officer might 'get shot' if he was not careful."

On Tuesday, at a hearing before Commissioner Boyce, Mrs. Loomis and Cornelia claimed that they knew nothing about the counterfeit money or postal currency that had been found in their home. Charles, who had told Filkins that he had "got it in different places," changed his story. "It was some my Uncle Wash gave me before he was killed," he admitted. The Commissioner decided "that there was not sufficient grounds for holding them," so they were released.

Plumb was arrested three days later for stealing a cloth cap from the store of Lewis W. and Marcus Rich in Canastota. Plumb, appearing before Justice of the Peace Edwin R. White, gave the name of his brother, Denio and waived examination on a charge of petit larceny. He was released on bail, pending action by the grand jury.

The Loomises did not let the repeated raids interfere with seasonal work. The middle of April found the sugaring season well under way. Extra help was needed at the Loomis sugar bush in Tinker Hollow. Isaiah Belfield drove over from Stockbridge with his low-slung sleigh and oxen. Henry "Banty" Brooks also helped. The syrup was drawn off into crocks and stored in the cellar of the homestead. Quantities of sugar were made for the table.

Mrs. Loomis served fresh syrup with pancakes one night for supper. Dr. Medina Preston, called hastily in the night, found the family and their help stricken with violent stomach pains and nausea. He saved their lives by administering antidotes. He took a sample of the syrup, tested it and found that it had been poisoned. The Loomises, having learned a lesson, kept their sugar bush guarded until the season passed.

Filkins received word in June that three associates of the Loomises, Tom Mott, Ezra Beebe and LaVergue Beebe, whom he wanted as suspects in the Crandall murder, had been apprehended in Iowa. He went to Crandall, who had partially recovered from his wounds, and talked the aged man into financing a trip to Iowa. Crandall gave him $354.

When Filkins applied to Governor Fenton for the necessary extradition papers, the Governor reminded him that he was under indictment for murder and could not leave the state without permission. The papers were sent to Sheriff Stone, who assigned his son to the task of bringing back the culprits. Filkins was permitted to accompany young Stone.

Filkins resented serving under the younger man. When Stone carelessly allowed LaVergue Beebe to escape as the train approached Girard, Pennsylvania, Filkins was out spoken in blaming the sheriff's son. He was still seething with rage when he and Stone arrived in Morrisville with Mott and Ezra Beebe. When he got to Waterville his wife informed him that a man giving the name of Jones had told her that several men Filkins wanted had arrived at the Loomis farm the previous night with a stolen horse.

"I left Waterville for the Loomises about 10 o'clock Saturday night with Constable Sanford," he said later. "Inquiring along the way I learned that there were other parties at the Loomises that Deputy Sheriff Conger of North Brookfield had warrants for. Sanford and I went down to North Brookfield and informed him of the fact. Conger and Constable Hibbard of North Brookfield then accompanied Sanford and me and four other men to the Loomis house in the southwest part of the town of Sangerfield."

Filkins and his companions pounded on the door of the home of Isaac Terry, about a quarter mile from the Loomis farm, at 2 A. M.

"Who's there?" Terry called from an upstairs window.

A figure stepped forward. "Why, don't you know Filkins and my party?"

"What do you want, Mr. Filkins?"

Filkins explained that they were going to raid the Loomises and asked if Terry wanted to join them.

"No," Terry replied. "I ain't got nothin' against them. They never done me no harm."

Terry permitted the posse to stay at his house until dawn, when they moved on the Loomises in a body.

"All of us surrounded the Loomis house a little after daylight Sunday morning," Filkins later testified. "Mrs. Rhoda Loomis, the mother, was at the back door feeding ducks. As soon as she saw us she hollered out to the men in the house, 'Here is Filkins and a lot of men.'

"We then entered the house and went upstairs. Seeing that the Loomis party had gone up to the garret, Conger and I went up together, Conger a little ahead as we started to go up the garret stairs. At this time someone, I cannot positively say who, stood at the top of the stairs with a gun and said, 'Go back, goddam you, or I will shoot you through.'

"Conger advanced and the unknown man struck at Conger with the gun, inflicting an ugly wound in the head. I now being some fifteen feet from the unknown man, shot at him with a revolver. I do not know whether I hit him or not, but I aimed for his breast. The man now attempted to strike Conger again and I shot at him the second time, taking aim at his head. I do not know whether or not I hit him. Someone then fired a gun shot down the stairs, but do not know that anyone was hit. As Conger and I started to go downstairs we met a stranger who, upon being asked his name, gave it but I now forget it. I asked him if old Bill Alvord was upstairs. He said there was someone there whom they called Bill; that he came from Canada a night or two before.

"Conger put the handcuffs on the Canadian. As Conger his prisoner, and some men went out of the house towards the road, the party in the garret fired upon them several times. The prisoner was hit in the shoulder and breast with buckshot, wounding him considerably, though not dangerously. Another man, named Lord, was also shot. Conger and his party then went away for help. I stayed there with the others to watch the house.

"Soon we saw a man come out of the house with a gun and start for the woods. We followed him and he fired at us with his repeating Minnie rifle. He fired at us several times as we followed him and at last hit me, inflicting a wound on the arm and leg. I do not know who the man was. I do not remember after this."

The bullet had entered the outer side of Filkins' left forearm about two inches below the elbow, passed out of the inner side of his forearm, traveled about five inches, fracturing the bone. It then tore through the fleshy part of his right thigh for about six inches. Though his wounds bled freely, the constable managed to crawl behind the clump of bushes opposite the house before he lost consciousness.

Grove Loomis told The Hamilton Republican: "I was awakened by a furious shooting in the vicinity of my house which was soon followed by the attacking party rushing in and shooting in the house. When I first came from my room Filkins and some others were upstairs. I had got word before this by a person who came here that it was the intention of the attacking party to shoot everyone they could find on the premises. My informant requested me and my brother to fly from the house to save our lives. My brother immediately left in such haste that he left his boots, not finding time to put them on.

"When I went downstairs, leaving the men up there, one said to me, 'Here, we want you.'

"I paid no attention to him and went on. When downstairs I met Mr. Conger, who had been hurt in the affray at the head of the stairs and then we both passed out of doors. While we stood talking the chamber window was raised and Filkins fired his pistol at me, the ball of which took effect in the side of my coat. We then changed our position and soon after I went above the house a short distance to the shanty where I kept my horse. I found two men there firing their pistols into the shanty.

"I found I could not get my horse out so I left and went to a neighbor's—Mr. Welch's. The attacking party must have numbered seven or eight men at first, all armed with revolvers but not guns. During their firing outdoors before they came in they killed two hogs weighing about 150 pounds each, shot a good cow breaking the bone in her leg and also shot my watchdog which ran off into the Swamp and has not returned.

"After staying at Welch's a short time I went back to my horse with the intention of taking him to Sangerfield Center and leaving him in the hotel barn down there, but on coming back I saw as many as twelve or fifteen men in the field toward the Swamp. Some of them were armed with carbines. I harnessed my horse as soon as possible and started off, but when the men near the Swamp saw me they fired at me, resting their guns over stumps and fences to make more sure of their aim. The road to the Center being more exposed to their fire I went towards Oriskany Falls. On passing Mr. Mason's they came out to talk with me. While there some of Mr. Mason's people saw some men near the Swamp opposite to them aiming at me. They told me, so when I started up they would not be left directly in range if the men should fire at me. I had gone but a few rods when they did fire, the ball passing harmlessly over my head.

"I then went over to Mr. Abbey's where I left my horse. I was followed nearly there by the men with carbines, I having a greater distance to go on the roads than in the fields. I then went to Bridgewater to get a Blackhawk colt which I had sent for to Vermont and was gone four or five hours. When I returned my neighbors told me that the men had been in the woods and swamps all day firing frequently and they were afraid they would come and shoot me if I went home. I obtained a few neighbors to stay over night there as a guard for the premises and went home. There were from twenty to thirty shots fired in all. I think Filkins was wounded after he came out of the house while I was gone to Mr. Welch's. A Mr. Lord of Brookfield was also wounded, I heard."

Filkins was carried to his home in Waterville. Henry Bissell held him while Drs. Bailey and Cleveland removed five splinters of bone from the constable's arm. "Mr. Filkins, although quite severely wounded, was not considered dangerously injured, and probably will get around again in the course of a few weeks," The Madison County Observer of Morrisville told its readers.

Jule Watson of Clarkville, who passed the homestead after the raiders had left, borrowed a rifle from Mrs. Loomis and, at her request, shot the wounded animals lying on the premises.

Hazen House, Henry House and Winthrop Allen of Clarkville searched the Loomis house late that afternoon for Bill Alvord and Shadrack Curtiss and other known desperadoes. They found splotches of blood near two beds in the attic.

Mrs. Loomis protested as they started to enter a bedroom on the second floor. "There is a sick woman lying in there at the point of death," she claimed.

"What is the matter with her?" asked Allen.

"Her sickness was occasioned by the shaking given her a day or two ago by Sheriff Conger for interfering with him while making a search of the house."

"Are you sure it isn't one of the murderers you harbor here?" Hazen House inquired bluntly.

Mrs. Loomis replied angrily that she did not hide murderers and barred their way. "First let me see if the poor thing is covered up," she said.

The men saw the figure of someone in bed, but they were unable to make an identification. A sheet was drawn up to the chin and a large sunbonnet covered the face as the person writhed in agony and vomited frequently. The three men hurriedly withdrew.

Bill Alvord, lying seriously wounded in the bed, narrowly escaped capture. Denio and Plumb later drove him to another hideout. The newspapers mentioned a rumor that Alvord had died and had been buried secretly. Deputy Conger did not believe it and had Alvord indicted for assault with intent to kill.

The gun battle made Filkins a local hero. Reporters thronged his home to obtain his version of the raid.

Praise also came from J. G. Patterson, president of the Travelers Insurance Company of Hartford, Connecticut, with whom Filkins had taken out a $5,000 policy on his life a few weeks before the raid. Newspaper notices of the fight sent to the home office by William B. Goodwin, local agent, brought these remarks in a letter from Mr. Patterson: "No apologies were needed for having insured Mr. Filkins, 'knowing' that the Loomis gang were not pleased with his ways. We only regret that the insurance was not larger, and if he had succeeded in killing the whole gang we would cheerfully have made him a pensioner for life. If the authorities of your county, after 20 years experience, cannot provide a safe residence for that Loomis family, we beg of you to insure all constables, and the Travelers Insurance Co. will provide for them.

"Never hesitate to insure a plucky fellow like Filkins for fear some scamp may kill him. If we could heal him as easily as we can pay him, our joy would be full. The custom of this company is to pay only on maturity of the claim. In this case, however, you are authorized to draw on us at sight, either weekly or monthly, (as may suit his convenience) for the amount of his compensation, twenty-five dollars per week."

CHAPTER XXIV

CLEAN OUT THE LOOMISES!

The second attempt to kill Filkins ignited the countryside's smouldering hatred of the Loomises. By dim lantern light the Sangerfield Vigilantes began gathering in their meeting places to discuss cleaning out the family. "A majority of the men had only been recently discharged from the army and they were toughened to scenes of violence and death," Hall said. "Many returned home to learn that the Loomises or their gang had run off their horses and cattle. In their fury they wanted to kill every member of the family and blow up the buildings."

Harold Mason claimed that Sheriff Asahel C. Stone of Madison County started the movement. "With him were his son, Undersheriff Asa Stone, and Hank Bissell, who were his lieutenants."

"Deputy Conger returned to Morrisville," Cummings wrote. "One of the Judges threw some documents before the Sheriff and told him it was his duty to serve them on the Loomises at all hazards. After the Judge retired, the Sheriff took a revolver from a nook in the wall and stated that it was the only document he would serve on the Loomises."

The documents included an indictment against "A. Plumb alias Denio Loomis," dated December 12th, 1865, for petit larceny, on a charge that he stole a cap valued at a dollar and a quarter from the store of Lewis and Marcus Rich in Canastota on April 5. The "judge" referred to by Cummings was possibly County Judge John Mason. Loomis had pleaded not guilty, and had forfeited his bail by failing to appear for trial. A new indictment had been issued against him.

A caucus of citizens was held at Nigger City (North Brookfield) to discuss the raid. Conger finally weeded out eleven men whom he felt he could trust out of two hundred who turned out.

"Conger hired a member of the gang to poison the dogs the night before the raid was to take place," Mason stated. "The Loomises had fifty dog kennels surrounding the house. The night the poisoning was to take place, the hired man failed to do the job and kill the dogs, so the raid couldn't take place. Two weeks later the member of the gang poisoned the dogs and the Vigilantes made their raid."

The Loomis family had received adequate warning of the caucus. Mrs. Geneva Main (Aunt Neva) Watson of Brookfield stated, "My father, Samuel Main, and old Bill Chesebro went to the Loomises and told them they were to be raided, but they would not listen." This fact was later confirmed by Mrs. Rhoda Loomis, who thoughtfully omitted the names of their informants.

On Saturday night, June 16, 1866 Deputy Conger and Constable Hibbard started for the Loomis farm with their posse. Constable Gay Sanford and Cort Terry led another group from Waterville. A third party in charge of Constable Hess left Hamilton. At Morrisville the yard of the Exchange Hotel was filled with carriages. Nearly all the county's deputy sheriffs were on the hotel porch with Undersheriff Stone and Sheriff Stone. "The party started out from Morrisville about dusk," a spectator wrote for the Oneida Daily Dispatch. "With the officers were several citizens of Morrisville, among them Alexander Cramphin, counsel for the sheriff. It was generally understood that one of our Supreme Court justices had suggested to Sheriff Stone that as all legal means for punishing the Loomis gang had failed, it was about time they were wiped out."

The rendezvous was held on a lonely road about a mile from the Loomis farm. The number of raiders has been variously estimated between 60 and 250. Every man was well-armed and expected a gun battle. Some of the more fanatical had brought kegs of gunpowder in their carriages to blow the house and its occupants up, and others carried ropes for a hanging. The men spread out and surrounded the Loomis farm to prevent the escape of the occupants.

The officers entered the house and put the family in irons. "Mrs. Loomis recognized Deputy Sheriff Stone of Madison County, Sheriff Conger of Madison County, Constable Hess of Hamilton and Hibbard of North Brookfield, also an official from Canastota named Cole," The Waterville Times reported. "And this Cole, she stated, informed her that they (the officials) had a bench warrant for Plumb, who stole a cap in Canastota last winter and was indicted at the recent session of court in Morrisville, Madison County, but who did not recognize his bail, and that they had come to arrest him. Mrs. Loomis complained that herself and Cornelia were rudely treated by the officers, and put in irons."

Grove and Plumb Loomis were also handcuffed and pushed out into the yard. Other occupants were not arrested, but a close watch was kept on them. These included Adeline Glazier, Plumb's girl; John Stoner, "the Dutchman"; John Smith, an Irishman; Esther Crandall, Elizabeth Hawkins, the family's drudge; and Charles Loomis, Wheeler's twelve-year-old son.

The mob rushed into every room of the big house from cellar to garret; under the pretext of searching for stolen goods, men looted everything of value. Cupboards and bureau drawers were torn open and their contents dumped in heaps on the floor. Mattresses on the beds were slashed open and torn apart. Windows were broken, the finest of furniture smashed to kindling wood, and even the floor boards were ripped up to see if anything was hidden beneath them. Gallon jugs of maple syrup and jars of honey were thrown from the cellar into the yard.

Two Waterville merchants began looking over some bolts of silks and other goods which they claimed had been stolen from them. A fire had been kindled in the closet of one of the upstairs bedrooms.

Mrs. Loomis dashed a bucket of water over the flames. In an adjoining room someone had set fire to a torn straw-tick.

The valiant old lady quickly doubled the tick over and smothered the flames. The cry rose that the house was on fire. Smoke began eddying up through the floors.

Cornelia went upstairs, dragged her Saratoga trunk to the window, lifted it in her strong arms and threw it out. As it struck the ground the raiders pounced on it, ripped off the lid and took possession of her best clothes and $836 she had secreted in the trunk.

The smoke became thicker in the upstairs rooms and the crackling of the flames below could be plainly heard. The officers plunged through the smoke down the stairway. Cornelia and her mother looked for the last time on their furnishings and rooms and hurried into the yard, where they were pushed into the circle of men guarding Grove and Plumb and the other prisoners.

The Loomis women and their help were quickly handcuffed. Young Charles Loomis suddenly dashed through the crowd. Some men started after him, but one of the officers said, "Let him go, let him go," and he escaped.

Sheriff Asahel Stone and Constable Cole conversed for a few minutes. Hall stated, and then talked with young Stone and Conger. "The sheriff and Cole then walked up the road over the hill and didn't come back until the affair was over with."

John Stoner was dragged from the family group. A rope was put around his neck and he was pulled up on the limb of the maple tree in the front yard. When let down he stated that Bill Alvord was at Loomis' the ninth and tenth. Alvord was the notorious outlaw who had shot Filkins in the gunbattle at the Loomis farm on the ninth.

Stoner was released when the men were unable to obtain any more information from him. Plumb Loomis was then dragged forward.

All bravado had departed from him. Hall recalled that he cried, "Don't hang me, don't hang me! You wouldn't hang poor, honest old Plumb that never did you no harm."

According to eye-witness accounts collected by Hall, Carter, Mason and others, Plumb stretched out on his tiptoes as the rope tightened about his neck. When his feet swung clear of the ground his body threshed wildly and his face contorted until it seemed as if his eyes were ready to pop from their sockets. His tongue thickened and protruded from between empurpled lips. His urine ran down his legs, soaking through his pants. When his struggles lessened Stone spoke to the men holding the rope. They let it slacken and Plumb fell to the ground, where he lay gasping for breath. At length he stirred and finally sat up.

"Are you ready to talk now?" Conger demanded.

Plumb closed his eyes and shook his head.

"When was the man Alvord here?" Stone demanded.

"I ain't seen Alvord for five years."

"Who shot Filkins last week?"

"A brother of Tom Mott."

"Who fired my hotel at Sweet's Corners?" Conger shouted.

When Plumb refused to answer, he was suspended from the maple limb again. His body twitched and then went limp.

The Loomises turned their heads away. Rhoda fell to her knees and lifted her face to the sky.

"I've never prayed before," she said. "But I'm going to pray now." Her lips moved. "Almighty God. . . ."

At Conger's orders Plumb was lowered to the ground and the noose removed from his neck. The rough rope had torn through the tender flesh. Someone brought a bucket of water and doused him with it.

"Are you going to talk now," Conger demanded, "or have we got to finish the job?"

"What do you want to know?" Plumb gasped. His voice was little more than a whisper.

"What do you know about the Crandall murder?"

"I don't know nothing about it."

"When did you last see Bill Alvord?"

"Last Sunday."

"Who shot Deputy Filkins?"

"Tom Mott."

"Who was the man Filkins shot on the garret stairs?"

"Bill Alvord. Filkins shot him twice. The reported sick woman in our garret was Alvord. Grove took him away last Saturday."

"Where was Alvord taken?" demanded Stone.

"I don't know," Plumb answered. "I don't know."

Deputy Stone, infuriated at Plumb's slow, elusive answers, nodded to the men holding the rope. He placed the noose around the outlaw's neck for the third time.

"Don't hang me again." Plumb groveled into the grass. "Shoot me and get it over with."

"Talk fast then," Conger demanded. "Who burned my hotel?"

Plumb closed his mouth sullenly. Seeing that this form of questioning and the two previous hangings had not broken his spirit, Undersheriff Stone ordered him hanged for the third time.

Plumb did not struggle. His feet were barely off the ground when he went limp. He was held there for a few minutes before Stone ordered him lowered.

He sank forward on his face. Conger turned his body over and placed his ear to Plumb's chest. He smiled grimly at Asa Stone.

"He is still alive."

"Bring me another bucket of water," Stone directed.

He seized the pail and again drenched Plumb. This time he was revived with great difficulty. He appeared willing to answer.

"Alvord shot Filkins," he whispered, "He was here a few days, but Grove took him away. Tom Mott fired the barn of Mr. Terry's in Waterville last fall and Mr. Conger's buildings at Sweet's Corners some time ago. We paid Mott to do it. Yes, Alvord was shot twice last Sunday morning by Officer Filkins. Mott and those others you have the papers for are away now, but we'll help you find them if you let me go. Spare our lives and, if you'll permit us, we will strive henceforth to be honest, peaceful and law-abiding citizens."

"Send Grove here," Conger demanded.

Grove was hustled forward. His face was pale and drawn. All of his superb arrogance had departed.

"What do you want with me?" he asked.

"You saw what happened to Plumb," Stone said grimly. "If you don't want a sample of the same, you had better talk."

"Everything my brother has told you is the truth," Grove admitted. "We can't be blamed for what the men who hung around here have done. If you will give us the chance, we will help you bring them to justice. We will no longer harbor outlaws and criminals."

Both Conger and Stone seemed satisfied. Their hatred had abated with the hanging of the two men. Sheriff Stone and Constable Cole had returned from the hills. Cole placed Plumb under arrest for larceny and started for Morrisville with him in his carriage.

The hollow shell of the once stately mansion crashed inward with a muffled roar. The wind was blowing from the southwest and this had saved the line of maples, including the one on which the hangings had taken place. As the officers in charge seemed satisfied with Plumb's confession, some of the men ran with blazing torches into one outbuilding after another, setting them on fire. One kinder than the rest thoughtfully turned Grove's prize black stallion loose from its shed before applying the torch. No barn had replaced the shed destroyed when Wash was killed, but the shanty hastily erected to house the livestock was touched off. Several feet south, on the opposite side of the road, stood the large hop house, surrounded by haystacks. It was the last building to be fired.

By this time the law officers had quietly departed. The Loomises sat dejectedly about on the fences, surveying the desolate scene about them. One by one the participants also went home, but throngs of sight-seers were arriving to view the conflagration.

As soon as Grove was able to get safely away he caught his horse and drove to Hamilton. John Stoner took the train to Syracuse, where he journeyed to Bardeen's Corners by stage to inform Denio of the tragedy.

The Loomis' hired girls and other laborers scattered. Mrs. Loomis and Cornelia had no place to go and apparently didn't care. Risking criticism, Decatur Welch, their neighbor, opened his house to them. Mrs. Loomis admitted that they had been advised of the raid, but did not expect it at the time it occurred. They were taken completely by surprise, she revealed.

Plumb was taken to Morrisville and placed in jail.

Stories of the raid circulated as far north as Utica and Rome by sundown, and west to Syracuse and Oswego. Reporters from a dozen city and country papers descended upon the Loomis farm.

The Utica Morning Herald told this story the following Tuesday: "We reached the Loomis place yesterday about three P. M. All the way thither from Waterville, we met people returning from the ruins, indeed, whatever rose to the dignity of a vehicle of any kind, at Waterville, and vicinity appeared to be pressed into service. At the place itself, teams were hitched at all eligible places, and the people, full two score at that time, were looking with evident interest at the scene before them.

"All that remained of the Loomis house was the charred and blackened cellar walls, a pile of bricks in the center, which appeared as if it might have answered for a chimney and timbers still burning showed with what intensity the flames raged. The fence situated some feet in front, alone remained unscathed. Across the way, an equally desolate scene marked the spot where once stood the hop house."

A few young men from Knoxboro visited the ruins Monday morning, the 18th. As they poked about one of them discovered a washtub that had been saved from the flames. In it, all washed, were three feed bags. Each bore a name, "H. Goff," 'Henty" and "J. Goodson," all identified as the property of three Knoxboro farmers who had lost the bags, full of flour and provender, when the gristmill at Augusta Valley had been broken into ten days earlier.

On the following Tuesday morning Mrs. Julia Banton Mason set down in her diary the general temper of the countryside.

"Mr. Welch notified if he did not leave Mrs. Loomis and Cor. removed from his house before sunset, his house would be burned over his head before morning. People continue to visit the ruins. It is thought over two thousand people visited the ruins."

On Wednesday, the 20th, Mrs. Mason observed: "Strangers from a distance continue to visit the scene of ruin. Hundreds with a knife take a chip from the limb Plumb was hung upon. Some seem as eager to get a chip as people did of the willow at the head of Napoleon's grove."

Plumb Loomis pleaded innocent upon arraignment on the petit larceny charge, and was allowed to give bail. He returned to the farm and with his brothers, cleaned up the pioneer home on the hill, made a few repairs and moved in. Wheeler sold his one-ninth share of the Sangerfield property to him on September 13th for $850. Where the money came from, if Wheeler was paid, is not known. The family admitted they were broke. Their land holdings throughout the state were large, but the loss of the homestead was a serious blow. The family carried no insurance. Mrs. Loomis had begged several insurance companies for protection, but all had refused the risk. In addition to the buildings there were individual losses of cash, jewels and personal belongings. Grove claimed a note for $3,000 he held had also been destroyed.

The town and county taxes on the property in Sangerfield had not been paid, and in November it was seized and the "three hundred and fifty-five acres of land" and tenements owned by Wheeler, Plumb and Denio were advertised by Sheriff David B. Danforth of Oneida County to be sold on January 5, 1867 at the American Hotel in Waterville.

At the Court of General Sessions on December 12, Plumb was arraigned before Judge Mason at Morrisville on the charge of larceny. He promptly pleaded innocent. On the motion of District Attorney S. B. Kern, the jury was ordered impaneled. The next day the jury returned a verdict of guilty. Judge Mason then ordered Plumb to serve thirty days in jail and pay a fine of $100 or sixty additional days. Loomis, unable to pay the fine, accepted the ninety-day sentence.

CHAPTER XXV

FILKINS STANDS TRIAL

Though eight months had elapsed since Filkins had been indicted on five counts for arson and murder, he was still free on bail. He had not been deprived of his deputyship nor temporarily suspended until his case could be tried. Despite all the enemies he had made, the wounds he had suffered in the June raid on the Loomis farm had aroused sympathy. The fight also had doomed the Loomises in the public eye.

District Attorney Jenkins knowing that Filkins would have to stand trial for Wash's murder or have the grand jury nullify the indictment against him, called a special term of Oyer and Terminer in Rome for the 27th of August. There being no legal excuse for a special term of court, proceedings were postponed until the regular term in November.

At these sessions Filkins was represented, not only by Senator Roscoe Conkling, but by J. Thomas Spriggs, who had defended the Loomises for years. The trial was postponed until February because Spriggs was unable to produce his star witness, John Garvey, who had left the area, "saying he was going to Mexico or Idaho, to the gold mines."

A further postponement in February showed the masterly touch of Spriggs, who had used this procedure so often in defending the Loomises.

The large courtroom in Rome was filled to capacity on June 3, 1867 when Judge Henry Foster opened court. Filkins, seated well in front, appeared a forlorn, diminutive figure in contrast to the tall, blond, immaculately dressed Conkling and the dark, heavy-set Spriggs. He sat through numerous cases quietly, with head bowed, as if he were drowsing.

When the constable's case was called at four o'clock Conkling moved "to set aside what is called the indictment in this case on the grounds that the same was never legally found and that the paper purporting to be an indictment was unlawfully obtained from the grand jury." Spriggs claimed that the affidavits of George Jones and Charles Bird, the two principal witnesses, "were produced and read before the grand jury, instead of being themselves produced as witnesses and sworn before the grand jury." He also read an affidavit in which Jones stated that he had not told the Loomis lawyers Filkins had struck Grove in the head. According to this affidavit Jones had not been subpoenaed to appear before the grand jury which indicted Filkins.

The District Attorney, claiming that the question of illegality of the indictment could not be raised, asked the Court to give him until the next day to prepare affidavits to answer the questions raised by the defense.

The court was again crowded when the case was resumed the following morning. Attorney General Martindale opened the argument by insisting that the affidavits produced by Spriggs were unlawful. District Attorney Jenkins produced the minutes of the testimony gathered by the grand jury, which he claimed showed abundant testimony upon which to sign an indictment without taking into account all the affidavits of Jones and Bird.

Conkling arose to review the case in detail. He pointed out that some of the lodgers at the Loomis home had not appeared before the coroner's jury. He also mentoned the fact that no person had appeared on behalf of Filkins. He claimed that the verdict in the case was thus left shrouded in mystery upon the partial and ex-parte showing of the Loomis family themselves. He told how William Loomis had sworn out a warrant against Filkins alone, charging him with the murder of Wash Loomis. He pointed out how the Loomises had failed to appear to press charges at the first session of the grand jury.

At a second session of the grand jury he disclosed that "one witness only, of all those lodging in the house, was found to be examined, and one other witness to collateral matter, and then the counsel who said he appeared 'at the request of the Loomis family' attempted to out wit and circumvent the justice and 'rested.' Finding that the magistrate knew his duty and meant to do it, the counsellor left the court in darkness by withdrawing.

"Attachments were then sent out, and every effort made during the residue of the week, to command the presence of the witnesses, but by trick and fraud, and defiance, the witnesses were spirited away or concealed, and so the law was baffled, and the proceedings defeated. The case was thus smuggled into the secrecy of the grand jury room, and the counsel of the Loomises associated with the District Attorney."

Senator Conkling firmly expounded the fact that the whole proceeding had been a matter of haste and that the matter had been introduced at the opening of the grand jury session on Monday, November 13th, and all the witnesses and testimony which had been deemed judicious had been produced during the two days the jury heard the case, which he said was insufficient. "The statements of the witnesses were inconculsive or incredible, or else the witnesses themselves appeared unworthy of belief," he said. "The probable guilt of the accused was not made out, and the attempt to indict must fail for want of proof."

Time after time the Senator referred to the disputed affidavits of Jones and Bird and pointed out that the jurors had commented on their absence after they claimed they had been in the Loomis homestead when the alleged homicide occurred. He said their failure to appear was suspicious and they must have been able to make important disclosures. The jury had been told that they were away and no one knew where, yet during this time they were "actually in the bailiwick, at Rome, only fifteen miles off, and the Loomises and their counsel knew it." He stressed the fact that the District Attorney had been kept in ignorance of the fact, if not by fraud, then by falsehood. "Jones at least says he was advised and prompted not to appear because his testimony would not be of a desirable character."

The Senator bluntly labeled the affidavits of Jones and Bird as false. After pointing out where they failed in the truth, he said, "The conclusion is forced upon us, that the instrumentalities of public justice have been seized upon and perverted, not only to bring one man to trial by forbidden means, but also to suppress the truth in other respects, and to screen the guilty and favored."

After thoroughly discussing and denouncing the manner in which the grand jury had accepted the one-sided evidence, he turned to the matter of the indictments against Filkins, and admitted "a motion to 'quash' an indictment in the ordinary sense is not looked upon with favor." He said the indictments against Filkins were not legal and cited numerous similar cases of the past to put over his point. He admitted, "An enormous crime seems to have been committed and it concerns the public that it should be thoroughly and impartially investigated, not to satisfy the vengeance of anyone..... The object is to vindicate law and order . . ."

Cleverly, he began to tear at the foundation of the plaintiff's characters as if the Loomises were on trial and not Filkins. "The court cannot close its eyes to the fact, but must take judicial notice of the fact that for a series of years numerous crimes have been committed in this county and vicinity, some of them very grave crimes, some even atrocious crimes, which, with abundant evidence of their authors, have been left forever unpunished and forever veiled in mystery, and this not in consequence of any of the ordinary failures of justice," he said.

The Senator cited each act of terrorism that the countryside had heard of: a public building containing indictments had been burned to the ground at a time when the statute of limitations was ready to halt second indictments; the District Attorney of the county had been seized after midnight by two men and relieved of twelve counterfeit bills which constituted the evidence to sustain indictments; the office of another District Attorney had been broken open at night when indictments against the same parties were there. "Many indictments mysteriously re-appeared, other papers came back mingled with forest leaves," he stated, "but the indictments against whose conduct is in issue never came back.

". . . Common fame has long published that certain criminals not only escape conviction, not only protect their confederates, not only bring to punishment their betrayers, not only wreak barbarous vengeance upon those who dare to oppose them, or even to testify against them, not only break through all the meshes of the law, but the bail and bail bonds, bench warrants, and search warrants, indictments and the civil process of the court, do their office or stand still at the beck and nod, not of innocence, but of guilt. This subject has become a matter of record in the legislative proceedings of the State.

"Here is a report to the Legislature, made by the Prison Association in January, 1866." The Senator picked up a bound pamphlet from his nearby desk. "From page 145 onward will be found a narrative of instances in principle and character like the doings now before the court, and the actors there are the actors here.

"The report shows how they organize victory by laying crimes at the doors of the innocent, by manufacturing and destroying evidence, by instituting false prosecutions, by stifling and evading investigations, by polluting the foundations and defiling the ministrations of justice. This is the statement the Legislature of New York has published, and similar presentations have appeared in the public press of the whole country. It is not consoling to know that the foreign press also, has given the subject to the world.

"Here is the London Quarterly Review for January, 1867," he said, holding up a magazine for the judges to see, "a publication of much ability and influence, and as old as the century. It is not fond of republican government; it does not believe in democratic institutions; it has little faith in the security of life and property in an organism like ours, operating by universal suffrage. It is not friendly to America. It has an article giving reasons for its skepticism in the wisdom of our government. The article is entitled 'Crime in The State of New York.' It narrates events already referred to, and upon the doings of this family and their accomplices, and the impotency of the laws to resist or punish them, or to protect honest men from their accusations, it grounds an appeal to the British people to say whether they would change places with the people of Central New York!"

Finishing his denunciation of the Loomises and their gang, the Senator returned to the duties of the grand jury and cited the right manner in which indictments should be found. "Oneida County has suffered imputation for lax practices of her political, judicial and ministerial tribunals. Here is a glaring instance of lax and dangerous administration. The court can put its hand upon it and the occasion is of more value to the public than the life or death of any culprit whose name is bórne on the roll of accusation."

Attorney General Martindale launched into the rebuttal. Observing that, due to the short notice the state had to prepare affidavits in answer to those read by the defense, he listed four points on the questions of the legality of the indictments that Conkling had raised: that after a defendant had entered a plea to an indictment, it was too late to make a motion to quash or set it aside; that the grand jurors cannot legally give the public any opinions on matters coming before them; that if the affidavits of Jones and Bird were improperly received as evidence, it was no ground for setting aside the indictment; and that if there was evidence to support an indictment, it was conclusive and no inquiry could be made.

The Attorney General took an hour and a half to argue his case before Judge Foster and the Justices of the Sessions took the matter for consultation. They did not deliberate long. "I regret that, in a case of this magnitude and importance, more time cannot be afforded for deliberation," Justice Foster said apologetically. "The Court is ready to give the decision now and take the responsibility for its correctness."

After all the questionable points that had been raised were discussed, Justice Foster gave the Sessions' opinion, stressing the four points of law. In each one they were in complete agreement with Senator Conkling. "The indictment is accordingly set aside," he announced.

Applause and shouts of approval rocked the audience, but they were quickly supressed by Justice Foster.

Some twelve years later, while Amos Cummings was doing extensive research for The New York City Weekly Sun, he brought up the subject of Wash Loomis' murder. "I asked Filkins his theory of the murder," he wrote. "He said that Richard Loucks, one of the Loomis negroes, told him that Jones and Bird killed Wash.

"They came there with a fine turnout that they had stolen in Vermont. They gave Wash the wagon and harness, and wanted him to give them $75 for the horse. He told them that his negro had seen Filkins spotting them, and refused to purchase the animal. Jones went up to the negroes' shanty and asked Loucks where he saw Filkins. The negro replied that he had not seen him at all. Jones then returned to the house and accused Wash of trying to swindle him out of the animal.

" 'You thought,' he said, 'that we would get scared and run away, and you would get the horse for nothing.'

"Jones then threatened to cut the throat of the horse and leave the carcass on the farm. He was about to put his threat into execution when Grove appeared and offered him $30 for the animal, which was worth $300.

" 'Give us $35,' said Jones, 'and take us to the nearest railway station, and we will close the bargain.'

"Grove said he would have to run the horse to the next station before he could get the money, and Jones and Bird agreed to wait. Grove returned after midnight, as sworn to by the old lady before the coroner, without the horse and without the money. A fight ensued in which Wash was killed and Grove sent to the verge of the grave.

"I asked Eph Conger and Wm. V. Durfee if they had ever heard this story. Eph winked at Durfee, and replied that he thought it was very plausible."

CHAPTER XXVI

THE CONFESSION

Sterry H. Simmonds of Boonville was the only horse thief who left a confession of the experiences he gained with the Loomis Gang.

It was published under the heading of "Nabbed!" in the Waterville Times on Thursday, September 30, 1875, and is self-explanatory.

The Times said: "We have received the following confession of Sterry H. Simmonds from Sheriff S. N. Bennett of Alleghany County through Deputy Sheriff Filkins. As the fellow has operated in these parts, and has been connected with the Loomises and other notorious characters hereabouts; and as his confession implicates other parties well known to officers in this locality, we deem it of sufficient interest to our readers to give it space:"

Having been arrested and convicted here on a charge of which I am guilty, I wish to make a full and voluntary statement and confession of this, and all other crimes, of which I am guilty. I feel sure that it will be manifest to all that it is not in the hopes of pardon that I do this; for I am bringing charges against myself that otherwise would never be brought up or proven against me. But my sins are many, and I wish to make all the atonement that I can; and I know of no other way of doing so, but by confessing my own crimes, and helping to bring other criminals to justice.

"My right name is Sterry H. Simmonds. I was born in the Town of Boonville, Oneida County, N. Y., in the year 1847, of honest, hard working parents. Till June, 1871, I was respected by all that knew me. It was then that I fell into bad company and it soon proved my ruin.

"Eugene Gowdy was the first to hint such a thing to me, but I did not think much about it at the time. About this time I went to Oneida and fell in with two men, who told me their names were James Petra and John Sullivan. I went with them to a house about a mile from Higginsville, and after getting me there they informed me then where I was and in what company.

"They told me I was at the notorious Bill Loomis', and in company of the hardest set of men in the state. By drink, coaxing and threats I was led on and put up to all kinds of crime. While there Petra and Sullivan took me over to a boot and shoe store on the canal, about two miles from Oneida. They tried to make me enter the store, and put out a lot of boots to them. I refused to do it. After we had some high words I left them and went back to the Loomises. They came in before morning and threatened to put up a job on me if I did not do something. I went home the next day, and Gowdy wished me to join him. I finally took a horse from one Henry Densilow, and hid in the woods till there was a reward offered for him, and then I let him go in the road and Gowdy took him back to Mr. Densilow and received the reward. In a few days after we took a horse of one William Courtney.

"I had my arm in a sling at that time, and Gowdy took the fetters off the horse and took down the fence, and I took the horse to Loomises. He (Bill) told me to turn the horse in his swamp pasture, among a lot of other horses, and to help him a few days with his haying, and if no one came looking for the horse, that he would buy him. I stayed there, I think, for about a week. I don't remember just how long. He then offered me $25 for the horse. He said it was too close by and too much risk to give more. Petra then coaxed me to take the horse and go with him to DeRuyter. I did so and we traded him with a man by the name of Scott for another horse and $10.

"Petra had half the money. We took the other horse to Loomises and I left him with Petra and I went back to Forestport and Alder Creek.

"Thursday night Gowdy took a buggy from the barn or shed of Samuel Mailbach and drew it down across the bridge out of the village, and I met him with the same horse, that we had taken the reward from Densilow's before. We put the harness and robe in the buggy and Gowdy went home and I went to Loomises with the rig. It was after daylight when I got there and I hid the things in the swamp lot and went up to the house for my breakfast, and told Bill what I had. He told me to take them to Sanford Gleason's after dark for they were not safe where they were. I took them to Gleason's about twelve or one o'clock that night. (I) had to call him up (and) told him Loomis sent me there. (I) put the buggy and harness in his barn (and) turned the horse in the back lot. Next night Loomis told me to move them again to a man's barn about a mile from the Loomises — have forgot the name — did so."

"I tried to make a bargain with Loomis that day. (I) met Gleason at the swamp lot in the afternoon. He told me I would be beat out of the rig; told me that Loomis had got two men to act as officers to try and scare me out of the rig (and) advised me to take it away as soon as dark.

"I heard Loomis talking of L. D. Snell of Central Square. (I) met Gleason near South Corners (and) gave him the double harness. He gave me a revolver and told me if they followed me not to be scared out.

"I called Snell (a tavern keeper at Central Square) out of bed about daylight. (I) told him my name was H. G. Locke. He said if I would say before a man that he brought around to his barn that there was no claim on the property, that he would trade for it.

"He gave me a black mare and $25 in money and agreed to pay me $50 more in three or four weeks. I traded the buggy I got of Snell with another man for a skeleton (sleigh) and I believe, $10. I traded another man the black mare and skeleton sleigh for another horse, a silver watch and $15. I then traded this horse with the man I got the skeleton of for a $45 watch, and, if I remember right, $5. S. D. Snell went down to the cars with me and I returned home. I was arrested on suspicion as soon as I arrived, but proved myself clear on examination.

"About three or four weeks after I met Snell by appointment at Rome. It was early in the evening. Gleason and John Sullivan, who was then going by the name of George Loring were present. Snell let me have a horse as payment for the $50 in our former trade. He said it was safe property for it came a good ways. I took the horse home to my brother's, only twenty-two miles from there, for I thought that it was, as I was told, from a long ways off.

"I was arrested at Gowdy's house a few nights after for stealing this horse. I then found that it had been stolen only a few miles from Rome, where it was given to me.

"Now I think it evidence that I did not steal this horse, for no one in his right mind would take a horse only twenty-four or five miles and hitch him up and drive and ride him around into the village and elsewhere if he had stolen him. It will be shown that such was the case. He was driven into town and ridden about most public roads every day that I had him.

"I waived examination and gave bail to appearance at court, and swore out a warrant for Snell. I intended to make a clean breast of the whole affair. This I think was on Saturday, and Monday I was to be at Rome to testify against Snell. I started for Rome Monday in good faith, but at Remsen I met Sullivan, alias George Loring, and he told me that it would only get me into deeper trouble, for that the Loomises had men to swear me away, and that Gleason would swear for Snell, and farther, that if I went on, that my life was not worth a cent. He gave me some money to make the bail up to my brother if I would go into Canada and let all drop. I finally did as he wished me to, for I saw plainly that my single evidence would do no good against so many. I went to Canada and worked for about a year in the lumber woods. I then went to Perth and met Sullivan there. He called himself there John Smith, and in a few days he had me in trouble again. It was for stealing a horse. Sullivan slipped out of it. and I had to serve two years in the Kingston Penitentiary."

CHAPTER XXVII

DENIO ASSUMES LEADERSHIP

Fire and a rope did not purge the Loomises of their deep-rooted criminal instincts. Constable James Filkins had almost completely recovered from his wounds by Sunday, August 28, 1866 when Philip H. Cowan, a farmer of Geddes, Onondaga County, drove to Waterville with a deputy sheriff to enlist his aid in recovering a horse that had been stolen from him the previous April. While there had been no clues to the horse's disappearance, the Onondaga County officer felt certain it had been stolen by the Loomises.

Filkins procured the necessary search warrants and recruited twenty-four residents for a posse to raid the Loomis farm. The scars of the June raid were clearly visible, as neither the homestead nor the barns had been rebuilt. Weeds were slowly covering the blackened cellar walls with a green carpet. Farming implements scattered about the farm were rusty from exposure. Despite the decay and neglect horses, cattle and sheep ranged over the pastures and men were at work in the hay fields. They offered no resistance as their guns and knives were taken from them. Young Charlie Loomis, who was carrying a seven-shot revolver in his pocket submitted meekly when he was disarmed.

Some of Filkins' posse rounded up the horse for Cowan to look over while the constable and the remainder made their way to the weather-beaten, two-storied house and dilapidated barn sitting in the midst of the apple orchard. The Loomises had cleaned up their original home and had moved in with the few possessions they had saved from the fire. Filkins arrested Denio, who was there with his mother and Cornelia.

Cowan could not find his horse on the Loomis farm. The Loomises dropped a hint that Richard Gorton in Stockwell had been seen driving a horse answering the description. The officers went to the Gorton residence and found the stolen horse.

"I did not know the horse was a stolen one," Gorton told Filkins. "The Loomises let me have the use of it for its keep."

Denio, arraigned before Justice Holl in Baldwinsville for grand larceny, pleaded innocent and was ordered held for action of the Onondaga County grand jury, which failed to agree and he was released.

A new trial was ordered, but it did not come before the court until June 1868. Filkins, who had been arresting officer, was summoned as a witness for the People. Although he had been acquitted of the murder of Wash Loomis, the Loomis family decided to halt his appearance in court to testify against Denio. William Loomis obtained a warrant from Justice of the Peace Coville of Fish Creek, charging the constable with murder. Grove Loomis wired his brother William to proceed with Officer Joseph Vincent to Oneida and arrest Filkins.

Bill and Vincent boarded the train and the Verona officer told Filkins he was under arrest for the murder of Wash Loomis. Filkins, knowing the Loomises did not want him to testify against Denio, refused to be taken into custody. When the train reached Canastota, Loomis and Vincent appealed to the passengers to help them handcuff and remove "the murderer" from the coach. Filkins identified himself and as soon as he told the passengers the Loomises were up to their old tricks, there was no interference.

At Syracuse the constable agreed to go before Judge H. A. Foster, who had presided at his trial in Rome. Foster set bail at $10,000, which was posted by friends. Vincent and William left empty-handed. Filkins testified at Denio's trial, but the jury disagreed and he was freed. The grand jury was unable to find an indictment against Filkins for murder, as he had been tried in Oneida County and acquitted.

Wheeler, Grove and Plumb also made the news for stealing. In May Wheeler, in company with Clark Wheeler and an unidentified man, drove into Mexico with one horse and left with a team. A deputy sheriff traced them to Pulaski, where Wheeler Loomis was arrested. In the satchel of his carriage the officer found a horse blanket, parts of a new harness and a surcingle that had been stolen from Lawrence Frank in Durhamville. A search of Wheeler's pockets turned up $270, a part of which was counterfeit. He was locked up in the county jail in Pulaski, while the officer searched for the other two men.

The Madison Observer reported: "At the May Oyer and Terminer, 1868, he was indicted for grand larceny and gave bail in the sum of $1,000 for his appearance at the June Sessions, William W. Loomis and Henry Hilliard being his bondsmen. At the June term the case was moved by the District Attorney, but Loomis was not present. It was claimed that he fell from the hay loft in the barn of one Gray a day or two previous, striking on a mowing machine and injuring himself so severely as to render him unable to be present. The affidavits of two physicians setting forth such inability to attend were presented. The court ordered the bail to be prosecuted. The falling from the hayloft was testified to and the two physicians were present. They testified that they belived him unable to be present. There were no marks on his body, though one of them thought he did discover a trifle of a bruise on his back, and he appeared to be sore and his pulse was excited and fluctuating. Both physicians thought this might have been caused by medicine. The judge in his charge to the jury laid down the law in pretty strong terms and, after a few minutes deliberation, they returned with a verdict of $1,000 for the People."

A horse belonging to W. E. Conger and a buggy and harness owned by Isaac Terry were stolen by Henry Burton and Frank Jones and abandoned in Monticello. The thieves returned to the Loomis home, where they were arrested. Upon arraignment before Justice Church in Waterville the youths made complete confessions implicating Grove and Plumb Loomis. In default of bail Burton and Jones were commended to the county jail to await grand jury action.

Grove and Plumb Loomis were arrested on the complaint of Conger and Terry. They waived examination when brought before Justice Church and were also sent to jail when they could not obtain bail. The Loomises were never brought to trial but their men were sent to jail.

Early in November, 1870 a three year old colt was stolen from an unidentified man in Montrose, Pennsylvania and was traced to Sangerfield. The publisher of The Times sent him to Grove's home in the Swamp, where he had dinner. He informed Grove of the loss of his colt and offered a reward for any information concerning it.

He returned to Pennsylvania without his three year old, but immediately telegraphed to Waterville that he was certain he had eaten dinner with the thief at the Loomises. He returned to Waterville with two witnesses.

Michael Gowen, an employee of Grove's, was arrested for horse stealing and was hustled out of the state before Grove obtained a writ of habeas corpus. Accompanied by Everett Terry and several other residents of Sangerfield, Grove drove to Montrose. Loomis proposed giving bail after Gowan was arraigned, but the justice would not accept the money and postponed the trial until January.

"Enraged citizens there believed we were all members of the same horse-stealing gang," Terry said later, "and discredited our testimony. The judge ordered Mike locked up in jail. This made Grove furious. Before I could stop him he had leaped to his feet.

" 'This man is innocent,' he shouted. Turning to where Mike stood handcuffed near an officer, he continued, 'I'll make them pay well for every day you're in jail, Mike.'

"This display made the Judge angry and he fined Grove heavily for contempt of court. Mike was taken to jail, but before he was brought to trial the real horse thief was caught and confessed to the crime. The stolen colt was also recovered. Mike was released from jail, but was a sick man for nearly a year afterwards."

Another published account reveals that shortly afterwards Montrose suffered the most disastrous fire in its history and the origin of the fire was never discovered. This appears to be entirely false, as court house records in Montrose disclose no such disastrous fire between the years 1863 and 1886.

Denio Loomis, his sister, Cornelia, and mother were permanently settled in their home at Bardeen's Corners across the road from the Bardeen's District School in 1870. The home became the center for the gangs of thieves in the area, and Denio was called the leader by the newspapers.

When Dr. Fayette F. Elphick, a respected physician and postmaster of Stockbridge, turned horse thief, sawed the bars of his cell window in the Morrisville jail and escaped on Saturday night, October 1, 1870, he fled to the Loomis home in Bardeen's Corners.

"Elphick swore that he was at Denio's house ten or twelve days in November," The Syracuse Daily Standard disclosed. "He came there with a rig, which he sold to Denio and Bill Loomis on consideration that Bill should pay him $20 and Denio $15, and that Denio should show him where he could bet another just as good—that bargain being made at Bill's house (near Higginsville)—and also map out a safe route for him into Pennsylvania where he could sell it. They talked about several places where Elphick should go for the rig—Mexico, Oswego and Syracuse—but after visiting one Jacob Hartman, who lived about eight miles from Denio, and talking with him about a bay horse and new buggy owned by (Edward) Lynch, it was determined that Elphick should go for that.

"Elphick was introduced to Hartman under the name of Curtis. He and Denio went to bed at Hartman's and talked it over, and Loomis advised Elphick to get the Lynch rig. On the way back to Loomis's, Denio pointed out the best road for Elphick to take to Parish and told him he'd better walk beyond Hunt's Corners and then get on the stage as by doing so they would not suspect that he came from Denio's.

He told him to hire the rig and go to Amboy that night, and drive to Bill Loomis's before morning where he could stay safely; then go to McIntyre's in Brookfield, Madison County, and thence make his way into Pennsylvania. Elphick hired the horse, drove to Amboy, thence to Bill's and thence to Stoddard's in Vernon, where he stayed over night.

"Next morning he pushed on to Augusta, stayed over night and thence to McIntyre's where his horse gave out. He took another and pushed on into Chautauqua County, where he traded the buggy for a sleigh. In January, 1871, he returned to Denio's."

Later that month a young man, Aaron Allen, who resided near Denio's, drove into Parish with a horse and cutter and offered the outfit for sale. Lynch had a suspicion that it was his. A posse of officers and citizens raided the Loomis farm at Bardeen's Corners. A thorough search of the house and barns was made without finding the man who had driven off with Lynch's horse. As the last of the raiders were leaving the house a member saw one bed that had not been searched. Under it, securely hidden by several bags of goose feathers, lay Elphick. Taken to the jail in Oswego, he was identified by Sheriff Edwin R. Barker of Madison County as the man who had escaped from the county jail. Oswego County officials would not release him. Brought to trial before Judge Foster, he was found guilty and was sentenced to four years and nine months in Auburn Prison.

Denio Loomis was arrested on February 18th as an accessory to the crime of grand larceny. As he was taken into custody he threatened to get even with Edward Lynch if he did not withdraw his complaint. Loomis quickly secured his freedom on $2,000 bail after pleading innocent upon arraignment. On Sunday morning the hotel and barns owned by Lynch at Parish burned to the ground at a loss estimated at $4,000. Said The Syracuse Daily Standard: "The charge is freely made that the work was that of a member of the Loomis gang named Denio."

He was indicted for grand larceny early in January, 1872, and also for being an accessory to grand larceny. Oswego County officials made extensive preparations for his trial. The Governor pardoned Dr. Elphick and restored his citizenship so that he might testify against Loomis. Aaron Allen, another important witness, was discovered in a Pennsylvania jail, where he had been taken by the gang and framed on a false charge. District Attorney Nutting went to Pennsylvania and obtained Allen's release.

The trial began in February, 1873 in the Oswego courthouse. Dr. Elphick, Allen Hartman, Lynch and other witnesses testified. Denio, through his attorney the Hon. S. C. Huntington, promptly denied all the accusations. When the case went to the jury, Denio and his attorney left the courtroom and went to Huntington's house nearby. In the jury room a unanimous agreement of guilty was found against Loomis. A juror suddenly complained of illness and asked for some camphor. A man hurried down the street to obtain it at the store, but stopped long enough to give Denio the jury's verdict.

District Attorney John J. Lamoree began to feel uneasy about Denio and went over to Huntington's house with a deputy. Denio was not in the house and Huntington suggested that he might be in the barn. Denio had fled on the fastest horse he could find. The Syracuse Daily Standard commented: "We are informed that a telegram was received in Pulaski today from a Canadian town saying that Loomis was in Canada, and if anybody wanted the horse he had used, they must come and get it."

The District Attorney took steps to have Denio's bail of $3,000 declared forfeited. The bonds had been posted by William Loomis, his wife, Martha, and Sanford Gleason. Denio sent word through his sister-in-law that he would appear in court to renew his bail, but insisted on another trial. Denio appeared before Special County Judge John Preston at Oswego to renew his bail, but the sheriff requested the Court to hold the matter open. Judge Preston heard the case and decided Denio would be better off in jail, so he was taken to Pulaski.

In March Loomis claimed he was in a debilitated condition from his long confinement in jail and had a fever sore on his leg. His attorney successfully argued the removal of the case to another county and the motion was granted by Judge Hardin at Utica. When the case again came to trial, despite Dr. Elphick's testimony, Denio was acquitted. The jury failed to believe such a fantastic story.

CHAPTER XXVIII

GROVE ENTICES CORA MAGWOOD

Constable Filkins found a note in his mail that demanded immediate attention when he went to the post office on Monday, October 6, 1874. It read:

"Mr. Filkins: Grove Loomis has a girl at his house by the name of Cora Atwood, to whom he lied to entice her there; and she has cried and taken on in the worst manner to get away; but all to no avail—they will not let her go. She is only sixteen years of age, and I should think people might take the matter in hand and rescue her from them, and have Grove and Plumb arrested for deceiving her. I think she is from Lee Center. Plumb met her on the cars and represented himself as a Mr. Baldwin, pretending that he lived in that village and wanted to hire her, offering her high wages. You know all they want of her is to ruin her; and I think something ought to be done immediately to save her."

The officer immediately investigated and discovered Plumb and Grove were keeping a girl named Cora Magwood of Lee Center in Grove's shack in the Swamp. He also wrote to the girl's mother, Mrs. R. J. Magwood, a widow, asking her to meet him in Waterville. She came to the village on Tuesday morning of the following week, accompanied by a Mr. and Mrs. Palmer of Lee Center, and James Rodenhurst, a relative who had formerly kept taverns in Vernon and Lowell. The constable told them everything he had learned and Mrs. Magwood immediately obtained search warrants for the Loomis home.

Leaving the women at the American Hotel, Filkins, Palmer and Rodenhurst drove to Grove's shack which stood in the middle of the swamp meadow in the Nine Mile Swamp within sight of the cellar ruins of the Loomis homestead. When they were near the shack they left their carriage and proceeded on foot cautiously to prevent the occupants from being warned. .

"Within they found Grove Loomis, Miss Nellie Smith, who has figured largely in the Loomis affairs in times past, three other desperate looking characters, and the maiden of whom they were in search," The Waterville Times reported. "Mr. Filkins made known his errand and told the girl, who at once recognized the other two gentlemen, that she could pack her trunk without fear and accompany him. While she was thus engaged quite a lively time ensued among those most interested. Grove, as usual, exhibited considerable spirit, but Filkins, calm and cool, after giving him the length of his rope or tongue, told him to 'mug up.' This he disliked to do, but Nellie, seeing he was likely to get himself into trouble, stepped in and entertained those present in a lively manner until the girl was ready to leave. While there Mr. Filkins learned that the desperadoes had, in some unaccountable manner, ascertained that he was on their track, and was informed that had he delayed in appearance twenty-four hours, the lady would have been beyond his reach.

"He subsequently ascertained, by questioning the girl, that they had informed her of a 'nice situation' in Oswego, where she was to have a 'nice time and big wages.' Filkins at once informed her that the nice place was the house of Denio Loomis where 'the wages of sin is death.'

"The party returned to our village at about noontime, and the meeting of the unhappy mother and rescued daughter may be better imagined than described. Upon taking his leave of them, Mr. Filkins cautioned the girl's friends to keep a sharp lookout or she would again be in the possession of the Loomis gang, as when they once set their mind on a piece of property they are bound to have it.

"The young lady, whose name is Cora Magwood, instead of Atwood, as Mr. Filkins' informant supposed, is about sixteen years of age, of medium stature, fair appearing, but not over and above bright. Owing to her youth and inexperience she was easily imposed upon when she first met Mr. Loomis alias Baldwin, and had not a disinterested person, as a friend, advised Mr. Filkins of the state of affairs, there is no telling what might have been her future history.."

The countryside was aroused over the newest Loomis escapade, and area newspapers asked J. J. Guernsey, the owner and editor of The Times for further details. Grove Loomis became alarmed over the furor that had been created and lost little time in giving Guernsey a letter signed with Cora's name for publication. It read:

"Lee Center, Oct. 26, 1874

To the Editor of The Waterville Times:

I noticed an article in your issue of the 15th inst. concerning myself which is very much to my discredit, as well as to those with whom I spent three weeks; and I therefore desire to have the truth published, not only in your paper but in all others which have copied the remarks referred to. The truth of the matter, substantially, is as follows:

After leaving home I went to Mr. Lewis' near Oriskany Falls, and picked hops for him for one week, at the expiration of which time Grove Loomis called and wished me to go with him. I told him I would go if Mr. Lewis was willing. I asked Mr. L. and he said he would go there as soon as anywhere else, adding that if I did not like it there I could come back to his house and return home. After I decided to go Grove told me that I had better leave my trunk at Mr. Lewis', as he lived somewhat retired, and as I had been living in the village of Lee Center I might get homesick, and if so he could bring me back to Mr. Lewis; or, if I was contented, he could get my trunk at any time. I went, and after staying at Mr. Loomis' a week, Mr. Lewis came over and paid me for picking hops. The next day I went with Grove Loomis to Oriskany Falls, and on our way back we stopped and got my trunk.

The next day, or soon after, Grove had carpenters and masons come to work for him. He said it was too much for

Nellie to do all the work while the workmen were there, and if I would stay and help her he would pay me well for it, and I agreed to do so. .

The Sunday before Mr. Rodenhurst and Mr. Palmer came after me, Grove told me that some person had written false letters to my mother or Filkins, and that Mr. Filkins was coming after me on Tuesday, and he would like to have me write my mother at once, as she might believe all she heard and be worried about me.

I wish it distinctly understood that Grove did not lie to me or entice me to his house; neither did I cry to get away from there, for I could go at any time I wished. I did cry after Filkins came and insulted me by breaking into the room Nellie gave me to dress in. He was the first and only one that insulted me while at Grove's house. It is also untrue relative to Grove being at or near the house at the time Mr. Palmer and Rhodenhurst, with Mr. Filkins drove up. He came some time after, and when he entered I introduced him to Mr. Rhodenhurst. After the usual greeting, Grove remarked that he was sorry Mr. R. was in such company, as he appeared to be a gentleman, after which he ordered Filkins out of the house, but he would not go.

The above are the facts in the case, which I am willing to take oath to at anytime.
                        Respectfully,
                            Cora Magwood."

The letter was immediately reprinted in The Utica Morning Herald and other area newspapers. A week later Constable Filkins received letters from Mrs. Magwood and her daughter which branded the one produced by Grove Loomis as forgery. Mrs. Magwood wrote:

                        Lee Center, Nov. 3, 1874
Sheriff Filkins, Sir:
I see by the Herald that Mr. Grove Loomis has written a piece for the Waterville Times to suit himself, and I wish it understood that neither Cora nor myself ever wrote or or-

dered written one word for that paper, or any other. Grove was here on the evening of the 25th of October, and wanted to see Cora, but he did not see her. On Monday he came where we were at work and wanted us to sign our names to an article which he would write. I told him I did not want anything more written, but he insisted that it should be done. I told him I would consult my friends, and if they advised me to do anything like that I would write a piece myself and send; but they advised me not to send a word, for we were unable to go down there again, if called to substantiate what I should write. Mr. Loomis was determined to see the letters that I got from there, and said, if I did not let him have them he should fetch us all down there again. He said that it was getting near election, and he wanted to find something against that murderer and thief Filkins to have him kicked out of office.

If he does that he will have to look in some other quarter. I have not time to write more.

Yours Respectfully
R. J. Magwood

P. S. If need be, I am willing to be sworn that both these letters are no more than the truth, and not the whole of that even. RJM."

The Times editor explained that Mrs. Magwood referred to the letter she had received, which was almost identical to the one received by Filkins, but which advised her to employ the constable. Cora Magwood wrote under the same date as her mother:

"Deputy Sheriff Filkins, Dear Sir:

The last act of Grove Loomis only gives coloring to what his intentions were; for I never wrote such an article as that, nor did I authorize him to. He came up here and wanted—nay insisted—that we should affix our names to a statement he would write, which mother refused to do. He said if she did not he would have us both down there, and compel her to show the letter so he could find out the author of all the mischief. Judging from his insolence, mother thinks he will have to go a good ways to do that. He wanted me to say that I staid there willingly and that no one insulted me but you when you looked in on me. In fact, he wanted me to contradict the article you had published in The Waterville Times. He did not insult me—neither did his hired man —but Plumb did, and on such occasion I was so angry that I couldn't help crying. The first afternoon that I was there I wanted to come home, or go back to Mr. Lewis' but they were all at work, and so I could not. They used all the seductive arguments they knew of, telling me that it would not be lonely there after I was accustomed to the place, and that Mr. Baldwin would be down that day certain, but he did not come that day nor the next. On Friday he was there and Nellie called me and said, 'Mr. Baldwin is here.' I went and found Plumb hid behind his horse. He denied ever having seen me, and I being naturally quick tempered, told him I did not blame him for taking an assumed name for hiding such a disgraceful act, and added, the man that would do such an act would steal sheep. Grove came into the house in a few minutes and asked the cause of the 'fuss,' as he termed it, and Nellie told him. He then proposed that I should go up to his mother's, saying that she was a good old lady, and Denio one of the best boys that ever lived. This I readily agreed to do. His nephew Charlie was on the hill and he was going back Monday, and I was going with him; but Plumb Loomis had some work to do that prevented our going that day, but we would go on the next day certain. Mr. Grove Loomis told me that he did not intend to come from Mr. Lewis' empty-handed when he came up there. He said he promised Mr. Lewis a horse and his daughter a gold watch if they would use their influence for him. This he told me himself.

This letter may be dull but you can't expect much from me as I am not very 'bright' but I hope I know a thing or two yet. Anyhow I intend to have the truth on my side, and if my word is not enough I don't mind swearing that every word of this letter is the truth, the whole truth and nothing but the truth.

My mother has looked this letter all over and thinks it all right.

Miss Cora Magwood

P. S. Mr. Filkins: I beg your pardon for the rude way in which I conducted myself when I was there. I could not help it for I felt just the way I acted. I didn't cry because you looked in on me when I was dressing. I don't remember crying at all; if I did it was because they were all talking so terribly that it frightened me.

Cora"

Filkins had the final word in the Magwood case. He gave Guernsey a card to publish in The Times: "No exceptions were taken by me to the strange manner in which Miss Magwood conducted herself while under my charge. I considered, at the time, the unpleasant circumstances in which she was placed, and did not blame her for being beside herself. No apology, therefore, is due me from either her friends or herself."

The Loomises had nothing further to say about the girl and they made no attempt at revenge, for they soon became occupied with family affairs of their own.

As the years passed the younger generation lost its fear of the Loomises and their gang. This was evident on Sunday, March 6, 1875 when Grove L. Loomis was forced to flee from a crowd of young men.

Loomis owned a house and some property at Congertown, near Sangerfield Center, which he rented to the Widow Chase. Many of the residents claimed his interest in the widow was more than platonic. Grove was fifty years old, still handsome, and dressed in exquisite taste. He had never married and was notorious for his love affairs.

The Widow Chase had two good looking daughters. The oldest who was about fourteen, was developed beyond her years. There were many of the youths, including several young married men, who were anxious to teach her about life. They persuaded the girl to go with them to a house in the neighborhood for a few days. The girl readily agreed, and had a neighbor girl ask the Widow Chase if her daughter couldn't come to her home and spend a few days. Mrs. Chase agreed.

Later that day the mother learned her daughter was not staying at the neighbors. The Widow Chase found her at another home with several young men and boys, and dragged her away.

The young men were incensed when the girl was taken home. They learned that Grove Loomis was at the Widow Chase's and immediately blamed him.

Shortly before eleven that night the youths gathered about the Widow Chase's. When Loomis left the house to get his team and buggy from the barn, the youths surrounded him. Some shouted, "Kill him! Kill him! We'll never have a better time!"

As he started to drive away, the crowd blocked his path. Thoroughly frightened, he returned the horses to the barn, and escaped through a back window.

The youths searched the barn until after midnight to satisfy themselves that Loomis was not on the premises. They also surrounded the house and refused to leave. Some of them carried pistols and rifles.

The next morning a newly painted sign, "Fresh Meat" hung from the widow's home.

The Waterville Times scoffed at the story, claiming it had originated with Loomis.

"There was no mob on the occasion spoken of, unless Grove L. Loomis constituted it," The Times reported. "Grove L. Loomis has no family 'towards whom the feelings of the people were manifest' unless unmarried females of doubtful chastity, and notoriously harbored by him, constitute his family. He is an unmarried man."

During the next week Loomis, Miss Nellie Smith, his mistress, and the Widow Chase went to Utica to procure warrants against several of the youths who had been recognized that Sunday night. They were advised to confer with the justices of the peace in Sangerfield.

The Times continued to sympathize with the young men. On Thursday, April 29, it said: "This alleged riot is the same matter of which we have heretofore spoken, and we now repeat what we said at the time, that the chief disturbance, and all the riot on that occasion were committed by Grove L. Loomis himself, and such will be proved, to the entire satisfaction of everybody."

The Times was right. Evidently the cases never came to trial. There are no court records or newspaper stories that give any further information.

CHAPTER XXIX

YOUNG GROVE LOOMIS

Rhoda Loomis never forgot Wash nor his brutal murder. She prized highly a gold signet ring she claimed he had made out of gold he had dug in California. She also did not forget that his son Grove, was approaching his fourteenth birthday, when he would inherit his father's share of the Loomis property.

Young Grove had been placed in the care of Mr. and Mrs. Richard Gorton of Stockwell Settlement, a small community east of the Nine-Mile Swamp, about two years after his mother, Hannah Wright, had died from a gunshot wound received in the Loomis kitchen. Wash himself had decided to place the baby with Mrs. Gorton, who was related to the child's mother. While Wash had been away on business the baby had committed some childish act which displeased one of his uncles. Young Grove had been given a severe beating. When Wash returned he had nearly killed the guilty brother, and had decided then and there that his child would not be brought up by the Loomises.

The Times reported: "He took the child away, placing it in the hands of Richard Gorton and wife, for their adoption and protection, making the request that they rear him in utter ignorance of his parentage, and teach him to call them by the endearing title of father and mother; promising at the same time to aid and assist them in providing for the child, which promise was faithfully and satisfactorily fulfilled up to the time of his death."

The Gortons, though very poor, were highly respected. They sent Grove to school and on Sunday to church. He grew up a fine, Christian boy. Phinnett Carter, who attended school with him, praised him, and Thomas Hall, a friend in later years, said, "He was one of Nature's noblemen."

According to The Times the family had tried for years, by flattery and otherwise, to regain possession of the child. As Grove's father died possessing property valued at from $8,000 and $10,000, including two shares in the homestead comprising 200 to 300 acres of valuable land plus personal property, the Loomis family spared no effort in trying to get possession of the boy's property.

On Saturday, February 6, 1875 Cornelia Loomis, by making false statements, succeeded in having herself appointed the boy's legal guardian by a surrogate in Clinton until he reached his fourteenth birthday on Tuesday, the ninth, when he could make his own choice. Cornelia, Grove and Plumb and an unidentified officer who was a friend of the Loomises broke into the Gorton home on Monday while the family was at dinner and demanded the boy. Young Grove ran to his foster mother for protection, crying for her to save him. The Loomises tore the child from Mrs. Gorton's arms and carried him screaming to their sleigh and drove away.

Mrs. Gorton notified friends and Constable Filkins that Grove had been kidnapped by his notorious relatives. A posse tracked the fleeing sleigh to Pratt's Hollow, but arrived there too late. The Loomises with the boy had boarded a train on the Midland Railroad and were on their way to Denio's home in Bardeen's Corners in Oswego County.

Residents of the area held a meeting and decided to take all action possible to find the boy and return him to Mrs. Gorton. A group of Waterville's most influential business men drove to Grove Loomis' shack in the Swamp and ordered him to produce the boy or they would see that the law took the full course. Grove was so frightened that he went to the sheriff and told him a crowd had threatened to mob him.. Deputy Sheriff Aurelius Benedict of Waterville, sent to investigate, found that Grove's accusations had been false. The deputy advised Grove that, although the county would try to protect his property, it had no jurisdiction over his person, and told him to act **accordingly.**

Justice of the Peace Orlando Stetson and Constable M. B. Cossett also advised Grove and ordered the boy returned.

Plans were made to visit the Loomis home at Bardeen's Corners, where Mrs. Loomis and Cornelia resided with Denio. No one was certain where young Grove had been taken. The Times repeated the general rumors: "Some of our people think he has been taken to Canada, where one of this depraved Loomis family resides; others think he has been taken to Vermont, where some members of this family have a sinful rendezvous; and others still, who comprise the greater number, think that he has been taken to the sea coast, and has been already, or soon will be sent out of country, and to some distant place, from which he will never be able to return. . . . This boy is an heir to a considerable portion of the Loomis estate; hence their anxiety to dispatch him under the pretext of giving him a moral and academical education."

Grove Loomis stopped in Waterville long enough to tell the editor of The Times that he had sent Plumb to Oriskany Falls to telegraph his family to return his nephew. The Times discovered that Plumb had telegraphed his family, not to return the boy, but to take him out of the country. The message Loomis sent read, "Hurry up the appointment!" Plumb then took the train to Rome, rented a livery and drove to William Loomis' farm near Higginsville. From there he drove to Bardeen's Corners, arriving about seven o'clock.

As soon as Filkins learned that the boy was at Denio's home, he telegraphed Officer E. G. Lynch of Parish and gave him instructions to raid the place and save the boy.

Lynch, accompanied by Officers Brown and Schuyler and several others, descended on the Denio Loomis some at eleven o'clock Monday night, February 22. Brown and Schuyler broke into the house while Lynch and the rest of his men surrounded the building to prevent anyone from escaping. Young Grove was there, together with his grandmother, Aunt Cornelia, and uncles, Denio, Plumb and Bill Loomis. The family, agitated over Plumb's arrival a few hours earlier, were arguing over taking the boy to nearby Mexico and having one of the family appointed his guardian. As soon as Brown and Schuyler showed their warrants Plumb demanded to know if "that murderer Filkins" was with them. When they told him he was not, Loomis asked if Lynch was with them. Told that Lynch was outside Plumb buckled on a gun belt that held two revolvers and snatched up a bowie knife.

"That one-armed son of a bitch!" he shouted and rushed out of the door with the knife in his hand. "He'll never leave here alive."

Lynch drew his revolver and aimed it at Plumb's eyes, and cocked the trigger. Plumb said nothing but backed into the house and slammed the door.

"The officers then told the gang they must give up the boy, or some one would get hurt, at which a contest ensued, lasting until 3:00 A. M., during which Cornelia and the old woman ordered the boy to feign sickness and go to bed," The Syracuse Standard reported, "which they forced him to do, throwing his sox in a tub of water and secreting the rest of his clothing. After a good deal of parleying on the part of the gang, the officers proceeded to take the boy, and finding no clothes, took some of the bedding to wrap about him. The Loomises, seeing that they meant business, finally gave up his clothing, and the lad was taken to Parish.

"Filkins arrived there Tuesday night, and was heartily welcomed by the lad, as he knew he was then in the hands of one who would protect him from his enemies. He seemed to understand, from the conversation which ensued prior to the arrival of the officers, that Plumb's team had been harnessed and fed preparatory to pushing on to some unknown point with him immediately.

"On the following morning, when Filkins and the boy took the cars at Parish for home, they discovered Cornelia Loomis and an officer already aboard the train. As soon as seats were secured, the officer served papers on Filkins which purported to be a writ of habeas corpus, and informed him that said papers were to restrain him from taking the boy out of the county.

"The service of the papers not being made in a legal manner led Officer Filkins to believe them to be a fraud, and that in giving them no heed he was not laying himself liable, or disobeying the order of any court. He therefore told the individual that he did not wish him as his counsel, and pocketing the papers proceeded on his way homeward. Since his arrival here he has consulted able counsel, who have informed him that he pursued the proper course, as the papers were worthless."

Filkins and young Grove arrived in Waterville Wednesday noon and on Thursday visited Mrs. Gorton, who was overjoyed to see the boy alive and well. On Friday Mrs. Gorton, accompanied by Filkins, the boy, and Egbert and Lorenzo Stetson went before a Surrogate. Young Grove selected his foster mother as his legal guardian. The Stetson brothers became her sureties and posted $4,000.

The Loomises made no further attempt to molest young Grove.

"Aunt Cornelia and Grandmother Loomis thought I did not have good enough clothes to wear as befitted a Loomis." the youth said, "so they took me away from Aunt Lydia Gorton. They never threatened me the short time they had me with them."

Young Grove inherited the family's love for horses. "When about seventeen he had a good young bay horse and a good carriage," his friend Hall recalled. "He liked horses. He patted and smoothed them as he talked of them to me. He had a born love for horses and animals."

CHAPTER XXX

THE FAMILY QUARRELS

The death of the boy's uncle, Grove Lawrence Loomis, on Monday, March 11, 1878 marked the beginning of nearly a quarter of a century of family quarrels, violence and court litigations that eventually drove the Loomises from the Chenango Valley. Grove had been seriously ill for several months and when he realized that the end was near, he requested the Rev. Mr. Lamb, pastor of the Congregational Church at Sangerfield Center, to visit him. Remembering the scathing sermon that had been preached at his brother Wash's funeral, Grove chose part of the 18th verse of Revelations I: "I am he that liveth and was dead and behold am alive forever more."

"He (Grove) confessed to this minister that he was a sinner and wanted God to forgive him," Carter recalled. "When he died that minister preached his sermon and said, 'I have no doubt but what Mr. Loomis is in heaven with the angels. There are many evil people that have been floated to Heaven at the eleventh hour of forgiveness, I've heard some men say. If I've got to go and live with that crowd I might as well be in hell.' "

The service was held at one o'clock Thursday in the church. Grove had been laid out in a heavy metallic casket. The chief mourners were Mrs. Ellen Kelloway of Hamilton, the former Nellie Smith, his mistress; his brothers Plumb and William Mrs. William Loomis, friends and enemies from the surrounding area. Grove was buried in the family lot in the Sangerfield Cemetery. His mother, Cornelia, Wheeler and Denio did not attend the funeral.

Grove's will generously provided for his ex-mistress, giving her the life use of his fifty-five acre farm, a span of fine horses, five cows and other personal property. As he had also owned a share in the family estate, he provided that she was to have $1,000 from it whenever she wanted the money. William Hathaway, Deansville Justice of the Peace and lifelong friend of Grove, was appointed executor of his estate.

The Loomis family, furious over the terms of the will, were determined to have it broken in their favor. Plumb Loomis took the first action. He made repeated threats against the lives of Nellie and Hathaway unless they cleared out. The Deansville justice, fearing Nellie would be harmed, sent her away and took possession of the property. He hired a few men, including Charles Nash of Deansville, to guard it.

"We understand this act of Mr. H.'s further increased the wrath of the survivors of the Loomis family," reported The Waterville Times on Thursday, May 2, 1878, "and threats have repeatedly been made against their lives. Notwithstanding this, Mr. H. went on and rented the place, selling some of the stock, and turning over the balance to the new tenant who took possession Tuesday. This act so incensed Plumb Loomis and his help, that they visited the place in the swamp Tuesday, to obtain satisfaction. Hathaway was there, and ordered the gang off the premises, but before leaving they again made threats to return and 'clean out' the legal holders of the property. Hathaway accompanied Plumb some distance on his way home, advising him to remain away and cautioning him against returning.

"But all in vain—for about six P. M. Plumb Loomis, Gary Penner, Tom Riley and another member of the gang, whose name we did not learn, accompanied by Plumb's wife, made their appearance armed to the teeth and commenced acts of lawlessness. They were again ordered off the premises by Hathaway and Nash, but refused to go. Penner, more bold than the rest, approached the house and endeavored to remove some property belonging to the estate, which Nash gave him strict orders not to touch. Penner then turned upon Nash, with an axe in his hand, and allowed he would kill him at the first opportunity. Nash was armed with a revolver, which he drew and again cautioned Penner, who again repeated his threat, whereupon Nash shot him twice, one ball only taking effect. This looked like business, a kind of business, too, which the Loomis family never fancied, and put an end to their depredations for that day. They left with the wounded man, Hathaway accompanying them home.

"When he and Nash came to our village, the latter surrendering himself to Deputy Sheriff (George) Dearflinger, who took him before Justice Church, but owing to the late hour the Justice put the matter over until Wednesday, allowing Hathaway and Nash to return to the swamp and guard the property until morning against further depredations of the gang. While here, he summoned Drs. G. W. Cleveland and F. T. Gorton, the latter as coroner, to take an antemortem statement of the wounded man, while Plumb posted off to Oriskany Falls and telegraphed District Attorney (Milton) Barnett of the proceedings.

"The physicians repaired to Plumb's house, but found Penner was not seriously wounded, the ball having entered the left shoulder, and remaining so near the surface that, although bleeding profusely, the wound was not dangerous, and was left until morning before endeavoring to extract the ball."

District Attorney Barnett, who arrived in Waterville the next day, heard the testimony concerning the shooting and stated that he could not find any reason why Nash should be arrested.

"The Deansville men were justified in protecting their property," he ruled.

The shooting of Penner did not lessen Plumb's attempts to obtain hold of his brother's property. In July he gave Isaiah Belfield a forged order for one of Grove's guns. Using the name of George Belville, Belfield went to the little house in the Swamp and presented the order to a Mr. Denfield, who was in charge of the property. Denfield gave Belfield the gun, but became suspicious after he had left. Justice Hathaway was notified and learned that no order had been given for the weapon. Belfield was arrested on a charge of forgery and pleaded innocent upon arraignment. He was taken to the county jail in Rome to await action of the grand jury.

During the twelve years that had passed since Mrs. Crandall had been murdered in her home in Coontown and her husband, Dennison, seriously wounded, it had become habitual for county officers to drive the elderly man to the various jails and lock-ups to examine the prisoners.

As soon as Crandall saw Belfield in jail he recognized him.

"That's one of the men who killed Phoebe," he stated. "Those eyes—I have seen them in my dreams a hundred times."

As the only charge against Belfield was for forgery Justice Hathaway took Nellie Smith to visit the prisoner in jail. She recognized him at once.

"How do you do, Nell?" Belfield asked, adding thoughtfully, "You have not changed much."

"Nor have you," Nellie replied, "except your hair is different. I should have known you if I had seen you in a pudding dish."

They talked over the past for a short time. Before Miss Smith left Belfield had promised he would give up the gun he had obtained with the forged order. He did not keep his promise and Miss Smith visited him again a few weeks later.

"Why haven't you fulfilled your promise about the gun?" she inquired.

Belfield refused to talk about the matter. "As long as you have been so mean enough to tell what you know about the Crandall murder, you can find out about the gun the best way you can," he said.

"I have not told anything about the Crandall murder," the woman protested.

"Who has then?"

Nellie said she did not know.

On October 11, 1878 Belfield was transferred from Oneida County to Madison County, where he was wanted on the murder charge. He was indicted for the first degree murder of Mrs. Phoebe Crandall by the grand jury. The trial was postponed repeatedly and Belfield languished in the county jail at Morrisville. Confined for nearly eight months in a dark cell on the lower floor, he grew pale and thin, causing his features to sharpen. His hair gradually returned to its normal darkness as the dye wore off. Sheriff Milton Delano said he was well behaved.

The trial began before Justice C. E. Martin of Binghamton at two o'clock Wednesday afternoon, May 7, 1879. Belfield was represented by Garrit A. Forbes of Canastota, while District Attorney John E. Smith of Morrisville appeared for the People. During the three days of the trial Belfield's connection with the Loomises was thoroughly explored. Mrs. Kelloway was one of the principal witnesses for the People. Her character as the former mistress of Grove Loomis and a member of the Loomis household was laid bare by Attorney Forbes. John Stoner, Henry Brooks and other members of the Loomis gang, ex-Constable Filkins and others who knew Belfield, testified. Forbes centered his attack on Dennison Crandall, the only eye-witness to his wife's murder. The attorney flayed at the elderly man's failing eyesight and memory. Belfield had numerous witnesses, including many members of his family, who gave testimony of his character and activities.

The bell on the courthouse began to toll at eight-thirty o'clock Saturday evening, announcing that the jury had reached an agreement. Belfield was found not guilty. During the following week he was taken to Utica and tried for forging the order to obtain Grove Loomis's gun. He pleaded guilty and was sentenced to one year in Onondaga Penitentiary. The editor of The Madison Observer commented wryly: "Considering all the complications which have surrounded him lately, Belfield may consider himself lucky in getting off so lightly."

Two months later Mrs. Rhoda Loomis and her remaining children brought suit against the estate which Grove had left to his former mistress in the amount of $20,000 they claimed was due for the rent of the Sangerfield farm and for borrowed money. The case never came to trial, as Grove's will was proved valid.

Mrs. Loomis did not press her claim, as Denio suffered another paralytic stroke early in September that made him hopelessly demented. Two years earlier he had suffered a stroke while milking. It paralyzed him completely for almost a year. He recovered sufficiently to move about. Miss Minnie Ladd of Oneida, who taught school at that time in the Bardeen's District School across the road from the Loomis home, recalled, "Denio had a shock and was, I believe, in bed for a short time. I can remember seeing him walking with a cane and he had a vacant-looking face. I think he started to raise his hat and failed and Mother said he showed traces of his former manners."

Denio died on January 7, 1880. The funeral was held in the Loomis home with the Rev. Phinney officiating. His body was buried in the family plot in the Sangerfield Center cemetery. The newspapers commented briefly on his passing. Said The Syracuse Herald: "Denio Loomis, a leading member of a gang of outlaws, is dead, and central New York, especially Oswego county, breathes more freely. The Loomis family has been a terror to the inhabitants of this section for years, and as they die off one by one the people feel relieved." The Waterville Times was more blunt: "Denio Loomis, who has been more dead than alive for several months past, shuffled off his mortal coil recently, and was planted at the Centre, Tuesday (Jan. 13th) of this week. What shall the harvest be?"

CHAPTER XXXI

THE LOOMIS EMPIRE FALLS

The closing years of the ninteenth century found the remaining members of the Loomis family struggling desperately to hold onto the rapidly disintegrating remains of their empire. The law suits Mrs. Rhoda Loomis and her remaining children had brought against Nellie Smith Kelloway and William Hathaway to gain possession of Grove's meager acreage and share of the Sangerfield farm and against Oneida County for the attack and burning of the homestead in 1866, both failed. The Oneida County Supreme Court ruled in May, 1872 ". . . while the Loomises knew their lives were threatened and that a raid was planned on their place . . . they did not notify the authorities or seek police protection."

The Sangerfield farm, once valued at $35,000, was heavily mortgaged. The fortune the family had accumulated had been swept away thousands of dollars at a time each year over half a century as the brothers forfeited their bail bonds to escape trial. The Loomis' attorneys obligingly accepted mortgages on the family property as fees and as sureties. The hotel the family owned at Higginsville had been taken over by Pomeroy and Spriggs and property in Rome and West Monroe went to other lawyers. Plumb Loomis sold his birth right on September 2, 1875, according to a Supreme Court record that stated, "The said Amos P. Loomis duly executed and delivered to Milton D. Barnett and Joseph I. Sayles a mortgage of his interest in said property. That afterwards the said mortgage was duly foreclosed and the interest of said Amos P. Loomis conveyed by said mortgage was duly sold to the defendant Adelbert P. Sayles."

Plumb lived on the hill in the old home with his wife, Adeline, and children and continued to enact the role of a lord of the manor. Criminals still made his home their headquarters, but they were no longer those who had remained faithful to the family through the years. The older men like Bill Alvord were in prison, others had left the state and some, like LaVergue Beebe, had died. Among the newer members of the gang were William Comstock, Garrison Penner, George W. Thomas and Jerry Riley.

Comstock, a seventeen-year-old youth, burglarized the home of Isaac Terry, a neighbor, and stole a sewing machine, clothes, bed clothing and gold beads. Arrested, he pleaded guilty, named Plumb as his accomplice, and was sentenced to the Western House of Refuge for juvenile delinquents in Rochester. Comstock and Plumb also stole 1,500 pounds of hay from the barn of Welcome Welch, another neighbor. Plumb pleaded not guilty on all charges when he was arrested. There are no records that the cases ever came to trial.

Thomas, a twenty-one-year-old canaler employed by Loomis, and Riley, a farmer who had been employed for a season by John Mason, were arrested for stealing a trunk owned by a daughter of E. H. Mott that had been dropped off the train at Sangerfield Center. Thomas was arrested at Deerfield and Riley at Newport. Both pleaded guilty. Part of the contents of the trunk were found hidden in a pillowcase under a barn below the Loomis farm.

Gary Penner, a frequent guest at the Waterville lock-up for his habit of stealing chickens, made his home with Plumb when he was at "liberty." His cousin, Norva Sturdevant of Brookfield, who proudly claimed he was the "last of the Loomis gang" also stayed with Plumb.

"When my cousin, Gary Penner, was working there Plumb called him 'Gary Goshin,' " Norva recalled. "Plumb always had a nickname for everybody. I got drunk for the first time to win a twenty-five cent bet he made with me. He dared me to drink a quart of cider. I did, but it knocked me cold. When we worked and pleased Plumb he would give us hard cider or beer, so many glasses to the men he thought had earned more. He would line us up and say, 'One glass to so and so, two glasses to him, and so on.' One man he called the 'three-legged man.'

"I remember Plumb called us one day and said he had some lumber for us to move. Plumb had hitched up his team and we got on the wagon and went off to the lot. We brought one load home and went back after another. Eli Hibbard, the constable, was there when we returned and he told Plumb he couldn't take the lumber as it didn't belong to him. Plumb swore and said that it did and told Gary and me to load up the wagon.

" 'I'll shoot the first one that touches that lumber,' Hibbard said.

" 'Go ahead,' Plumb ordered us. 'He won't shoot.'

"Gary reached out and picked up a board and Hibbard shot him in the wrist.

" 'Try that again,' Hibbard warned, 'and next time I'll shoot to kill.'

"So Plumb didn't get the lumber. All the way home he praised my cousin for his courage.

"Plumb had ten or eleven cows when he was living on the hill. He used to take the milk to the cheese factory in North Brookfield. He sure had a funny way of talking. Plumb always swore by saying, 'By Christ,' talked, "Tween me an' you,' and 'By God, by God.' He said his brother Wash was a fine man and the whole family had thought a lot of him. His sisters, he said, were pretty smart. He told me about Cornelia stealing the muffs by drawing them onto her legs. Plumb didn't say much about his mother, only that he got along fine with her, but she had an awful temper.

"Plumb said to me one day, 'Norvy, I'm kind of hungry for chicken. I notice a lot of our neighbors have some mighty nice chickens in their hen houses. How about going out some night and getting some?'

" 'I'll be damned if I'll do it,' I said. 'I'll get drunk for you, but I'll be goddamned if I'll steal.' "

John Greenman, who lived near Brookfield and worked for Plumb when he was a young man, related that Plumb was a good farmer. "He stayed home most of the time,' Old John recalled. "Cornelia kept house for him for awhile and was a fine cook. His nephew, Grove Collins, was there, a little boy, about two feet high. His mammy, Charlotte Collins, Plumb's sister, died on the farm in Hastings of T.B. They had two rooms in the shanty where they lived. Later Plumb made it bigger. Cornelia slept on the floor and Plumb slept with me. George (his son) and Bill slept on the other side of the room. Plumb had a horse saddled all the time and bridled, in case he had to leave in a hurry."

W. H. Weller of the law firm of Weller and Smith of Waterville, who served as counsel for Plumb Loomis in his declining years, stated he had visited his client's home on the hill and found it neat and clean. He said he was well treated and Mrs. Loomis insisted on serving him a piece of her excellent cake. Mr. Weller said Plumb was well versed on law.

Plumb bore a charmed life that a cat might have envied. He had been shot at and badly wounded and hanged three times during his earlier years, and during old age survived two serious accidents. Early in September, 1874 he and another man were driving past the Park House in Waterville when his horse shied and the carriage was thrown upside down into the ditch. Both men were uninjured. A bull badly gored Plumb early in September, 1878. The Times reported, ". . . his physician thinks he may recover."

Plumb lived to hold neighborhood children like Harold Mason on his lap and show them the rope scar around his neck where he had been hanged. He never lost his sense of humor, Sturdevant recalled. Once he put a large sign, "Beware the Loomis Gang," up behind his stove. A peddler came in the home one day and spread out his goods. Plumb pointed to the sign and said, "Read that." The peddler grabbed his pack, rammed in his wares and made a flying start for the door.

"There is more than one way to deal with these peddlers," Plumb stated.

George Eddy Olin of Madison, who took a threshing crew to Plumb Loomis's farm in the fall of 1896, described his experiences several years later to his daughter-in-law, Mrs. Willard (Marian) B. Olin, now of Liverpool. Olin did custom threshing and silo filling, Mrs. Olin recalled. He owned one of the first "oil pulls" in Oneida County.

Plumb's little farm was overgrown with brush.

The men were threshing oats. In the afternoon there was some excitement, when Plumb ordered the men to stop their work and go home. They had threshed more oats than he had planned, and found several harnesses and saddles hidden in the grain.

The threshers went home. The next day when they returned to finish their work, the oat bin was empty.

Olin recalled that Plumb was smaller than most of the Loomis men. Adeline Glazier was very short and stout.

Their son, George Loomis, who was about 30 years of age, helped the men thresh.

George Olin and the threshers remained for the night, as was customary in those days. The house had no staircase, but there was a ladder leading to the loft. The rungs were built in a corner of the room, so the ladder was corner-wise.

The men slept in the loft on beds made up on the floor, in the one large room.

"There was corn drying, hanging from the rafters, and shotguns hanging on the walls," Olin remembered. "There were more guns than any of the men or myself had ever seen before."

During the night one of the men, who was already drunk, got up and went down the road to a neighbor's place where he obtained a jug of whiskey. As he came back into the house, Adeline met him at the door and tried to get the jug. The thresher slipped away from her and they started running around the room.

Plumb entered the room and after watching the efforts of his wife, called encouragingly, "Get him Adeline! Kill him! Kill him!"

All the men in the loft were awakened by the noise, and they crowded around the ladder hole watching the fun below, cheering both their comrade and Mrs. Loomis. Adeline managed to get hold of the jug at last, and threw it on the floor where it broke.

"I've worked all over the country," Olin told his daughter-in-law, "but I'll never forget the time I threshed for Plumb Loomis."

Like his brothers and sisters, Plumb usually tried to outfox the peddlers who visited his home. Most of them were known as "pack peddlers" from the wrapped bundle they carried on their backs as they walked the long dusty roads. Others drove a horse or team if their wares were too large to carry on their back.

According to Greenman, who often worked for the Loomis family, an Irishman, Jimmy Doyle who was fresh from the "Auld Sod" came along one day with a pack on his back and stopped at Plumb's.

Loomis was not at home, but his sister, Cornelia was staying there a few days. She was not too interested in seeing what Doyle had to sell, and insisted that he leave. The Irishman stubbornly refused to budge until he had shown his wares.

Miss Loomis told Jimmy she would look as his goods, providing he could out-jump her. She said she was a good jumper. The peddler said he would try.

Cornelia jumped and Jimmy leaped, beating her, Miss Loomis's next jump took her out the open door of the house. The Irishman's next leap carried him further into the yard.

Cornelia quickly ran into the house and threw out Jimmy's pack and locked him out.

After Plumb Loomis was put out of the old home on the hill, he finally moved into the house his late brother, Grove had built in the swamp.

Norman Cowan of Stockwell, a historian of the Town of Sangerfield, told this story concerning Plumb. He said he had heard it from James Grover of New Berlin, who with his partner, a man named Madison, drove a horse and buggy through the countryside.

Grover and his partner bought cattle from the farmers along the way. At night they would stay with some family and turn their cattle into a lot on the farm. They would continue on their way the next morning until they reached the nearest railroad point. If they had collected enough cattle for a carload or two, they would ship them to the city markets, and then start out to buy another herd.

"On one of their trips south of Waterville the men came to a farm in the Nine-Mile Swamp and bought a few head of cattle," Cowan said. "As it was late afternoon, they asked the farmer if he would put them up for the night. He told them travelers were always welcome at his home.

"After turning their 20-odd head of cattle into a nearby pasture, and putting their horse in the barn, they were called into the house for supper. It was a fine meal. Later they went out to smoke and congratulate themselves on the fine place they had found to stay for the night.

"A hired man came by and Grover inquired what their host's name was. The man said they were at Plumb Loomis's, and he proceeded to tell them some yarns that scared the two visitors.

"After the hired man went on into the house, Grover and Madison talked it over and decided they would stay, as they were afraid to leave. They took a sled stake from a bob sled in the yard, and one of them concealed it under his clothes and they went into the house. The men decided one would sleep, while the other remained awake, and then change off. However, neither was able to sleep a wink," Cowan said.

"The next morning, bright and early, they were called by their host to a hearty breakfast. When the two buyers were ready to leave and wanted to settle up with Plumb, he refused to take any money from them for their lodging or meals. He said he was glad to have company, and if they ever passed that way again, they were welcome to stay.

"Plumb and his men helped to get their cattle from the pasture and onto the road through the swamp. It was not until they were well on their way again, that they breathed easier.

"Jim said he never stayed at a place where he was used better than at Plumb Loomis's," Cowan related.

Advancing age and the death of Denio Loomis mellowed the fierce spirit of Rhoda Loomis, the mother. For several years after Denio's passing she continued to live across from the Bardeen's District School with Cornelia. Charles Loomis, Wheelers' eldest son, resided with them most of the time. Frequently Wheeler's other good looking boys and girls came to visit their grandmother. Neighbors claimed they never talked about their home in Canada but, when questioned, would answer that they "lived ten miles back in the woods."

Mr. and Mrs. Arthur Dunn, who were neighbors, and Miss Minnie E. Ladd, the "schoolmarm," remembered that old Mrs. Loomis was friendly and Cornelia "standoffish," but believed neither cared about having visitors. "Don't think they cared to have people come and respectable folks did not want to be thought 'in with the Loomises,' " Miss Ladd explained. "Never heard of people calling there except when he (Denio) was first ill and when he died."

Old Mrs. Loomis was over ninety years of age, but she looked much younger, Mrs. Dunn said. A slender little woman, with "snapping" black eyes. Mr. Dunn recalled that the Loomises kept a large dairy of cows and Mrs. Loomis made excellent sage cheese. He considered it a treat when she made one of her rare visits to his parents, bringing a piece of her cheese and an apron full of pears. "She wore a lace cap on her head and dressed in fine silks and satins," Mr. Dunn said. "As a child I felt sure that people must be mistaken about her being one of the Loomis gang as she was so nice."

Miss Ladd remembered Mrs. Loomis visiting the school when her mother, Mrs. Joseph Ladd, was a teacher and she was a student. "She would criticize politely and sometimes remark how different teaching was than when she had taught school in her younger days," Miss Ladd said.

"We most often spoke of her as Grandma Loomis," Mrs. Caroline H. Baratier of Parish, RD1 said. "She was a very beautiful looking lady and was always busy doing things and was a good cheese maker. I only wish now I had a piece of the delicious cheese she made, full cream cheese, also brandy and sage cheese. She was very free-hearted when she cut one and she did not forget to bring or send a sample of it."

Mrs. Loomis was ninety four years of age when she died on October 2, 1887 in the home across from the school. Dr. Myron Woodruff of Central Square gave the reason of her death as old age. Gabriel Traub, the undertaker at Central Square, was called, and Mrs. Charles Ladd and Mrs. Clark H. Hoesington helped to lay her out. Cornelia Loomis wanted a metallic coffin for her mother, the best that money could purchase. Mr. Traub drove her to the Marcellus Casket Company in Syracuse and Cornelia selected the coffin she wanted. The price was $140. "That was quite expensive in those days and the man making the sale was a little doubtful of the pay on account of the poor appearance of Cornelia," Mr. Traub's grandson, George G. Traub of Central Square, recalled. "Grandpa told him to let her have what she wanted. After making her selection she dug down in the front of her dress and pulled out a roll of bills and paid $100 immediately."

The actual bill of sale in Mr. Traub's possession shows that $100 cash was paid, a cow valued at thirty five dollars, and wood, five dollars.

Mrs. Loomis was laid out in her best silk dress. The funeral was held on Sunday in the Bardeen's School with the Rev. A. P. Phinney officiating. Floral offerings were not in vogue, but the traditional sheaf of wheat reposed on the mantel.

William and Martha Loomis and Cornelia were her only children present, along with several of the grandchildren. After the funeral the body was taken by train to Sangerfield for burial in the family plot.

Shortly after her mother's death Cornelia and Charles moved into a little box-shaped, unpainted house a few yards down the road. She did not mingle with her neighbors. "Cornelia was tall, rather fleshy and mannish in her ways," Miss Ladd disclosed. "Apparently did not care to make friends. I guess sloppy might describe her dress. She was reported to be a poor housekeeper and untidy. I think she helped with the outdoor chores. We would just bow or say a word or two when meeting, but during my first term as teacher in that District she crossed the road in the rain to bring me an umbrella and rubbers to wear home as she knew I had always been sick much. That was kind, although I did not need them as father was coming for me."

Cornelia was working in her kitchen on Tuesday morning, November 24, 1893 when she suffered a cerebral hemorrhage and paralytic shock. Her nephew, Charles and two of his half-sisters managed to get her into bed. Dr. N. W. Bates of Central Square was sent for, but there was little that he could do. She died without gaining consciousness the following Friday.

Her body was taken to the Traub Undertaking Parlors in Central Square for the night. Mrs. Martha Loomis was sent for and she accompanied her sister-in-law's remains to Sangerfield, where the Rev. Mr. Cossitt read the burial service before she was laid to rest beside the other members of her family.

Cornelia passed away ten months after the Loomis' archenemy, James L. Filkins, died of blood poisoning at his home on Sanger Street in Waterville on January fourth. He was sixty-nine years of age. A controversial figure nearly all of his life, he was feared and hated by all criminals and enemies, and admired but never loved by his few friends. Older residents of the Valley who knew him, as well as law officers who worked with him, claimed that he was one of the greatest detectives who ever lived but received very little pay for his work. This is substantiated by frequent notations in court records of "Jas. L. Filkins pd. $- as a poor witness." The amount usually ranged from four to eight dollars.

After Wash Loomis' murder and the burning of the Loomis homestead the business men who had paid Filkins to break up the gang withdrew their support, as the objective had been accomplished, Historian Hall recorded. He also disclosed that Filkins tried to blackmail some of his former supporters and then burned their barns. There are no official records or newspaper accounts to confirm this. The Tower barns did burn and in September, 1878, Morris Terry's hop house was destroyed by fire and the home, barns, hop-kilns and hop house of his son, Cort, together with the forty-three bales and 1,000 pounds of hops, were destroyed in a fire that was definitely the work of an incendiary. The cases were never solved. Filkins, who was still a deputy sheriff, but no longer a constable, did solve several other arson cases. Working with Victor B. Stewart of Utica, an insurance detective, he arrested George E. Woodruff and D. K. Pierce of Waterville late in December, 1875 for setting fires that nearly destroyed Waterville. Both men were sentenced to life imprisonment in Auburn. On May 13, 1876 he arrested John O'Brien and Alexander Smith of Cooperstown for arson and secured convictions. Filkins said O'Brien, under an alias, had been employed by the Loomises.

Filkins left Waterville after family troubles broke up his home as he stubbornly refused to allow a fourteen-year-old daughter to marry. For several years he was employed as a night watchman in Head's Foundry on Broad Street in Utica. He returned to Waterville after his health began to fail. He died at his Sanger Street home of blood poisoning on Wednesday morning, January 4, 1893. His funeral was held from his home on Friday with the Rev. William Williams officiating. He was interred in the Sand Hill Cemetery at

Sweet's Corners. His grave looks out towards the Loomis Pinnacle across the Swamp.

Over in Higginsville, where William W. Loomis resided on the Side Cut Canal, the neighborhood children looked upon him as a "kindly, gentle old man" and were unaware that he had been involved with his parents and brothers in crime. His reformation was a credit to his wife, "Aunt Martha Ann," a fine, saintly woman who remained faithful through the long years of their marriage and raised an excellent family, shielding them from all the notoriety of the Loomis family escapades. During the last fifteen years of Bill's life there is no evidence in either the court records or upstate newspapers to indicate any connection with crime. He was the only brother who did not take an active part in the violent quarrels that split the family over their Sangerfield property.

Mrs. Helen Kilts Clifford of Blossvale, who lived on the Side Canal near the Loomis home in the 1890's, remembered Bill and his family well, according to Miss Jean Loomis, also of Blossvale, who began collecting stories and interviews while in school. "Mrs. Clifford said she visited the Loomis home often," Miss Loomis recalled. "She said Bill was a short, thin old man with a long gray beard. He had arthritis and was forced to use a cane when walking. His wife, Martha, was a sweet little woman and very well educated. Their children were neat and well behaved. Mrs. Loomis was a good housekeeper and their home always looked cozy and in order.

"Mr. Loomis kept a few cows and regularly every morning took his cans of milk to Doxtator's Cheese Factory in a little wagon drawn by a stout little black horse. 'He had to pass the one-roomed school I attended,' Mrs. Clifford stated, 'and if I was lucky enough to be at the corners when he came by, he always stopped his horse and courteously asked me to ride. As soon as he had helped me onto his wagon and I sat down primly on the seat beside him, Mr. Loomis would ask, "And how is your father?" or "How's your father been lately?"

" 'I would always answer, "Fine, Mr. Loomis, thank you."

" 'Then he would say, "Good."

" 'As the little black horse trotted along the dusty road, Mr. Loomis would chide me gently on school girl pranks or show deep interest in the stories I told him about my studies or work. When we reached the school Mr. Loomis would stop his horse and gravely help me out. After bidding me a cheery good-bye he would cluck to his horse and continue on towards the cheese factory, sitting proudly erect on the seat of his wagon.

" 'I never heard anything against him that I can remember. I only remember Mr. Loomis as a gentle old man who always had time to give a little girl a ride to school and treat her as if she was a princess.' "

Mrs. Charles Ruggles of Oneida recalled Bill driving through the city streets with his horse and wagon, and that his daughters were considered the most beautiful women in the area. Other old residents admitted Bill liked his beer, but when he became badly crippled with arthritis he was unable to dismount from his wagon seat. He would stop at the Higginsville Hotel that he and Denio had once owned and the bartender would bring the beer out to him. When he died in his home on July 3, 1896, the newspapers were kind in giving him only a brief notice without reviewing the history of the Loomis gang. He was buried in the Grove Cemetery near Higginsville.

Only Amos Plumb Loomis carried on the traditions of the Loomis' high-handed methods to the last. Many residents said he was acting. Nellie Smith Kelloway obtained a judgment against William Hathaway, the executor of Grove's estate, on September 1, 1884 and for the sale of his share in the original estate. After considerable litigation Nellie's property was granted her. Plumb, his wife and children resided in the old house on the hill through the courtesy of Harry Morgan of Madison, who purchased several acres, including the site of the homestead, in 1888. Morgan later sold sixty-eight acres to Morris E. Mason, who owned the adjoining farm north of the Loomis home for $2,350. After the remainder of the farm came into Mason's hands in 1900, following a suit against Plumb and all the other heirs by Grove Loomis Collins, Charlotte's son, Plumb was ordered to move off the hill. He refused. An unidentified newspaper clipping in the Harold Mason collection, reviewing Loomis' fight to retain his own, stated: "Some hold that although he has sinned he has also been much sinned against. It is seriously and confidently stated that one of the foreclosures he fought so stubbornly was on a real estate mortgage given to secure a person who had consented to go bail for him in some criminal suit that went against him, provided the bondsman was secured as indicted . . . . It is said there was nothing in the mortgage that showed it was not for money actually loaned although it was really only for the purpose stated. If this is true Mr. Loomis has had reason for fighting in the courts."

Norva Sturdevant disclosed that Plumb said it was the old family home and he had lived there in his youth, so he wouldn't budge from the hill. "Dell Rice, who was a lawyer, finally got Plumb off," Norva said. "He drove up one day and told Plumb he had to leave or he would throw him off if he had to kill him. Plumb got off and moved down into Grove's old home in the Swamp."

Actually Justice Andrews issued a writ of possession and it was served on Plumb by the constable, but Loomis did need persuading to move.

Plumb was involved in lawsuits almost up to the time of his death. One of the last indictments ever found by the Madison County grand jury was on February 4, 1889 for obtaining the signature of Evan Davis of Madison to a promissory note for $450. He was arraigned, pleaded innocent and placed on bail of $1,000. The case was brought to trial December 7, 1892, but unfortunately there is no record of the disposition.

Plumb made such a lasting impression on Waterville during his final years that he will always be remembered. William Doyle, business manager of the Rome Sentinel Company, who was a Waterville newspaperman at the time, recalled Plumb "as an irascible old cuss with a vicious tongue."

"My grandfather, Patrick Doyle, a powerful six-foot, two-inch Irishman of most fearless type, often told Plumb that he was the meanest old son of a bitch that ever escaped a deserved hanging," Doyle wrote, "and he used to brag to Plumb how he (Doyle) helped to hang him on the night of the big raid on the Loomis stronghold. Loomis replied that he knew my grandfather helped to hang him and that while he might have deserved hanging he never got low enough to deserve hanging at the hands of a goddam Irishman. My grandfather often would run into Plumb in the tavern at Waterville and there they would put on a verbal show that entertained the natives. No name was bad enough to suit either one in speaking of the other and they would stand together at the bar and damn each other by the hour. As each grew older they grew more mellow and were almost good friends towards the end."

"When Constable Jim Filkins was alive Plumb was equally pleasant to him," George P. Bissell of Waterville related. "Plumb met Filkins in the hotel one day but seemed to let bygones be bygones," Bissell said. "Plumb shouted to Filkins, 'Jim, you old son of a bitch. I know you murdered my brother, but come and have a drink with me.'"

Filkins did not drink or smoke.

There was also one other side to Plumb that very few people saw. John P. McNamara of New Hartford remembered seeing Plumb about once a week in Fritz Brand's Columbia Music Hall in Utica in the late 1890's and often talked with him. "He was over sixty years of age and his dark hair was streaked with gray," said McNamara. "He was always dressed neatly and wore a heavy gold watch chain across his vest front. Anyone would have taken him for a business man or a banker. His choice of words was good. He usually sat alone to watch the girls on the stage, but I have also seen the little

Dutchman, Fritz Brand, sitting with him. Plumb drank very little. I never saw him touch anything but beer."

Plumb was ill for several months with what was called "rheumatism of the chest." He died at his home in the Swamp on Wednesday, August 26, 1903 from neuralgia of the heart.

"I drove to the house the night he died," William Doyle recalled. "His body was lying on an old-fashioned couch in the front room of the house of some squalor. Everything looked old and was originally cheap, and the interior showed the rundown and uncared-for appearance of a home occupied by a very old couple. The wife was probably too old to do much more than to keep a path open and cook a little food.

"The house was small and rather dilapidated on the outside and as lonesome and God-forsaken surroundings as could be found in that section.

"Plumb's body was lying on the old couch with his bristly, bushy whiskers pointing towards Heaven where Plumb may have gone to, if one was optimistic. Apparently he had been moved from the small bed in the little room off the kitchen where he died, to the couch to await the attention of the undertaker. I recall his wife was there with three or four other people, among whom was (his nephew) Grove Loomis, a fine upright fellow."

A short time later Lysle Dunbar (now of Oneida) who worked for Bissell's Undertaking Co. in Waterville, drove to the home to care for the body.

Doyle, who was a country correspondent for The Syracuse Post Standard, made a drawing of Plumb from a family group picture in the home and a drawing of the home's exterior, to illustrate his story. He wrote a history of the gang, laden with inaccuracies. Later he said he wrote "on space" and needed the money, so drew some on his imagination.

Plumb was buried in the Sangerfield family lot. A stone that has since disappeared was placed on his grave. It bore the words, "Gone, But Not Forgotten."

Only Wheeler Loomis remained of the once powerful family, and he was a legendary figure to the residents in the Valley. Under his assumed name he lived quietly on his farm "Lot seven in the third Concession" of the Township of Kenyon, County of Glengarry, Canada. Having fled from standing trial in the Madison County Court, he shied away from the glare of publicity that made his brothers so notorious. The brief mention of his connection with any crimes in Oswego County as reported in the newspapers may have been the work of his brothers, who were adept at assuming each other's personalities. Wheeler even allowed his wife to swear falsely that he was dead before the Supreme Court in 1900 when the final disposition of the Sangerfield farm was being made to the heirs. Considered a good farmer and of excellent character by his neighbors in Kenyon Township, he raised a large family who became highly influential and respected citizens.

The record of his death on file in the office of the Registrar-General of Ontario revealed that he died on March 20, 1911 from cancer of the stomach and bowels, and heart failure, according to D. D. McDonald, M. D. of Alexandria.

The body was brought to Waterville where the funeral was held from the home of a daughter, Mrs. Frank Roberts on Hanover Street at 3 o'clock on Thursday afternoon, March 24. His body was taken to the cemetery in Sangerfield Center and laid to rest beside his family.

The Loomis Empire had fallen!

CHAPTER XXXII

THE GHOST OF WASH LOOMIS

The Loomis name had vanished from the Valley and their once-powerful stronghold was owned by the Mason family. Only a few acres were held by a Loomis descendant and this was the "Collins Piece" on the sloping hillside of Tinker Hollow. The land was all that remained to Grove Loomis Collins, the son of Charlotte Loomis Collins, from his mother's family inheritance.

The whole farm was cursed, some of the Loomis descendants claimed, and the curse was made by Wash Loomis before he died in 1865. The official coroner's report stated Wash never regained consciousness, but family descendants claim he murmured, "Violent death will come to anyone not of Loomis blood whoever has this farm."

Mrs. Anna Collins, the widow of Grove, who resided in Utica for many years, told of the workings of the curse.

"The Loomis farm was always one of the most productive in the Valley," she said, "but new owners found it almost impossible to raise crops on its soil. Sheep and cattle graze today where the family grew hops, grain, corn and potatoes.

"My husband had often told me that the ghost of Wash Loomis appeared at the old farm shortly before someone came to a violent death. I thought he was merely trying to scare me.

"One afternoon he put on his coat and hat and said he was going over to Sangerfield Center. The afternoon passed. I finished my housework and sat on the front porch to await his return. Dusk fell and I rose to go inside and prepare supper. Suddenly I heard the sound of footsteps coming down the eastern slope near the house. I looked up and saw a man, head bent as if in deep thought, slowly making his way past our home. He was dressed much as my husband had been when he left several hours earlier.

"Certain that it was Grove, I cried, 'Heaven's sake, man, where have you been? You said you were coming straight back from town, and here the whole afternoon has passed.'

"The man did not answer me. Without looking right or left, he continued down the slope towards Tinker Hollow. I called again, but received no answer. I went into the house and slammed the door angrily, thinking it was a fine thing when a woman's husband wouldn't even speak to her.

"An hour or two later I heard footsteps on the porch. I was still angry and did not bother to go to the door and raise the curtain to see who was there. The door opened and Grove walked into the kitchen. He spoke cheerfully to me, but I would not answer him.

" 'What is the matter with you?' he asked. 'Here I have been gone all afternoon and when I come home I find my wife won't speak to me. What have I done?'

"I turned on him furiously. 'You're a fine man to talk. I sat out on the porch almost all afternoon. I saw you walk by me and when I spoke to you you wouldn't even answer me.'

" 'But I didn't pass this house this afternoon. I can prove that I've been in Sangerfield and Waterville ever since I left here.' Suddenly his face went white. He questioned me closely on the appearance of the man whom I had seen. He listened carefully to my description of the man. 'You have seen the ghost of my Uncle Wash.' he said. 'My people have told me I look a lot like he did. Whenever he walks across the old farm someone is about to die.'

"I was unable to sleep that night. I am not a superstitious woman, and Grove's stories of the Loomis curse had often made me laugh; but, after my experience, I'll frankly admit I was worried.

"Grove came home two days later to tell me that Motty Mason, who lived on the Swamp Road and owned most of the original Loomis farm, had committed suicide. His body had been found near the line fence in the back pasture.

"I have often asked myself, had Motty Mason, who was a fine man and a good neighbor, also seen Wash Loomis' ghost?

"Upon Motty's death, the farm passed into the hands of his two nephews, Ed and Harold Mason. In the early 1940's, while Harold Mason was in Sangerfield Center on business, he stepped from the curbing into Route 20 and was struck and killed by a passing automobile. Surely, it was an accident, but somehow it seems related to the Loomis curse."

The late Harold Mason never believed in curses. An excellent farmer and a keen student of local history, he never tired of telling about the Loomis gang. His knowledge came from parents and grandparents who had been close neighbors of the notorious family almost from the time George W. Loomis bought the farm in 1806.

Wash Loomis' son, Grove, who lived in Stockwell until his death in 1937, usually visited Mason when he came across the Swamp.

"We often walked over the old Loomis farm and talked about his folks," said Mason. 'I wish people would forget about the Loomises,' Grove often remarked. 'We have been maligned enough. I want to tell you something, though. It has nothing to do with you personally, for your family has always been friends of mine. You'll never have any good luck—you or anyone else who doesn't have Loomis blood—who owns this farm.' "

People in the Chenango Valley will never forget the Loomis family. On windy October evenings they listen closely for the sound of the ghostly horsemen gathering at the deserted farm overlooking the Nine-Mile Swamp.

BIBLIOGRAPHY

Reference

Histories of Madison (Mrs. L. M. Hammond) and Oneida (Henry J. Cookingham, 2v.) Counties.

Annals and Recollections of Oneida County, Pomeroy Jones, 1851.

Oneida County, N. Y. edited by Daniel E. Wager, 1896.

Documentary

Records of the Courts of Oyer and Terminer, General Sessions, Common Pleas and Supreme Courts of Madison, Oneida and Oswego Counties.

Wendell's and Barbour's Supreme Court Cases.

Judgments found for George Washington Loomis, Sr. (1816-17), in personal papers of his attorney, Othniel Williams of Clinton.

Corporation records of the Town of Alexandria, Ontario, Canada.

Genealogy

Descendants of Joseph Loomis in America and His Antecedents in the Old World, 1875.

History of Union, Conn., 1893.

Unpublished family records in possession of Dr. Elisha S. Loomis of Cleveland, Ohio.

Statistical records from Towns of Hastings and Sangerfield.

Records of William Walter Loomis and family of Higginsville.

Newspapers

Issues of twenty-six separate newspapers variously published in Chenango, Madison, New York, Oneida, Onondaga and Oswego Counties.

Unpublished Material

Journal, letters, diaries too voluminous to list in detail. Particularly noteworthy:

Journal, kept by L. Sherwood Fitch of North Brookfield, now owned by his nephew, Raymond Burdick, Brookfield. Although undated, Fitch wrote first-hand observations from about 1840-1870.

Recollections and letters of John I. Mulligan, Sherburne. Mulligan, who was an intimate friend of Grove Loomis Collins, son of Charlotte Loomis Collins, wrote down many of Collins' reminiscences of life in the Loomis household, where he lived for many years.

Diary of Mrs. Julia Banton Mason for 1866 in possession of Mrs. Harold Mason's family, which resides on the Swamp Road, Town of Sangerfield.

Letters and interviews collected for a book on the Loomises by Miss Jean Loomis of Blossvale.

Book of Sangerfield Earmarks for 1797 and leaves from account book of Dr. Erastus Munger, recording professional visits to Loomis home.

Interviews with Mrs. Kelly (Helen Louisa Loomis) Hyland of Higginsville, youngest daughter of William Loomis; the grandchildren of Plumb Loomis in the Sauquoit Valley, Mrs. Grove (Anna) Loomis Collins of Utica and some of the children and grandchildren of Wheeler T. Loomis.

Interviews with Herbert Bissell of Waterville, who was in the raid when Wash Loomis was killed; his son, George Bissell, also of Waterville and the many wonderful men and women, already mentioned, who gave me their time, their memories and told me the way life was in those days.

REONGE
SHARPJV

Jeanne Galster
8547 Morgan Rd Apt 116
Clay, NY 13041